Your Pregnancy After 30

Your Pregnancy After 30

Glade B. Curtis, M.D., FACOG

Illustrations by David Fischer

FISHER
er
BOOKS™

Publishers:	Bill Fisher	
	Helen Fisher	
	Howard Fisher	
Editors:	Judith Schuler	
	Sarah Trotta	
Book design:	Deanie Wood	
Cover design:	B. Josh Young	
Cover photo:	©1996	
	COMSTOCK, Inc.	

Published by Fisher Books
4239 W. Ina Road, Suite 101
Tucson, Arizona 85741
(520) 744-6110

**Library of Congress
Cataloging-in-Publications Data**

Curtis, Glade B.
  Your pregnancy after 30 / Glade
B. Curtis; illustrations by
David Fischer.
     p. cm.
  Includes index.
  ISBN 1-55561-088-9
  1. Pregnancy in middle age—
Popular works. 2. Patient education.
I. Title.
RG556.6.C87   1996
618.2—dc20   96-22165
                              CIP

Note: The information in this book is true and complete to the best of our knowledge. This book is intended only as an informative guide for those wishing to know more about pregnancy. In no way is this book intended to replace, countermand or conflict with the advice given to you by your own physician. The ultimate decision concerning care should be made between you and your doctor. We strongly recommend you follow his or her advice. The information in this book is general and is offered with no guarantees on the part of the author or Fisher Books. The author and publisher disclaim all liability in connection with the use of this book. The names and identifying details of people associated with events described in this book have been changed. Any similarity to actual persons is coincidental.

Acknowledgments

It is a joy for me to be able to share the excitement and anticipation of a couple expecting a baby. I want to thank my patients and their families for allowing me to share this important time with them. A special thanks to all the "older" pregnant women I see in my practice who helped me with their insights. Their questions and comments helped me pull together what I believe is valuable information for any woman over 30 who is expecting a baby.

My thanks to my wife, Debbie, and our family who have supported me in the pursuit of a profession that requires me to give a lot of time and energy to my patients. Their unfailing support, which is an inspiration to me, has continued during this and other projects. My thanks also to my parents for their endless love and support.

Judi Schuler's insight, persistence, commitment to excellence and accuracy continue to inspire and challenge me. I appreciate her drive and ability to "pull things together" and keep me focused.

About the Author

Glade B. Curtis, M.D., is board certified by the American College of Obstetricians and Gynecologists. He is in private practice in obstetrics, gynecology and infertility in Sandy, Utah.

One of Dr. Curtis' goals as a doctor is to provide patients with many types of information about gynecological and obstetrical conditions they may have, problems they may encounter and procedures they may undergo. In pursuit of that goal, he has written several books especially for pregnant women, including *Your Pregnancy Week-by-Week* and *Your Pregnancy Questions & Answers*.

Dr. Curtis is a graduate of the University of Utah and the University of Rochester School of Medicine and Dentistry, Rochester, New York. He was an intern, resident and chief resident in Obstetrics and Gynecology at the University of Rochester Strong Memorial Hospital. He lives in Sandy with his wife and their five children.

Contents

Part 1

Congratulations, You're Pregnant!

Chapter 1

Positively Pregnant

Pregnancy is an exciting time. The new life you carry is a source of joy for you, your partner and your family.

More women every year are happy to find they are pregnant in their 30s or 40s. If you waited to start a family, you are not alone. Many couples choose to postpone having children until careers are on track or relationships are firmly established.

In the 1980s, births to women in the 30- to 44-year-old age range nearly doubled. First births to women in their 30s in 1990 accounted for about one-fourth of all births to women in that age group. Every day in the United States, nearly 200 women who are 35 or older give birth to their first child. Researchers believe that by the year 2000, one in every 12 babies will be born to a mother aged 35 or older.

When an older woman has a baby, her partner is usually older, too. A growing number of births are to couples who divorced and remarried and are starting a family together. Some couples have experienced infertility and do not achieve a pregnancy until they have gone through a major workup and testing or even surgery.

❧❧❧❧

Susan, a 38-year-old recently remarried woman with two kids, had a new partner who had not fathered any children. Susan came to the office concerned about their chances of conceiving. I gave her some suggestions and laid out a plan for the next few months. An ecstatic Susan called me two weeks later. She was pregnant and was probably a few weeks along when we had discussed the possibility of infertility.

Your Health

Today, many healthcare professionals gauge pregnancy risk by the pregnant woman's health status, not her age. Pre-existing medical conditions are the most significant indicator of a woman's well-being during pregnancy and the baby's health. A healthy 39-year-old is less likely to develop pregnancy problems than a woman in her 20s who suffers from diabetes, for example. A woman's fitness level has a greater effect on her pregnancy than her age.

Most women who become pregnant in their 30s and 40s are in good health. A woman in good physical condition who has been exercising regularly usually goes through pregnancy as easily as a woman 15 to 20 years younger. An exception: Women in a first pregnancy after 40 are somewhat more likely to encounter complications than women the same age who have had children. But most healthy women will have a safe delivery.

Some health problems are age related—the risk of developing the condition increases with age. High blood pressure and some forms of diabetes are age related. You may not know you have these conditions unless you see a doctor regularly. Either condition can complicate a pregnancy and should be brought under control before pregnancy, if possible.

Play it safe. If you haven't had a checkup recently, get one. If you are 35 or older and haven't had a mammogram yet, get one before pregnancy. Eat healthfully and follow a regular exercise program as you prepare for pregnancy.

Achieving Pregnancy When You're Older

Age affects fertility; fertility begins to decline when a woman is 20, and declines faster after 35. Partners older than 35 may take twice as long to conceive a child as a younger couple (1-1/2 to 2 years). A woman over 40 may take longer to conceive because ovulation is less frequent. The good news is that advances in fertility and reproductive technology have helped women conceive who might never have conceived before.

Older women may also find it somewhat harder to conceive, based on the declining number and quality of eggs in the ovaries. Your doctor can learn more about your ovulatory cycle by administering a test called the *clomiphene challenge.*

Other factors can affect fertility. Caffeine can affect a woman's ability to conceive. One study showed that drinking even one alcoholic beverage can lower a woman's chances of getting pregnant.

Some older couples turn to assisted reproductive technology (ART) to achieve pregnancy. ART includes in-vitro fertilization and gamete intrafallopian transfer (GIFT; a donor egg is paired to the partner's sperm). Success relates to the woman's age. For women at 34, the success of in-vitro fertilization is about 20% per menstrual cycle. At 44, a woman can expect a 5% success rate with this procedure.

The Question of "Higher Risk"

Some patients ask me why having a baby when a woman is in her 30s or 40s is considered "higher risk." Medical professionals originally chose the age of 35 as the dividing line between normal risk and high risk because of risks associated with the amniocentesis test. (See page 125 for a detailed explanation of the test.)

When amniocentesis was first developed, researchers found a 0.5% risk of having a miscarriage after the test. They compared this risk to that of giving birth to a baby with a chromosomal disorder, which increases with the mother's age. At 35, a woman has a 0.5% chance of giving birth to a baby with a chromosomal disorder. When the risk of having the test was equal to the risk of giving birth to a baby with problems, the test was advised. Thus 35 became the age at which healthcare professionals recommended testing.

The age of 35 is no longer meaningful because amniocentesis is much safer now. The estimated risk of a miscarriage after amniocentesis is about 0.3%. Perhaps more important, two-thirds of all babies born with Down syndrome (the most common reason for a woman to have the test) are born to women *under* 35.

Still, pregnancy in your 30s and 40s slightly increases the risk of some problems:

• birth of a baby with Down syndrome
• likelihood of a Cesarean-section delivery
• problems with diabetes and high blood pressure
• a harder, longer labor

I have found older pregnant women are often well informed about pregnancy. They are typically interested in what's happening to them and their developing babies and are willing to ask questions. They want to be part of the decision-making process in their health care. They usually seek prenatal care early and often prepare for pregnancy before getting pregnant. For these reasons, many researchers now believe risk does not increase greatly just because a woman is older. Other factors also influence a woman's health risks during pregnancy.

☙ How Your Healthcare Professional Treats You

Healthcare professionals often treat older women with more caution. Your healthcare provider may recommend more office visits, more testing, genetic counseling and screening for problems associated with pregnancy in older women.

Labor and delivery options may be more limited; you might be discouraged from using a birthing center because your age "puts you at greater risk." However, good prenatal care can significantly reduce obstetrical complications associated with age. Most women can have healthy pregnancies and deliver healthy babies into their 40s.

Genetic Counseling

If you or your partner is older than 35, genetic counseling may be recommended, which can bring up many questions. An additional concern is the impact the baby's father's age can have on a pregnancy.

Genetic counseling brings together a couple and healthcare professionals who are trained to deal with problems associated with the occurrence or risk of occurrence of a genetic disorder. Through genetic counseling, information researchers have about human genetics is applied to a particular couple's situation. Healthcare providers interpret the information so couples or families can understand it and can make informed decisions about childbearing. For futher information on genetic counseling, see pages 82 to 88 and 255 to 258.

Father's Age

When a pregnant woman is older, risks to both mother and child increase somewhat during pregnancy. At this time, we have no clear indication that a man's age can affect a pregnancy because when a mother is older, the father is often older, too. It can be difficult to determine whose age—the mother's or the father's—matters the most in pregnancy.

However, some studies demonstrate that men 55 or older are more likely to father babies with Down syndrome. These studies indicate the risk is higher still when the mother is also older. We estimate that at the age of 40, a man's risk of fathering a child with Down syndrome is about 1%; that rate doubles at age 45 but is still only 2%.

When both parents are over 35, genetic counseling is recommended. The risk of chromosome abnormalities exceeds 5% in this situation.

Some researchers now recommend that men father children before the age of 40. This is a conservative viewpoint and not everyone agrees with it. More data and research are needed before we can make definite statements about a father's age and its effect on pregnancy.

Common Pregnancy Problems

Problems that doctors see more often in older pregnant women include pregnancy-induced diabetes, high blood pressure and placental problems. (See chapter 16 for further information about these potential problems.) Older women do have more miscarriages, more Cesarean births and are at a slightly higher risk of giving birth to a baby with genetic or chromosomal abnormalities. But most older pregnant women have uncomplicated pregnancies and deliver healthy babies.

Beginning in their late 30s, women are more likely to develop medical conditions associated with reproductive organs, such as uterine fibroids. After 40, a woman may feel the physical strains of pregnancy more readily. She may be more bothered by hemorrhoids, incontinence, varicose veins, muscle aches and pains, and back pain.

Two serious pregnancy risks increase for women in their 40s—miscarriage and birth of a child with Down syndrome. Miscarriage ends about 40% of pregnancies in women who give birth after 40. Miscarriages are discussed on pages 243 to 246; a discussion of Down syndrome begins on page 258.

The national average for Cesarean deliveries is close to 25%. The rate rises slowly with age, to 30% for women in their 40s.

The risk of a pregnancy ending in stillbirth (the baby is dead upon delivery) has fallen for women of all ages in recent years. For a mother older than 35, the risk is about 7 in 1000. The risk of some birth defects does not increase for older mothers. These include spinal-tube defects (spina bifida), cleft palate and club foot.

As a pregnant woman in your 30s or 40s, you can expect pregnancy to be an exciting time for you and your partner. You may feel the physical and emotional effects of being pregnant a little more than a woman in her 20s, but you will find that there are many positive steps you can take to help ensure your pregnancy will go as smoothly as possible for you and your baby. This book can help you.

Chapter 2

First-time or Repeat Pregnancy?

When greeting a pregnant patient for the first time, I ask, "Is this pregnancy good, bad, exciting or scary for you?" I get answers ranging from "Yes" or "No" to "All of the above." Being pregnant can be scary and wonderful at the same time. It's a time of learning and spiritual, intellectual and physical growth. It's also a time to be open about your concerns.

Your First Pregnancy after 30

During any pregnancy, you may experience fatigue and emotional mood swings. Your changing body takes some adjusting to. People will give you advice and share stories about their own pregnancies, labors and deliveries. You will receive a lot of attention, sometimes unwanted.

You can't avoid some of these experiences. However, knowing the facts about pregnancy can prepare you to accept or ignore advice. Knowing how the female body reacts to pregnancy can help you understand the changes you will experience and help you make intelligent choices as the need arises. If you're willing to adapt and adjust your lifestyle for the sake of your health and that of your growing baby, you can do a lot to make your pregnancy a happy, fulfilling experience.

❧ You'll Receive a Lot of Attention

A positive (or negative) side to a first pregnancy is the attention you receive. At times you may be irritated by people who ask you how you feel and what you're experiencing.

❧❧❧❧

Debbie was tired of wisecracks from co-workers about her pregnancy. She turned it back on them by asking them the same questions. When asked about her weight gain, she might reply with a grin, "My doctor says I'm doing great with my weight gain. What has your doctor said about yours?" Her friends took it in good humor and got the message.

Allow people to help you and to do things for you. I've had patients tell me that they really didn't appreciate how much others were willing to do for them during their first pregnancy until they became pregnant again. Helpful attention is a luxury not always available in subsequent pregnancies, so take advantage of it!

❧ Sharing the News

You may feel a little awkward telling family members, friends and co-workers that you're pregnant. Some people thoughtlessly offer their advice or opinions on "being an older mother."

If others are critical or do not have your best wishes in mind, ignore them! Focus your attention on staying healthy and having a happy pregnancy. Your pregnancy is your business—you don't need the good opinion of anyone else to make it a positive experience for you.

When you announce to co-workers and supervisors that you're pregnant, be prepared for a range of reactions. Be clear that you have made the right decision. Assure co-workers that your pregnancy is just one aspect of your life (a very important aspect), and you plan to continue your job as long as you are able.

Repeat Pregnancy

First-time pregnancy is unlike any other pregnancy you experience. Everything is new. In later pregnancies, things are different. Many women assume their second pregnancy will be just like their first. Often it isn't—your emotions in a repeat pregnancy may not be the same as a first pregnancy. However, you may feel more relaxed.

In a repeat pregnancy, you are often seen as a "pregnant mother." You may be reluctant to ask for extra attention, although you may need it more. A second pregnancy can be more stressful because of the extra demands on your time and energies. You must attend to your family's well-being, take care of yourself and maybe a career as well. You may wonder where you will find the energy to satisfy everyone else's needs. Physical discomforts may bother you a bit more.

On the plus side, women usually have a shorter labor with their second child, often only about half as long as with a first baby. Pain does not lessen, but because labor is usually shorter and you know more of what to expect, it may be easier to handle.

⁓ Physical Changes

With a repeat pregnancy, you may "show" sooner because your muscles and skin are more stretched. Some women think they are further along than they really are because they look pregnant sooner than they did the first time.

You may experience backaches more frequently because the ligaments that hold the uterus in place were stretched with your first pregnancy. You may carry your second pregnancy lower, which adds pressure to your back and sometimes to your bladder.

Be careful when lifting, especially young children. Bending over to pick up a toddler can cause back pain. To help with backache, practice the exercises you learn in childbirth-education classes. A hot-water bottle or a light maternity girdle also helps relieve backache.

⁓ Some Challenges with This Pregnancy

Because of demands on your time and energy, fatigue may be one of your greatest problems. It's a pregnant mother's most common complaint.

Rest is essential to your health and to your baby's. Seize every opportunity to rest or nap. Nap when your child does, or put up your feet. Don't take on more tasks or new roles. Don't volunteer for a big project at work or anywhere else. Learn to say "No." You'll feel better!

Moderate exercise can help boost your energy level and may eliminate or alleviate some discomforts. Consider choosing an activity you can do with your child. Check with your healthcare provider before starting an exercise program. Exercise is discussed in depth in chapter 13.

Stress can also be a problem. To alleviate feelings of stress, exercise, eat healthful, nutritious meals and get as much rest as possible. Take time for yourself. Don't let mood swings control you. If you feel one coming on, remember it won't last forever.

Some women find a pregnancy support group is an excellent way to deal with difficulties they may experience in a second pregnancy. Check with your healthcare provider for further information. You and your partner might want to take a childbirth refresher course.

✣ Involving Your Children

Being pregnant when you already have children is different from a first pregnancy. You'll probably feel anxious about how the new baby will affect your older children and your relationships with them.

Explain in simple terms how pregnancy affects your body. Try to help your children understand any problems you may experience, such as morning sickness. If you're too tired to do some regular activities with your children, let them know it's because of how you're feeling, not because of them. Reassure them over and over that as soon as you feel better, you will do as much as possible with them.

Let your children help prepare for the new baby. Older children might help choose the baby's name or decorate the nursery. A picture drawn by a big brother or sister adds color to the baby's room and makes the older child feel very important.

Delay telling very young children about the baby until they can see for themselves it is growing inside you. Even then, it may be better to wait until close to the baby's birth to tell a very young child (under 3). Time passes much more slowly for young children, and a couple of weeks seems like forever! If possible, use a familiar reference point for the birth, such as Christmas or when school gets out.

Ask your healthcare provider if it's all right to bring one child with you to a prenatal visit, so the child can listen to the baby's heartbeat. Or take your child to the hospital nursery to see the new babies. Many hospitals offer preparation classes for siblings of an expected baby; choose one suited to your child's age.

❧❧❧❧

Abbie didn't know how much to tell her kids about her pregnancy or how to explain things about it. She took Rob and Ian with her to the library to look for books in the children's section. She was amazed at how many excellent books were available, many with tasteful pictures and simple explanations. They took books home and spent time together going through them and talking about the new baby.

When your child asks questions, it's probably a good idea to keep answers simple. For example, if your young child wants to know how the baby eats while it's growing inside you, an explanation such as "the baby gets its food from Mommy" will probably suffice. To your young child, your pregnancy isn't very important.

You may need to provide older children with more information. Answer their questions honestly, but even with older kids, don't provide more information than they need. Most important, provide them with extra love and attention during this time, and plan time alone together with each of them after the baby is born.

❧ Prepare Your Children for Your Absence

Let them know in advance who will be caring for them. If possible, include them in making this decision. While you're in the hospital, it may be a good idea to have your children stay with someone they know and trust. If possible, allow your children to stay at home, where things are familiar. This is a time of great upheaval for your children—make it as easy as possible on them.

❧ Making Changes in Your Child's Life

Encourage your child's independence from you. Let your partner take over part of your regular childcare duties so they can spend time together without you. It'll help when you go to the hospital or are busy after the baby is born.

If you must make changes in your child's routine, such as putting him in a new room or taking away her crib, do it before the baby comes. If the change occurs near the time of the baby's birth, the child may feel more displaced. Wait awhile to give your older child's toys, clothes or bottles to the new baby, or it could cause resentment.

Don't try to make life easier on yourself by pushing toilet training or making your child give up the bottle. It can cause more problems than it resolves. Encourage your child toward independence in small steps at the appropriate time.

❧ When You're Expecting More than One Baby

Older women are more likely to have twins. For older children, welcoming one baby into the family is hard enough. Making room for more than one baby can be that much more difficult. Make sure the older child has his own familiar place and keeps his own things. Reassure him of your love frequently, and give him plenty of attention.

If you'll need help after the babies are born, especially childcare, have the helper start work before the babies are born. Your older children get to know the caregiver beforehand, and it provides a sense of continuity after the babies come home.

Encourage your older child to express his or her feelings about the upcoming birth of the babies. Let your child know you understand why she might feel negative; help her find positive ways to deal with her feelings.

Establish a regular, uninterrupted time with your older child before the babies are born and continue it after their birth. This might be story time in the evening or preparing for bed or bath time. These routines contribute to the child's sense of security. Tell your child this time is important to you, and you will continue it after the babies are born. Then make every effort to do so.

Chapter 3

Your Career and Your Pregnancy

Working during pregnancy is an established concept today. More than half of all women work outside the home. Many women work until the day they deliver.

Whether you work throughout your pregnancy depends on your particular circumstances; it's a subject to discuss with your healthcare provider. No matter what kind of job you do or whether you work full- or part-time, expect to modify some daily activities. If your profession is especially demanding, set priorities and establish guidelines with co-workers about how much you can work during pregnancy.

ବ୍ଲ-ବ୍ଲ-ବ୍ଲ-ବ୍ଲ

Delfina never had much to do with the human-resources person at her workplace. At her husband's urging, she made an appointment with the woman to discuss her pregnancy. She found a friend and an advocate in Irene. With her help, Delfina made a lot of changes at work, including her work hours and breaks, so she could lie down. With these changes, she was able to work through her entire pregnancy.

If you are concerned about whether your workplace is a safe environment during your pregnancy, discuss the situation with your healthcare provider. It may be difficult to know the specific risks of a particular job; the goal is to minimize any risks to you and your baby while enabling you to work. A normal, healthy woman with a normal job should be able to work throughout her pregnancy.

Work Precautions during Pregnancy

If you work during pregnancy, bear in mind a few precautions. You will probably have to slow down and lighten your duties. Expect to take things a little easier at work and at home—you may not be able to do some of the things you do when you aren't pregnant. Ask for help when you need it.

❧❧❧❧

Kelly had an especially demanding job; some days she worked 10 hours. She came to see me at the end of her sixth month looking terrible and hardly able to move. I told her that her pregnancy really had to come first, not her job. Her emphasis on work could have a negative effect on the health of her baby. She wouldn't last another week the way she was going, and I told her so.

We decided she would set some boundaries at work, and we devised a plan—8-hour days that would decrease to 4-hour days over the next three months. When she came in a month later, Kelly reported that things were much better at work. She had begun to train her temporary replacement. I told Kelly what I tell others about work and pregnancy—I wanted her to be able to work, but her pregnancy had to come first.

❧ Making Changes

Your center of gravity is changing, so you may have to change the way you do certain tasks—lifting, for example. Do most of your lifting with your legs. Bend your knees to lift; don't bend at the waist. As your abdomen grows larger, don't lift anything weighing more than 20 pounds.

Avoid activities that involve climbing and balance, especially during the third trimester. Talk to your supervisor about eliminating these activities. If you stand or sit all day at your job, you may have to make changes.

With a "sit-down" job, get up and move around regularly to stimulate circulation. Sit in a chair that offers good support for your back and legs. Don't slouch or cross your legs while sitting.

❧ Work Risks Associated with Pregnancy

If your job includes two or more of the following risks, talk with your healthcare provider. He or she may want to monitor your pregnancy more closely. Work-related pregnancy risks include:

• standing more than 3 hours a day
• work on an industrial machine, especially if it vibrates a lot or requires strenuous effort to operate
• strenuous physical tasks, such as lifting, pulling, pushing or heavy cleaning
• repetitious work, such as an assembly-line job
• environmental factors, such as high noise levels or extreme temperatures
• long work hours
• shift changes
• exposure to infectious diseases
• exposure to chemicals or toxic substances

გგგგ

Aimee was a cashier at a large discount department store. Before pregnancy, her legs would ache after standing for an 8-hour shift. At her 6-month visit, she was miserable. She had just finished a shift and couldn't get her shoes off because of the swelling. She needed to make some major changes.

Aimee changed to a 6-hour shift, with two breaks, during which she rested on her side on a couch for 30 minutes. She was able to sit on a stool while she worked. She found running shoes were very comfortable and maternity support hose helped a lot. Her boss was happy to work with her to make the changes possible.

Many women work at a computer or a video-display terminal (VDT) and wonder if it can harm the baby. To date, we have no evidence that working at a computer terminal can harm a growing baby. However, if you work at a VDT, be aware of how long you sit and the way you sit, to keep good circulation in your legs. Get up and walk around frequently.

Some substances in the workplace can harm a developing fetus. If you think you may be exposed to hazardous substances, discuss it with your physician. Substances may also be brought into your home on your work clothes or those of someone else in your family. A discussion of hazardous environmental substances begins on page 70.

Job Stress and Fatigue

Some women experience stress on the job during pregnancy. Nearly every pregnant woman I know feels tired and fatigued at some time while she's pregnant.

❧ To Relieve Stress

Some muscle exercises can help you relieve stress; you can do them at home or on the job. I have a couple of favorites. The first one I recommend is to relax each muscle group in turn with a deep breath. Start with the feet and work up through the legs, hands, arms, torso, shoulders, neck and face. Continue for 10 to 20 minutes. (This exercise also works when you're lying in bed and are having trouble getting to sleep.)

The second exercise is also easy. Do this: Inhale slowly. Push your abdomen out as you breathe in. Count to 4 before exhaling. Let shoulders and neck relax as you slowly exhale while counting to 6. Repeat as often as needed.

❧ Feeling Fatigued

Feeling fatigued can be a sign of pregnancy. For some women, the feeling lasts throughout pregnancy. For others, stress on the job or at home can cause fatigue during the day or sleeping problems at night.

If possible, lie down during breaks or on your lunch hour. Even 10 or 15 minutes of rest can make you feel better.

Do some leg-stretching foot exercises several times each hour, whenever you can. Remove your shoes before doing the following exercise. Extend your legs in front, then point your toes and flex your feet. Repeat 4 or 5 times. This exercise helps circulation in your feet and may prevent some swelling in your legs. Stress and fatigue are discussed in depth beginning on page 38.

Travel during Pregnancy

Many women travel as part of their job. Traveling during pregnancy can be tiring and frustrating, but if your pregnancy is normal, you should be able to travel in the first and second trimesters without too much trouble. Consult your physician if you're considering travel in your third trimester.

The best time to travel, if you can choose, is during the second trimester. You'll have more energy, and you'll feel better. Complications are less likely. In the first trimester, you may have morning sickness or feel very tired. In the third trimester, you may find it difficult to sit or to stand for long periods, and you may tire easily.

✋ Travel Tips

The most important travel tip I can give you is *don't overdo it*. Pregnancy does impose some restrictions. If your company requires you to travel, limit the amount of time you are away from home.

If you experience nausea when traveling, carry crackers or some other bland snack food to nibble on. Prop up your feet when you sit for any length of time.

Discuss travel plans with your physician. Most will tell you it's fine to travel at certain times while you're pregnant, but each situation is different. Keep in mind the following general considerations about traveling during pregnancy.

- Avoid areas in which good medical care is not available or where changes in climate, food or altitude could cause problems.
- Don't plan a trip during your last month of pregnancy.
- If you have any problems, such as bleeding or cramping, don't travel.

- If you're uncomfortable or your hands or feet swell, sitting in a car or on a plane or walking a lot may make matters worse.
- Take along a copy of your medical records when traveling.
- Keep your doctor's name and telephone number handy in case of an emergency.
- If your pregnancy is considered high risk, a trip during pregnancy is not a good idea.

๛ Ways to Travel

Flying should not present a problem. Most airlines allow preboarding for passengers who need extra time. Take advantage of the offer. Try to book an aisle seat, so you can stretch your legs and get up to walk more easily. Drink plenty of fluids, such as water and juice, because recirculated air in a plane is extremely dry.

Consider consulting with someone at the airline about your condition *before* buying tickets. I've heard of some airlines refusing to carry a pregnant passenger without the written consent of her physician.

If you haven't considered train travel recently, now might be the time to do so. Trains have wide aisles and roomy seats, and the ride is smooth. Moving around is easy.

Bus trips and sailing are probably not good choices. On a bus, leg room is limited and the ride is jarring, which could make you uncomfortable. If you are unused to it, the rolling motion of a ship or boat can be unsettling. Seasickness could add to pregnancy discomforts you may already have. If you do sail, most healthcare providers believe Dramamine® is safe against seasickness, but a seasickness patch is *not* advised.

Car travel may be comfortable or uncomfortable, depending on how far along you are. Limit car travel to not more than 5 hours a day (sitting longer slows circulation). Stop at regular intervals to take short walks and use the bathroom. When sitting in a car, tuck a pillow into the small of your back. Do ankle circles while riding to increase circulation in your feet and legs. Always wear your seat belt and shoulder harness.

☙ Risks to Consider

If you travel, your discomfort level is likely to increase, especially if you are cooped up in a car or plane for hours. You may have trouble sleeping in a strange bed. If you travel during pregnancy and develop a complication while you're away from home, those who have been involved in your pregnancy and know your history will not be available to care for you.

Avoid travel during the last month of pregnancy. Labor could begin at any time, your water could break or other problems could occur. Your doctor knows what has happened during your pregnancy up to now and has a record of tests you've undergone—information that is important. If you check into a hospital to deliver in a strange city, some doctors won't accept you as a patient because they don't know your medical history. It doesn't make sense to take any chances.

Many women want to know if their doctor can tell when they will go into labor so they can travel. Unfortunately, no one can predict when your labor will begin. Always discuss your travel plans with your doctor before you finalize them.

Health Insurance

Most employers offer some type of health insurance to their workers—private medical-and-hospitalization coverage, membership in an HMO (health maintenance organization) or a preferred-physicians plan (PPO). With private insurance, you can choose your own physician. With an HMO, you choose a physician affiliated with the group. With a PPO, you may choose any doctor on a list of acceptable physicians.

☙ Important Coverage Questions

You will need answers to some very important questions about pregnancy coverage under your insurance plan. Talk to the people in the personnel department or your employer's human-resource specialist. You may want your husband to ask these questions, if coverage is through his employer.

- What type of coverage do I have?
- Are there maternity benefits? What are they?
- Do maternity benefits cover Cesarean deliveries?
- What kind of coverage is there for a high-risk pregnancy?
- Do I have to pay a deductible? If so, what is it?
- How do I submit claims?
- Is there a cap on total coverage?
- What percentage of my costs are covered?
- Does my coverage restrict the kind of hospital accommodations I may choose, such as a birthing center or a birthing room?
- What procedures must I follow before entering the hospital?
- Does my policy cover a nurse-midwife?
- Does coverage include medications?
- What tests during pregnancy are covered under the policy?
- What tests during labor and delivery are covered under the policy?
- What types of anesthesia are covered during labor and delivery?
- How long can I stay in the hospital?
- Does payment go directly to my healthcare provider or to me?
- What conditions or services are not covered?
- What kind of coverage is there for the baby after it is born?
- How long can the baby stay in the hospital?
- Is there an additional cost to add the baby to the policy?
- How do I add the baby to the policy?
- Can we collect a percentage of a fee from my husband's policy and the rest from mine?

Laws that Protect You during Pregnancy

❧ The Pregnancy Discrimination Act

The Pregnancy Discrimination Act of 1978 requires companies employing 15 or more people to treat pregnant workers the same way they treat other workers who have medical disabilities and cannot work. The law prohibits job discrimination on the basis of pregnancy, childbirth or related disability. It guarantees equal treatment of all disabilities, including pregnancy, birth or related medical conditions.

Your employer cannot fire you because you are pregnant or force you to take mandatory maternity leave. You are protected in other ways, too.

• You must be granted the same health, disability and sick-leave benefits as any other employee who has a medical condition.
• You must be given modified tasks, alternate assignments, disability leave or leave without pay (depending on your company's policy).
• You are allowed to work as long as you can perform your job.
• You are guaranteed job security on leave.
• You continue to accrue seniority and vacation, and to remain eligible for pay increases and benefits.
• If your company does not provide job security or benefits to other employees, it does not have to provide them to a pregnant woman.

✷ Pregnancy Leave

Your pregnancy leave is the period during which your healthcare provider states you cannot work. This can range from 4 to 6 weeks after a vaginal delivery to 6 to 8 weeks following a Cesarean delivery. (Fathers are not covered under this law.)

If you have problems obtaining these benefits from your employer, tell your healthcare provider. He or she may be able to direct you to someone who can help you.

✷ The Family and Medical Leave Act

The Family and Medical Leave Act was passed in 1993. If you or your husband spent at least one year working for the company at which you are currently employed, the law allows either of you to take up to 12 weeks of unpaid leave in any 12-month period for the birth of your baby. Maternity leave may be taken inter-mittently or all at the same time.

Under this law, you must be restored to an equivalent position with equal benefits when you return. However, the act applies only to companies that employ 50 or more people within a 75-mile radius. States may allow an employer to deny job restoration to employees in the top 10% compensation bracket. Check with your state's labor office.

❧❧❧❧

Carol and Brett were first-time prospective parents with busy careers. Carol learned she could take 6 weeks off after delivery but wanted to go back to work after that. I suggested Brett ask what the policy was for paternity leave at his job. He hadn't heard of it and was skeptical.

Brett learned his company's policy covered leave for him. He got a week off after Carol delivered, which he later reported to me was "the best week ever." He was able to get another two weeks when Carol went back to work. Brett told me the time he had by himself with his new daughter helped him get to know her better than he would have any other way. The time also helped him understand what Carol was up against and eased the transition of leaving their daughter with a sitter.

❧ State Laws

At this time, about half the states have passed legislation that deals with parental leave. Some states provide disability insurance if you have to leave work because of pregnancy or birth.

State laws differ, so check with your state labor office or con-sult the personnel director in your company's human resources department. You may also obtain a summary of state laws on family leave from:

The Women's Bureau Publications
U.S. Department of Labor
Box EX
200 Constitution Avenue, NW
Washington, DC 20210

Preparing to Leave Your Job

Whatever your plans—leaving work a few months early, working until the day you deliver—be *prepared* to leave by the end of the eighth month. You'll need to prepare your replacement to step into your job temporarily, schedule times at which to call the office and take care of other details.

๛ Think Ahead

Think about how to be prepared in case your water breaks or you have some other problem at work. Keep a towel and some sanitary pads available. Carry medical-information cards and identification with you at all times. Check with the human-resources department to make sure paperwork for your maternity leave is in order.

Have your suitcase packed and ready at home, in case you need to go from your office to the hospital. I've seen some pretty weird stuff brought in by partners who had to pack a bag for the hospital when the woman didn't have the chance!

๛๛๛๛

Tina's water broke at work, and she went directly to the hospital. When she got there, she called her husband and asked him to pack some things for her and come right away. Tina's delivery went well. In her room later, she opened her overnight bag to look for a hairbrush. Was she surprised! She wished she'd taken the time to pack for herself. The nightgown Kevin brought was one of her flimsiest, as was the underwear he had chosen. And he had forgotten her robe. Luckily the hospital provided her with a toothbrush, toothpaste and a comb. She was able to get her sister to bring her a robe, some makeup and other things she needed. At least the orange and apple Kevin packed came in handy after the delivery.

❧ Prepare Your Replacement

Save yourself problems later by training the person who will handle your job to do the work the way you would. Initiate the relief worker to office procedures, rules and regulations, and particular ways to do your job efficiently. It's a good idea to have the person perform your duties while you're still on the scene so you can evaluate the work.

Before you leave, arrange to talk with your replacement, your boss and your co-workers one last time about details that must be taken care of while you're gone. Together, review the plans you have prepared.

Schedule times to call the office. Discuss with co-workers how to keep in touch with you. (Will you call them? When can they call you?) It's a good idea to schedule times to call the office. That enables your co-workers to have information available for you and have questions ready when you call. Few annoyances are worse than having various people at your office call you every day asking questions when you are trying to concentrate on your baby! Letting them know in advance when you will call sets guidelines and puts you in more control.

Chapter 4

Will You Be a Single Mother?

Many women, especially those in their late 30s and early 40s, choose to have a child without a spouse. The situations I have seen vary from woman to woman. Some women are deeply involved with their partner, the baby's father, but have chosen not to marry. Some women are pregnant without their partner's support. Still other single women have chosen donor (artificial) insemination as a means of getting pregnant.

I have come to realize that no matter what the personal situation for each woman, many concerns are shared by all of them. This chapter reflects many of the issues they have raised with me.

Information in the first part of this chapter is general and deals with situations single mothers face frequently. Questions I list at the end of the chapter have no absolute answers. They are of a legal nature that I am not qualified to answer. However, I include them because the decision to have a baby as a single woman has legal ramifications you should be aware of. If you are single and pregnant, use them as a basis for formulating questions about your own situation, then seek the advice of an attorney, a patient advocate, a hospital social worker, your healthcare provider or family members.

People may ask why you chose to be a single mother as your pregnancy begins to show. Answers to this question vary greatly.

Marriage doesn't meet the needs of many women, but their desire to be a mother—to give birth to a child and parent him or her—is very strong.

In many situations—whether a mother is single, widowed or divorced—a child's overall environment is more important than the presence of a man in the household. Eighty-six percent of single-parent households are headed by women. Recent studies indicate that if a woman has other supportive adults to depend on, a child can fare well in a home headed by a single woman.

Concerns about Your Decision

You may find people ask you the most intimate questions during your pregnancy, especially if you are single. If you believe you need to answer their questions, decide early how detailed an explanation you want to provide.

Some people may think your choice is unwise and tell you you're "crazy" to have a baby alone. However, your true friends won't treat you this way. Once they understand your situation, they'll be supportive. If anyone gives you a hard time, change the subject. Don't discuss your reasons for having a baby with anyone unless you want to.

Even if you are "alone," you're not really alone. Seek support from family and friends. Mothers of young children can identify with your experiences—they have had similar ones recently. If you have friends or family members with young children, talk with them. You would probably share your concerns with these people even if you were married. Try not to let your particular situation alter this.

Sometimes a single woman's family is against her decision to have a baby. If you are comfortable with your decision, ask family members to talk to you about the reasons they are uncomfortable with your pregnancy. You may not change their minds; you have no control over that. You *do* have control over your response; learn to live with their disapproval or ignore it.

Some women choose not to marry their partner. If this is your situation, you may find that people assume you and your partner are married, especially if you are pregnant and together. In most cases, it's nobody's business; however, do tell your doctor about the situation.

Emotional upheavals aren't uncommon for many women during pregnancy. If coping with emotions is hard for you, talk with your healthcare provider. Office personnel will know about support groups, or they can direct you to a counselor, if that is what you need. Check the resource section of this book starting on page 333 for the name and telephone number of a group you can contact that deals with the issues of single motherhood.

Deciding Who Can Help You

Finding someone to count on for help during your pregnancy and after your baby arrives is a concern for many single pregnant women. One patient told me that she thought about whom she would call at 2 a.m. if her baby were crying uncontrollably. When she answered that question, she had the name of someone she believed she could count on in any type of emergency—during or after pregnancy!

You will want to choose someone to be with you when you labor and deliver, and who will be there to help afterward. The only part of labor and delivery that might require special planning because you're single is your plan to get to the hospital to deliver. One woman wanted her friend to drive, but couldn't reach her when the time came. Her next option (all part of the plan) was to call a taxi, which got her to the hospital in plenty of time.

Finding a Labor Coach

Finding a labor coach probably won't be difficult. Not all women choose their partner for the job; you can ask a good friend or a relative. A woman who has given birth using the method you have chosen is an excellent choice. She understands your feelings and can identify closely with your experience.

If you can't think of someone, discuss the matter with your

healthcare provider. He or she may suggest other single mothers who might volunteer to coach you during labor.

❧ Other Sources for Labor Coaches

Professional labor coaches are available. Some members of Doulas of North America, an organization of women who help new mothers, are trained labor coaches. See the resource section of this book for listings (page 333).

Going Home from the Hospital

If you're a single mother without a partner, going home from the hospital may seem overwhelming at first. You'll be fine if you plan ahead and enlist a little help.

A new baby is an incredible challenge in any situation. You may need more support from family and friends because you will have total responsibility for your new baby. Ask for their help! If you feel you can't ask others for their time, consider hiring someone to stay with you at night for the first couple of weeks until you get on your feet.

Your "Unusual" Situation

Today, being a single mother isn't that unusual—many mothers are divorced, widowed or unmarried. Women of all ages have made the same decision you have. Some people may treat you differently; others won't care. Good friends and family members should draw closer to you.

Some women have chosen donor insemination to conceive a child. This can create unusual situations; however, families today are different than they were in the past. Many families are "unusual" now. Many children don't have a complete set of parents or grandparents, even in the closest family units. I've found in these situations that an older family friend can be just as loving as a grandparent. Encourage older friends to take an active part in your child's life. Support groups for single parents can also be a valuable source of information and help. Ask your healthcare provider for the names of groups in your area.

As a single parent, you do need an alternative childcare plan in case you become ill or there is an emergency. Plan ahead for this. Ask a family member or close friend if they can be called upon to help out in case this happens. Providing for this event should give you peace of mind.

Legal Questions

The following questions have been posed to me and other physicians by women who chose to be single mothers. I repeat them here without answers because they are legal questions that should be reviewed with an attorney in your area who specializes in family law. They can help you clarify the kinds of questions you need to consider as a single mother.

- A friend who's had a baby by herself told me I'd better consider the legal ramifications of this situation. What was she talking about?
- I've heard that in some states, if I'm unmarried, I have to get a special birth certificate. Is that true?
- I'm having my baby alone, and I'm concerned about who can make medical decisions for me and my expected baby. Can I do anything about this concern?
- I'm not married, but I am deeply involved with my baby's father. Can my partner make medical decisions for me if I have problems during labor or after the birth?
- If anything happens to me, can my partner make medical decisions for our baby after it is born?
- What are the legal rights of my baby's father if we are not married?
- Do my partner's parents have legal rights in regard to their grandchild (my child)?
- My baby's father and I went our separate ways before I knew I was pregnant. Do I have to tell him about the baby?
- I chose to have donor (artificial) insemination. If anything happens to me during my labor or delivery, who can make

medical decisions for me? Who can make decisions for my baby?

- I got pregnant by donor insemination. What do I put on the birth certificate under "father's name"?
- Is there a way I can find out more about my sperm donor's family medical history?
- Will the sperm bank send me notices if medical problems appear in my sperm donor's family?
- As my child grows up, she may need some sort of medical help (such as a donor kidney) from a sibling. Will the sperm bank supply family information?
- I had donor insemination, and I'm concerned about the rights of the baby's father to be part of my child's life in the future. Should I be concerned?
- What type of arrangements must I make for my child in case of my death?
- Someone joked to me that my child could marry its sister or brother some day and wouldn't know it because I had donor insemination. Is this possible?
- Are there any other things I should consider because of my unique situation?

Chapter 5

Concerns You and Your Partner May Have

At the beginning of your pregnancy, you won't know all the questions and concerns you will have. As your pregnancy progresses, many of the issues I cover here will become important to you. In this chapter, we'll look at some of the common concerns couples expecting a child often have.

The Due Date

Most women don't know the exact date their baby was conceived, but they usually know the day of their last menstrual period. Because ovulation occurs about the middle of a woman's cycle, or about 2 weeks before the beginning of the next period, a doctor uses the date of the last period and adds 2 weeks as an estimate of when conception occurred. By doing this, your healthcare provider can determine your due date.

You can calculate when your baby is due another way. Begin with the date of the onset of your last menstrual period; add 7 days and count back 3 months. This gives you the *approximate* date of delivery. For example, if your last period began on January 20, your estimated due date is October 27.

Gestational age or *menstrual age* is one way to date a pregnancy. If your doctor says you're 12 weeks pregnant, he's referring to gestational age. He means that your last menstrual period began

12 weeks ago; however, you actually conceived 10 weeks ago.

Fertilization age, also called *ovulatory age,* is 2 weeks shorter than gestational age and dates from the actual day of conception. This is the age of the fetus. In the case of "12 weeks pregnant," the fetus is actually 10 weeks old.

Your doctor may also refer to your pregnancy by *trimesters.* Trimesters divide pregnancy into three stages, each about 13 weeks long. This division helps organize stages of development.

The Emotions of Pregnancy

When a woman discovers she is pregnant, she may feel many different emotions—excitement, fear, anxiety, joy. You may be surprised by the emotions you feel when you learn you are pregnant. Even if you and your partner have been anticipating your pregnancy, the emotions you may feel may not be the ones you thought you would have.

If you aren't immediately thrilled about pregnancy, don't feel alone. It's common to feel conflict about the news and to question your condition. Some of this may be attributed to the anxiety you feel if you're not sure what lies ahead.

It's normal to become very emotional about many things during pregnancy. You may feel moody, cry at the slightest thing or daydream. Emotional changes during pregnancy are discussed in more detail beginning on page 98.

You may feel attached to your developing baby immediately, or it may not happen for a while. Some women begin to feel attached as soon as they know they are pregnant. For others, it occurs when they hear their baby's heartbeat, at around 12 or 13 weeks, or the first time they feel their baby move, at between 16 and 20 weeks.

Stress, Fatigue and Rest

High levels of stress during pregnancy can increase a woman's chance of having a premature baby or giving birth to a baby that has a low birth weight. Studies have shown the more anxious a woman was during pregnancy, the more prematurely her baby was born.

Making some lifestyle changes may help minimize the effects of stress on you and your baby. Eat a healthful diet. Practice stress-reducing exercises, such as yoga. Get enough rest.

You can't always eliminate stress, but you can learn to cope with it. The following suggestions may help you deal with everyday stressful situations.

Accept what you cannot change. Turn off your anger, resentment or impatience, and tune out. When you feel anxious or upset, practice deep breathing or relaxation exercises learned in childbirth-education classes.

Talk about it. Instead of acting out the next time you have problems, talk them out. Be specific, and listen to what others tell you in response. Work together toward practical solutions.

Take time out. When stress gets to be too much for you, take time out. Go into the bathroom or your bedroom—someplace quiet. Stretch, practice breathing exercises or listen to soothing music.

Let go of the little stresses. Do your best—then relax! If you make a mistake, acknowledge it and go on. Be kind to yourself.

Set realistic priorities. Manage your time with priorities in mind. Use a daily calendar. Learn to say "no."

Get some exercise. Exercise is a great stress reliever. Walk, swim or ride a stationary bike to deal with stress.

Seek help. You may need outside help to make it through a difficult time or to change behavior patterns. If necessary, ask your healthcare provider for a referral.

⁓ Fatigue and Rest

During the first stages of your pregnancy, you may find that getting enough rest is utmost in your mind. Do yourself a favor by taking it easy and resting when possible.

Try not to lie on your back or stomach when you sleep or rest. As your uterus grows, it presses on important blood vessels that run down the back of your abdomen. When you lie on your back, the pressure decreases circulation to your baby and to the lower parts of your body. You may notice it is harder to breathe when you lie on your back. Lying on your stomach puts a lot of pressure on your uterus, which can become a comfort problem later.

Learn to sleep on your side early in the pregnancy; you'll be glad you did as you get bigger. Elevate your feet to keep blood moving throughout your body, especially your legs. Rest your top leg on a pillow. Many women find "pregnancy pillows" that support the entire body are can offer great relief.

Use extra pillows to support your abdomen or your legs as your pregnancy progresses.

Some pregnant women can't sleep enough at night to make them feel rested. If you can, nap during the day. If you can't nap, sit down and relax—listen to music or read, if that helps. When you relax, prop your feet above your chest or lie on your side to help ease swelling and discomfort in your legs.

Childbirth-education Classes

Childbirth-education classes help you and your partner prepare for the birth of your baby. I have found that if a couple, especially the woman, is prepared for labor and delivery, the entire experience is usually more relaxed, even enjoyable. Childbirth-education classes have been developed for couples in their 30s and 40s to meet their specific needs.

ஃ What to Look for in a Class

Every class has a different style. The list below can help you evaluate if a childbirth class is right for you.

- Class was recommended by my healthcare professional.
- Class uses a philosophy shared by my healthcare provider and childbirth team.
- Class begins when I need it, in the seventh month of my pregnancy (earlier if you are having more than one baby).
- Class size is small; no more than 10 couples.
- Graduates are enthusiastic. (Locate some and ask about the class.)
- Class outline is informative and interesting.
- Class covers Cesarean delivery, different types of anesthesia, emotional issues.
- Class includes the time and the opportunity to ask questions, practice techniques and talk to parents who have recently given birth.

❧ How Classes Help Prepare You for Childbirth

Classes help prepare a woman and her partner for labor and delivery. Studies have shown that women who take childbirth-education classes need less medication, have fewer forceps deliveries and feel more positive about the birth than women who do not take classes.

Classes cover many aspects of labor and delivery, including vaginal birth, Cesarean delivery, hospital procedures, ways to deal with the discomfort and the pain of labor and delivery, various pain-relief methods and the postpartum or recovery period. Having this information available beforehand can make you feel more confident and prepared to cope with the birth experience. Nearly 90% of all first-time expectant parents take some type of childbirth-education class.

❧ Major Childbirth Philosophies

Patients often ask me if one type of delivery method covered in childbirth-education classes is better than another. Any method can be the right one for a couple, but I always suggest that both parties agree on the method. If the woman chooses a method that involves her partner greatly and the partner isn't able to provide that level of involvement, it could lead to disappointment and anxiety.

Childbirth preparation methods are usually divided among three major philosophies—Lamaze, Bradley and Grantly Dick-Read. Each philosophy offers its own techniques and methods.

Lamaze is the oldest technique of childbirth preparation. It conditions mothers, through training, to replace unproductive laboring efforts with effective ones. It emphasizes relaxation and breathing as ways to relax during labor and delivery. In recent years, partners have been included in Lamaze classes.

Bradley classes teach the Bradley method of relaxation and inward focus; many types of relaxation are used. Strong emphasis is put on relaxation and deep abdominal breathing to make labor more comfortable. Classes begin when pregnancy is confirmed and continue until after the birth. Bradley class members typically have decided they do not want to use any type of medication for labor-pain relief.

Grantly Dick-Read is a method that attempts to break the fear-tension-pain cycle of labor and delivery. These classes were the first to include fathers in the birth experience.

Choosing Your Class

At around 20 weeks of pregnancy, begin looking into classes that are offered in your area. You should be signed up or just beginning classes by the beginning of the third trimester (about 27 weeks). Plan to finish the classes at least a few weeks before you are due. The following ideas can help you and your partner find the right class for you.

Find out what classes fit into your schedule and your partner's. Talk to friends and relatives who have taken different childbirth classes. Decide whether you want a drug-free birth or whether you are willing to consider pain relief if it is necessary. Learn about the instructor's qualifications. Visit some classes in your area.

Childbirth classes are offered in many settings. Most hospitals that deliver babies offer prenatal classes on site. They are often taught by labor-and-delivery nurses or by a midwife.

Classes are not only for first-time pregnant women. If you have a new partner, if it has been a few years since you've had a baby, if you have questions or if you would like a review of labor and delivery, I encourage you to consider taking these classes.

Ask your healthcare provider to recommend classes in your area. He or she is familiar with what is being offered. Friends can be good sources, or look in the yellow pages under *Childbirth Education.* Some insurance companies and a few HMOs offer partial or full reimbursement for class fees.

Choosing Your Baby's Pediatrician

Choosing a doctor for your baby (commonly a pediatrician) is as important as choosing your obstetrician or the hospital where you will give birth. It's best to choose and to visit him or her before your baby is born.

❦❦❦❦

Willa asked friends for suggestions for a pediatrician and
finally decided on one. Willa wanted to meet her before the
baby was born. She wasn't prepared for the experience.
Willa had been used to reading a magazine in the relative
peace and quiet of my waiting room. The pediatrician's
waiting room was very different. In one corner, a new mom
was trying unsuccessfully to change a diaper. In another, two
brothers fought over a book, while their mom talked to
another mom.

Willa was beginning to think she was in the wrong place when
she was called to meet the pediatrician. She immediately felt
at ease with Dr. Summers, who was obviously busy but
seemed competent and open. Willa was able to ask questions,
and when she left the office she felt good about the choice
she made. But she was sure it would take awhile to get used
to that waiting room!

Ask your family practitioner, friends, co-workers and family
members for names of pediatricians they know and trust. Or
contact your local medical society and ask for a reference. Plan to
visit the pediatrician about 3 or 4 weeks before your due date. If
the baby comes early, you will be prepared.

The first visit is important, and your partner should attend
with you. This is the ideal time for the two of you to discuss any
concerns or questions about the care of your baby and receive
helpful suggestions.

At the meeting, you can discuss the doctor's philosophy, learn
his or her schedule and "on-call" coverage, and clarify what you
can expect of this physician. When your baby is born, the pediatrician will be notified so he or she can come to the hospital and
check the baby. Selecting a pediatrician before the birth ensures
that your baby will see the same doctor for follow-up visits at the
hospital and at the doctor's office.

❧ Questions to Ask a Pediatrician

I believe the questions below will help you create a useful dialoge with your pediatrician. You will undoubtedly have others.

- What are your qualifications and training?
- Are you board certified? If not, will you be soon?
- What hospital(s) are you affiliated with?
- Do you have privileges at the hospital where I will deliver?
- Will you do the newborn exam?
- If I have a boy, will you perform the circumcision (if we want to have it done)?
- What is your availability?
- Are your office hours compatible with our work schedules?
- Can an acutely ill child be seen the same day?
- How can we reach you in case of an emergency or after office hours?
- Who responds if you are not available?
- Do you return phone calls the same day?
- Are you interested in preventive, developmental and behavioral issues?
- How does your practice operate?
- Do you provide written instructions for well-baby and sick-baby care?
- What are your fees?
- Do your fees comply with our insurance?
- What is the nearest (to our home) emergency room or urgent-care center you would send us to?

❧ Analyzing Your Visit

Some issues can be resolved only by analyzing your feelings after your visit. Below is a list of questions you and your partner might want to discuss after your visit to the pediatrician's office.

- Are the doctor's philosophies and attitudes acceptable to us, such as use of antibiotics and other medications, child-rearing practices or related religious beliefs?

- Did the doctor listen to us?
- Was he or she genuinely interested in our concerns?
- Did the physician appear interested in developing a rapport with our expected child?
- Is this a person we feel comfortable with and with whom our child will be comfortable?
- Is the office comfortable, clean and bright?
- Is the office staff cordial, open and easy to talk to?

If you belong to an HMO, and there are a group of physicians in pediatrics, arrange a meeting with one physician. If you have a conflict or don't see eye to eye with this person on important matters, you may be able to choose another pediatrician. Ask your patient advocate for information and advice.

The Cost of Having a Baby

No doubt about it—it costs a lot of money to have a baby, no matter where you live in the United States. Costs vary depending on how long you stay in the hospital, what type of anesthesia you have, whether you or your baby have complications and where you live. Prices in 1995 ranged from $4,500 for an uncomplicated vaginal delivery in Arkansas to $8,850 for the same delivery in New York state. Cesarean deliveries are more expensive— $13,750 in New York compared to $7,750 in Oklahoma. The average 1995 cost in the United States was $6,500 for a vaginal delivery and $11,000 for a Cesarean delivery.

At your first prenatal visit, check with your healthcare provider about the fees for prenatal care, including delivery. Nearly every medical office employs someone who deals with insurance questions; he or she may know about things you haven't considered. Don't be embarrassed or afraid to ask questions about the financial side of your pregnancy. Every healthcare provider expects it.

You may also need to check with the hospital and your insurance company. When you communicate with an insurance company, it helps to have a list of questions ready. Write down the answers so you can refer to them later, especially if you need to discuss them with your healthcare provider.

Often the insurance person in your doctor's office knows the answers to these questions or can help you get answers. See the discussion of insurance on pages 24 and 25 which includes a list of questions to ask.

❧ Costs in Canada

The Canadian healthcare system is very different from the healthcare system in the United States. Canadians pay a health-care premium on a monthly basis, and pregnancy costs vary depending on the province you live in. The doctor who delivers your baby is paid by the government, not you.

Driving during Pregnancy

Driving a car is important to most women, but some wonder if it is safe to drive during pregnancy. It is usually safe to drive throughout pregnancy, but it may become uncomfortable for you to get in and out of the car as pregnancy progresses. However, your increasing size shouldn't interfere with your ability to drive.

Many women are confused about whether they should or should not wear seat belts and shoulder harnesses during pregnancy. These safety restraints are just as necessary during pregnancy as they are when you're not pregnant.

For your protection, and the protection of your developing fetus, *always wear your safety belt when driving or riding in a car!* There is no evidence that use of safety restraints increases the chance of fetal or uterine injury. You have a better chance of survival in an accident wearing a seat belt than not wearing one.

There is a correct way to wear your safety belt during pregnancy. Place the lap-belt part of the restraint under your abdomen and across your upper thighs so it's snug but comfortable. Adjust your sitting position so the belt crosses your shoulder without cutting into your neck. Position the shoulder harness between your breasts; don't slip this belt off your shoulder. The lap belt cannot hold you safely by itself.

Taking Others to Your Office Visits

If you want to bring your partner with you to your prenatal visits, do so. These visits can help him realize what is happening to you and help him feel that he's a part of your pregnancy. And it's nice for your partner and your healthcare provider to meet before labor begins.

It's all right to take your mother or mother-in-law, too. If you want to bring anyone else, discuss it with your healthcare provider first.

Many offices don't mind if you bring your children with you; other offices ask that you not bring children to your office visit. If you have a problem and need to talk with your doctor, it can be difficult to do if you're trying to take care of a young child at the same time. If you do bring children, observe the following rules of etiquette.

• Ask about office policy ahead of time.
• Bring only one child to a visit.
• Don't bring a child on your first visit, when you will probably have a pelvic exam.
• If you want your child to hear the baby's heartbeat, wait to bring her until after you have heard it.

- Bring something to "entertain" your child in case you have to wait. Not all offices have toys or books for kids.
- Be considerate of other patients; if your child has a cold or is sick, don't bring him.

Some Pregnancy Precautions

Your baby relies on you to maintain correct body temperature. An elevated body temperature in a pregnant woman for an extended period may harm a developing fetus. For this reason, avoid hot tubs, saunas, steamrooms and spas.

Most doctors agree douching can be dangerous during pregnancy because it can cause an infection or bleeding, or even break your bag of waters (rupture your membranes). It can also cause more serious problems, such as an air embolus. An air embolus results when air gets into your circulation from the pressure of the douche. It is rare but can be a serious problem.

There is some controversy about the safety of using electric blankets during pregnancy. Until we know more, stay warm other ways, such as with down comforters or extra blankets. Do not use an electric blanket.

Feeding Your Baby

It's never to early to think about whether you want to breastfeed or bottlefeed. Even after you decide on a method, you may have to make adjustments after your baby is born.

Early in life, most babies eat every 3 to 4 hours, although some babies feed as often as every 2 hours. It may help your baby get on a regular schedule if you time feedings. Or let your baby set the schedule; some babies need to nurse more often than others.

Sometimes a baby needs to feed more often than she normally does. See how often your baby wants to feed and whether she is growing properly. A baby usually waits longer between feedings and feeds longer at each feeding as she grows older.

A baby is usually the best judge of how much he should take at each feeding. Usually a baby turns away from the nipple when he is full.

We do know that breastfeeding is best for your baby. Breast milk contains all the nutrients a baby needs, and it's easy to digest. Breastfed babies have lower rates of infections because of the immunological content of breast milk. Breastfeeding can also give the baby a sense of security and the mother a sense of self-esteem. However, if there are reasons you cannot or choose not to breastfeed, be assured that your baby will do well if you bottle-feed her on formula.

℘ The Bottlefeeding Option

It won't harm your baby if you choose to bottlefeed. I don't want any mother to feel guilty if she chooses bottlefeeding. Sometimes a woman cannot breastfeed because of a physical condition or problem. Some women want to breastfeed and try to, but it doesn't work out. If breastfeeding doesn't work for you, please don't worry about it.

℘℘℘℘

At her 37-week visit, Lily wanted to talk about breastfeeding and bottlefeeding. With her first child, she had tried breastfeeding and had a miserable experience, giving up after 2 weeks. This time she planned to bottlefeed from the start and wanted to know if this was OK. Friends and family had been giving her a hard time about it. I reassured her that bottlefeeding was fine and not to feel guilty. I told her breastfeeding wasn't for everyone; it's an individual decision.

Lily left my office feeling better. She realized that giving birth to, caring for and rearing a baby carries a lot of decisions. Some aren't easy to make.

Statistics show that more women choose to bottlefeed than breastfeed their babies (about two to one). We know that with iron-fortified formula, your baby receives good nutrition if you bottlefeed. There are advantages to bottlefeeding.

- Some women enjoy the freedom bottlefeeding provides; someone else can help care for the baby.
- Bottlefeeding is easy to learn; it never causes the mother discomfort if it is done incorrectly.
- Fathers can be more involved in caring for the baby.
- Bottlefed babies are often able to last longer between feedings because formula is usually digested more slowly than breast milk.
- A day's supply of formula can be mixed at one time, saving effort.
- You don't have to be concerned about feeding your baby in front of other people.
- It's easier to bottlefeed if you plan on returning to work soon after your baby is born.

• If you feed your baby iron-fortified formula, he or she won't need iron supplementation.
• If you use fluoridated tap water to mix formula, you may not have to give your baby fluoride supplements.

✌ The Benefits of Breastfeeding

Breastfeeding is an excellent choice for feeding your baby. Breastfed babies contract fewer infections than those who are bottlefed because breast milk is bacteria free and actively helps newborns avoid disease. One study showed breastfed babies are much less likely to develop ear infections than bottlefed babies.

All babies receive from their mother some protection against disease before they are born. During pregnancy, antibodies are passed from the mother to the fetus through the placenta. These antibodies circulate through the baby's blood for up to a few months after the baby is born. However, breastfed babies continue to receive protection from breast milk.

Breast milk is easily digested by baby; for a preemie, it is often the best nourishment. It cannot become contaminated, be mixed incorrectly or served at the wrong temperature. There are also benefits for you—breastfeeding helps metabolize fat deposits your body laid down during pregnancy.

Breastfed babies are less likely to develop allergies and asthma; research has shown this protection can last until a child is a teenager. Studies show that babies fed only breast milk for 6 months had fewer instances of asthma, food allergies and eczema into their teens.

You can usually begin breastfeeding your baby within hours after birth. This provides your baby with *colostrum,* the first milk your breasts produce. Colostrum contains important factors that help boost the baby's immune system. Baby's breastfeeding also causes your pituitary gland to release oxytocin, which helps the uterus contract and decrease bleeding. Breast milk comes in 12 to 48 hours after birth.

❧❧❧❧

Jane was due to deliver soon and wanted to breastfeed, but she was scared she couldn't do it. She had read books, talked to friends and knew lots of information. I think her biggest fear was that she would be left alone with this new baby and wouldn't know what to do. I told her it didn't work that way, and there would be a lot of help available. One of the best places to learn to breastfeed is in the hospital after the baby is born. The nurses are experienced in helping new moms learn how to get started breastfeeding, and they're available to help after you go home. Patients have told me that after they went home, they called the hospital nursery and even went back for help.

Breastfeeding is an excellent way to bond with your baby. Closeness between mother and child can be established during the feeding process. Don't be discouraged if breastfeeding doesn't feel natural to you at first. It takes some time to find out what works best for you and your baby. Hold your baby so she can easily reach the breast while nursing; hold her across your chest or lie in bed. She should take your nipple into her mouth fully, so her gums cover the areola. She can't suck effectively if your nipple is only slightly drawn into her mouth.

For the first few weeks, feed your baby 8 to 10 times a day, for 20 to 30 minutes at each feeding. Take more time if your baby needs it.

You may be concerned about how much breast milk your baby gets at a feeding. You'll know your baby is getting enough to eat if he nurses frequently, such as every 2 to 3 hours or 8 to 12 times in 24 hours; has 6 to 8 wet diapers and 2 to 5 bowel movements a day; gains 4 to 7 ounces a week or at least 1 pound a month, and appears healthy, has good muscles and is alert and active.

❧ How Breastfeeding Affects You

The nutrients your baby receives while breastfeeding depend on the quality of the food you eat. Breastfeeding places more

demands on your body than pregnancy. Your body burns up to 1000 calories a day just to produce milk. If you breastfeed, you need to eat an extra 500 calories a day. You also need to keep up your fluid intake.

While you are breastfeeding, you may not have menstrual periods and you may not ovulate, meaning you won't get pregnant. However, don't rely on breastfeeding alone if you don't want another pregnancy right away. *Take precautions.*

Do not use oral contraceptives because hormones in oral contraceptives can get into your milk and be passed to your baby. Choose some other form of birth control until you are finished breastfeeding. You may choose a "minipill" or progesterone-only birth-control pill, condoms, a diaphragm or an IUD. Norplant® birth control is also safe to use if you nurse.

Most substances you eat or drink (or take orally, as medication) can pass to your baby in your breast milk. Spicy foods, chocolate and caffeine are some things your baby may react to when you ingest them. Be careful about what you eat and drink when you breastfeed.

❧ Pumping Breast Milk

Many women pump their breast milk for use at a later time, especially when they return to work. Many types of breast pumps are available; ask your healthcare provider which is best for what purposes. Pumps are hand, battery or electrically operated.

❧ Other Breastfeeding Facts

Many women are surprised when they experience milk letdown. Soon after a baby begins to nurse, a woman feels a tingling or cramping in her breasts; this means milk is flowing into breast ducts. It occurs several times during feeding; sometimes a baby chokes a bit when the rush of milk comes too quickly. You may also experience this letdown when it's time for your baby to nurse or when you hear a baby crying—your own or any other baby!

It's best to avoid bottles for the first month of breastfeeding for two reasons. Your baby may come to prefer feeding from a bottle (it's not as hard to suck), and your breasts may not produce enough milk.

Women who have had breast-enlargement surgery with silicone implants are often able to breastfeed successfully; ask your healthcare provider about it if this concerns you. You should also be able to breastfeed after a breast reduction. Milk production may be less after such surgery, but it is usually enough to satisfy the baby.

If you need help with breastfeeding your baby, ask friends and family members for help. Call your healthcare provider—office personnel may be able to refer you to someone knowledgeable. You can also look in the telephone book for the La Leche League, an organization that promotes breastfeeding. Someone from a local affiliate can give you advice and encouragement.

Part 2

Your Medical Health

Chapter 6

Your Health and Medical History

If possible, see your doctor before you become pregnant, so you can take care of any existing medical problems and routine exams. If you know you are in good health before you get pregnant, you'll feel more secure about your growing baby. You'll know your Pap smear is normal, your breast exam is all right and any medical conditions are under control. You can have a mammogram, if one is needed. If a preconsultation visit is not possible, make an appointment to see your doctor as soon as you realize you are pregnant.

Your health affects the health of your growing baby. Good nutrition, proper exercise, sufficient rest and attention to how you take care of yourself are all important to your baby. These matters also affect you and how well you tolerate being pregnant.

Prenatal Care

Prenatal care is the care you receive throughout your pregnancy. Special care from professionals during pregnancy is designed to help identify any pregnancy problems or conditions before they become serious. Always feel free to ask questions about your pregnancy at your prenatal checkups.

If you have confidence in your healthcare provider, you'll be able to relax and enjoy your pregnancy. Pregnancy really is a special time in a woman's life; good prenatal care helps ensure that you do everything possible to make it the best 9 months possible for your growing baby, too.

✤ Your First Prenatal Visit

Your first prenatal visit to your healthcare provider may be one of the longest. He or she will ask questions, order lab tests and give you a physical examination.

To take a complete medical history, your healthcare provider will ask about your menstrual periods, recent birth-control methods, previous pregnancies and other details. Tell him or her about any miscarriages or abortions you have had. Include information about hospital stays or surgical procedures.

Tell your doctor about any medications you take or those you are allergic to. Your family's past medical history may be important, as in the case of diabetes or other chronic illnesses. Tell your doctor about any chronic medical problems you have. If you have medical records, bring them. (See the discussion of your medical history on pages 88 and 89.)

On your first visit, you will probably have a pelvic exam, which helps your healthcare provider determine if your uterus is the appropriate size for how far along you are in your pregnancy. A Pap smear is done if you haven't had one in the last year, and other tests may be required. Tests are discussed in chapter 9.

✤ Normal Prenatal Care

In most cases, you will visit your healthcare provider every 4 weeks for the first 7 months, then every 2 weeks until the last month, then once a week. You may be scheduled for visits more frequently if necessary. On every visit, your weight and blood pressure will be checked to give your healthcare provider valuable information about how your pregnancy is progressing.

Choosing a Healthcare Provider

You have many choices when it comes to choosing a healthcare provider. You can choose an obstetrician, a family practitioner or a certified nurse-midwife to oversee your prenatal care.

An *obstetrician* is a medical doctor or an osteopathic physician who specializes in the care of pregnant women, including delivering babies. He or she completed training in obstetrics and gynecology after medical school.

A *perinatologist* is an obstetrician who specializes in high-risk pregnancies. Only about 10% of all pregnant women need to see a perinatologist. If you see a perinatologist, you may still be able to deliver your baby with your regular doctor. You may have to deliver at a hospital other than the one you had chosen because of its specialized facilities or the availability of specialized tests for you or your baby.

A *family practitioner,* sometimes called a *general practitioner,* is a physician who provides care for the entire family. Many family practitioners deliver babies and are very experienced at it. If problems arise, your family practitioner may refer you to an obstetrician or perinatologist for prenatal care.

A *certified nurse-midwife* is a trained professional who cares for women with low-risk, uncomplicated pregnancies and delivers their babies. These professionals are registered nurses who have additional professional training and certification in nurse-midwifery. Supervised by a physician, they will call him or her if care or delivery complications occur.

A *nurse practitioner* may serve as your regular healthcare provider at office visits, if your pregnancy is normal. Nurse practitioners are registered nurses with advanced degrees in this specialty area. They are certified by national organizations in their specialty and practice under the rules and regulations of your state, under the supervision of a physician. They can provide prenatal care and family-planning services. At delivery, a nurse-midwife, obstetrician or family practitioner delivers the baby.

If you have an obstetrician you like, you may be all set. If you don't, call your local medical society for a referral. Ask friends who recently had a baby about their healthcare providers.

Sometimes another doctor, such as a pediatrician or internist, can refer you to an obstetrician.

Make an effort to communicate with your healthcare provider so you can comfortably ask him or her questions about your condition. Read articles and books such as this one and my other books, *Your Pregnancy Week-by-Week* and *Your Pregnancy Questions & Answers*. They will help you prepare questions to ask your healthcare provider. However, never substitute information you receive from other sources for information, instructions or advice you receive from your own healthcare provider. He or she knows you, your history and what has occurred during your pregnancy.

Don't be afraid to ask any question. Your healthcare provider has probably already heard it, so there is no need to be embarrassed. Check out even the smallest details. Your doctor would be the first to tell you that it's better to ask a thousand "silly" questions than risk overlooking a single important one.

Your Health Affects Your Baby

Your health directly affects your baby's health and well-being. Some illnesses, diseases and conditions women experience during pregnancy can affect their babies; it's a good idea to be informed about them.

❧ Asthma

Most women with asthma have a safe pregnancy. If you have had severe asthma attacks before pregnancy, you may have them during pregnancy. Usually you can use the medication you are accustomed to, but discuss the matter with your healthcare provider.

I've found that many women feel better and have fewer problems with their asthma if they increase their fluid intake during pregnancy. Try it—you should increase your fluid intake during pregnancy anyway.

❧ Cytomegalovirus

Cytomegalovirus (CMV) is a member of the herpes-virus family. It is transmitted in humans by contact with saliva or urine. Day-care centers are a common source of the infection; CMV can also be passed by sexual contact. Most infections do not cause symptoms. However, when there are symptoms, they include fever, sore throat and joint pain.

Cytomegalovirus can affect a developing baby, causing low birth weight, developmental problems, jaundice, enlarged liver, enlarged spleen and anemia, among other problems.

❧ Diarrhea during Pregnancy

Diarrhea during pregnancy can raise concerns. If the diarrhea doesn't go away in 24 hours, or if it keeps returning, contact your healthcare provider. He or she may prescribe medication for the problem. Do not take medication for diarrhea without discussing it with your healthcare provider first.

One of the best things you can do for yourself if you experience diarrhea during pregnancy is to increase your fluid intake. Drink a lot of water, juice and other clear fluids, such as broth. (Avoid apple juice and prune juice because they are laxatives.) You may be happier eating a bland diet, without solid foods, until you feel better.

It's OK to avoid solid food for a few days if you keep up your fluid intake. Solid foods may actually cause you more gastrointestinal distress when you have diarrhea. Avoid milk products while you have diarrhea; they can make it worse.

❧ Epilepsy

Epilepsy can be a serious problem during pregnancy. If you suffer from the disease and become pregnant, call your physician immediately. Most medication to control seizures can be taken during pregnancy; however, some medications are safer than others.

During pregnancy, phenobarbital is often used to control seizures. Dilantin® is not recommended for seizure control because it can cause birth defects. Discuss this important issue with your healthcare provider as soon as possible.

Some people have expressed concern recently about the safety of taking phenobarbital during pregnancy. During pregnancy, phenobarbital is used mainly to prevent seizures in women with a history of seizures or at the end of pregnancy to treat pre-eclampsia (toxemia) and prevent seizures. If you take phenobarbital, do not stop taking it without first checking with your physician. In most cases, doctors will administer the lowest possible amount of phenobarbital to control seizures during pregnancy.

Fever

Fever commonly accompanies some illnesses. A fever, especially a high one, can be serious because your baby relies on you for its temperature control. A prolonged high fever, especially in the first trimester, may affect a developing fetus and cause limb (arm and leg) defects. To bring down a high fever, drink lots of liquids (1 pint of fluid a day for every degree above 98.6F [37C]), take acetaminophen (Tylenol®) and dress appropriately to help you cool down. If your physician prescribes medication for an infection or other illness that may be causing the fever, take it as prescribed.

Fifth Disease (Parvo Virus 19)

Fifth disease, also called *parvo virus 19*, received its name because it was the fifth disease to be associated with a certain kind of rash. Fifth disease is a mild, moderately contagious airborne infection that spreads easily through groups, such as classrooms or day-care centers.

The rash looks like skin reddening caused by a slap. Reddening fades and recurs, and can last from 2 to 34 days. There is no treatment for fifth disease, but it is important to distinguish it from rubella, especially if you are pregnant.

This virus is dangerous during pregnancy because it interferes with the production of red blood cells. If you believe you have been exposed to fifth disease during pregnancy, contact your healthcare provider. A blood test will determine whether you have had the virus before; if you have, you are immune. If you have not, your healthcare provider can monitor you to detect fetal problems. Some fetal problems can be dealt with before the baby is born.

✵ Group-B Streptococcus Infection

Group-B streptococcus (GBS) infection is found in 15 to 35% of all healthy women. GBS in a pregnant woman does not affect the fetus, but it is the most common cause of life-threatening infections in newborns, including pneumonia, meningitis, lung damage, kidney damage, loss of sight, hearing loss, cerebral palsy and developmental problems. The infection is transmitted to the baby during delivery.

GBS is often transmitted from person to person by sexual contact; it is found in the mouth or lower-digestive, urinary or reproductive organs. In women, GBS is most often found in the vagina or rectum. It is possible to have GBS in your system and not have symptoms.

We do not have an ideal screening test for GBS, but your healthcare provider may recommend taking a swab of your vagina or rectum toward the end of the pregnancy. The cultured test identifies 90% of all women who will carry the bacteria at the time of birth. (Faster tests that can be used during labor to detect GBS are not as accurate.)

If you become high risk during labor because of your symptoms or if you have had GBS recently or in the past, your doctor tests you at that time. He or she may administer antibiotics to help prevent transmission of the bacteria to your baby.

✵ Hepatitis

Hepatitis, a viral infection of the liver, is one of the most serious infections that can occur during pregnancy. Your doctor will probably test you for hepatitis antibodies at the beginning of your pregnancy. Hepatitis B is responsible for nearly half the cases of hepatitis in North America. It is transmitted from one person to another by sexual contact and the reuse of intravenous needles. Symptoms include flulike symptoms, nausea and pain in the liver area or upper-right abdomen. The person may appear yellow or jaundiced, and urine may be darker than normal. This form of hepatitis is transmitted to the baby during birth or through breastfeeding.

If a mother tests positive for hepatitis during pregnancy, the baby may receive immune globulin to treat hepatitis after it is born. This is different from hepatitis vaccine. Hepatitis vaccine is given to *prevent* hepatitis from occurring. It is now recommended that all newborns receive hepatitis vaccine shortly after birth. Ask your pediatrician if the vaccine is available in your area.

Lyme Disease

Lyme disease is an infection carried and transmitted to humans by ticks, and it crosses the placenta. Complications include preterm labor, fetal death or a rashlike illness in the newborn.

The disease appears in stages. In most people, a skin lesion with a distinctive look, called a *bull's eye,* appears at the site of the bite. Flulike symptoms appear next, and 4 to 6 weeks later, heart or neurologic problems may develop. Arthritis may be a problem much later.

Treatment for Lyme disease includes long-term antibiotic therapy. Many medications used to treat Lyme disease are safe to use during pregnancy.

To avoid exposure to Lyme disease, avoid places that are known to have ticks, such as heavily wooded areas. If you can't avoid these areas, wear long-sleeved shirts, long pants, socks and boots or closed shoes. Keep your head and hair covered with a hat or scarf. Check your hair for ticks; they often attach to the hair or the scalp.

Rubella (German Measles)

Rubella is a viral infection that causes few problems in the nonpregnant woman. It is more serious during pregnancy, especially in the first trimester. There may be no symptoms, or you may have a rash or flulike symptoms; the most common symptom of rubella is a skin rash. Rubella infection in a mother-to-be can increase the rate of miscarriage and cause malformations in the baby, especially heart defects.

One of the blood tests you have at your first or second prenatal visit is a rubella titer. It determines whether you have been vaccinated against rubella or if you previously contracted the disease. Most women have had rubella, but if you haven't, you will be vaccinated after pregnancy to safeguard you in the future.

Sickle-cell Anemia

Sickle-cell anemia occurs when a person's bone marrow makes abnormal red blood cells. It occurs most often in people of African and Mediterranean descent.

Sickle-cell anemia can cause anemia during pregnancy. It can cause abrupt pain in the abdomen or limbs of the pregnant woman, called a *sickle crisis*. (A sickle crisis can happen at any time in a woman's lifetime, not just during pregnancy.) In addition to a painful sickle crisis, the pregnant woman may suffer from infections more frequently and may even have congestive heart failure. Risks to the fetus include a higher incidence of miscarriage and stillbirth.

A relatively new treatment for sickle-cell disease relieves severe pain and is called *hydroxyurea*. It does pose some risk and is not for all sickle-cell sufferers. Because we do not know the long-term effects of the drug, women who are pregnant are advised not to use it.

Toxoplasmosis

Toxoplasmosis is a disease caused by the microbe *toxoplasma gondii*. It is spread by eating infected raw meat, drinking infected raw goat's milk, eating infected raw eggs, eating food that has been contaminated by insects or by contact with an infected cat or its feces. You can pick up the protozoa from the cat's litter box, from counters or other surfaces the cat walks on or from the cat itself when you pet it.

Infection in the mother-to-be during pregnancy can lead to miscarriage or an infected infant at birth. Usually an infection in a pregnant women has no symptoms. An infected baby may appear normal at birth. Between 80 and 90% develop serious eye infections months to years later. Some lose hearing, suffer from mental retardation, experience seizures or have learning disabilities. Babies whose mothers had toxoplasmosis in the first trimester are usually the most severely affected. About 1 in 1000 babies is born with toxoplasmosis.

To prevent transmission of the microorganism, cook foods thoroughly and use hygienic measures in the kitchen. Get someone else to change the kitty litter. Keep cats off counters, tables and other areas where you could pick up the microbe. Wash your hands thoroughly after every contact with your cat, and don't nuzzle or kiss it.

⁓ Varicella

Herpes is a family of viruses that includes the herpes-simplex virus, herpes varicella-zoster virus and cytomegalovirus. The word *varicella* is used interchangeably with chicken pox. (It is also used to describe the rash seen with chicken pox.) The term *herpes zoster* is used interchangeably with shingles.

When adults get chicken pox, they can become very ill. The most serious times for you to get chicken pox are during the first trimester or around the time of delivery. The baby can get the virus during delivery, which can cause a serious infection.

Shingles occurs mainly in adults whose immune systems are compromised. During pregnancy, shingles can be a severe illness, with sharp pain and even breathing problems. Fortunately, it rarely occurs then. Exposure during the first trimester, when major organs are developing in the fetus, can cause defects, such as heart problems.

Allergies

Allergy sufferers may notice their allergies change with pregnancy. They may improve or get worse. If you have allergies, drink plenty of fluid, especially during hot weather.

You may have to treat your allergy problems differently during pregnancy. Before taking any medication, ask your doctor or pharmacist whether it's safe to take during pregnancy; don't presume it's OK to take it. Asking before you use it is easier than fixing a problem it may cause later.

✍ Nasal Congestion

Some women complain of nasal stuffiness during pregnancy. We believe this occurs because of circulation changes and hormonal changes in pregnancy that can cause mucous membranes of the nose and nasal passages to swell and to bleed more easily.

Do not use decongestants or nasal sprays to relieve stuffiness without first checking with your healthcare provider. Many preparations are combinations of several medications that should not be used during pregnancy. Use a humidifier instead. Increase your fluid intake and use a gentle lubricant, such as petroleum jelly, in nasal passages. Discuss the problem with your healthcare provider if these remedies don't provide relief.

Anemia

Anemia is a common medical problem in pregnant women. Women who are anemic don't have enough hemoglobin in their blood. Hemoglobin, the iron-containing pigment of red blood cells, is important because it carries life-sustaining oxygen to all the body's cells.

If you suffer from anemia, you won't feel well during pregnancy. You'll tire more easily. You may become dizzy. If you're anemic during labor, you may need a blood transfusion after your baby is born. Pregnancy anemia increases the risk of preterm delivery, growth retardation in the baby and low fetal birth weight.

Anemia is a serious but preventable condition during pregnancy. If you are anemic, your doctor can prescribe a course of treatment to deal with the problem.

✍ Pregnancy Anemia

Iron-deficiency anemia is caused or aggravated by the fetus' demands on your iron stores. While you are pregnant, your baby uses some of the iron stored in your body. Your body makes red blood cells but not enough of them, and you become iron deficient.

Several factors can cause iron-deficiency anemia. These include:

• bleeding during pregnancy
• multiple fetuses
• recent surgery on your stomach or small bowel
• frequent antacid use
• poor dietary habits

Iron-deficiency anemia is easy to control; iron is contained in most prenatal vitamins. If you can't take a prenatal vitamin, you may be given iron supplementation. Eating foods high in iron, such as liver or spinach, also helps.

Blood-sugar Problems

Pregnancy affects your blood-sugar levels; high blood sugar (hyperglycemia) or low blood sugar (hypoglycemia) can make you feel dizzy or faint. Many doctors routinely test pregnant women for blood-sugar imbalances during pregnancy. A blood-sugar problem caused by diet can be avoided or improved by eating balanced snacks and meals, by not skipping meals and by not going too long without eating.

Diabetes is a much more serious blood-sugar condition. Doctors diagnose diabetes through a blood test called a *fasting blood-sugar* or *glucose-tolerance test.* If you are diagnosed with diabetes, you may be able to control it through dietary changes. A dietitian can help you. If diet changes alone aren't enough, you may need insulin, which helps the body process sugars. Your healthcare provider or another specialist, usually an internist, prescribes this drug. Also see the discussion of gestational diabetes that begins on page 239.

Environmental Poisons

Be aware of your environment's effect on your health and that of your baby. Environmental poisons and pollutants that can harm a developing fetus include lead, mercury, PCBs (polychlorinated biphenyls) and pesticides.

Exposure to lead increases the chance of miscarriage. Lead is readily transported across the placenta to the baby; toxicity occurs as early as the twelfth week of pregnancy. Lead exposure may come from many sources, including some gasoline (now regulated in the United States and some other countries), water pipes, solders, storage batteries, some construction materials, paints, dyes and wood preservatives. Workplace exposure is possible; find out if you are at risk.

Reports of mercury exposure have been linked to cerebral palsy and microcephaly. Exposure occurs with ingestion of contaminated fish; one report linked contaminated grain to mercury poisoning.

PCBs are mixtures of several chemical compounds used for industrial purposes. Most fish, birds and humans have small, measurable amounts of PCBs in their tissues. Humans are typically exposed through some of the foods we eat, such as fish. PCBs have been blamed for miscarriage and fetal-growth retardation.

Exposure to pesticides during pregnancy has been held responsible for an increase in miscarriage rates and fetal growth retardation. Pesticides include a large number of agents. Human exposure is common because of the extensive use of pesticides; those of most concern include DDT, chlordane, heptachlor and lindane. It's a good idea to stop using pesticides in your home and around your work area during pregnancy.

You may not be able to eliminate all contact with pesticides. To protect yourself against these agents, avoid exposure when possible. Thoroughly wash all fruits and vegetables before eating them. If you know you will be around certain chemicals, wash your hands thoroughly after exposure.

Hypotension

It is normal for your blood pressure to change somewhat during pregnancy. It often decreases slightly during the second trimester and increases toward the end of pregnancy.

Hypotension (low blood pressure) during pregnancy can cause dizziness. The problem usually occurs during the second trimester for two reasons. First, an enlarging uterus puts pressure on the aorta and vena cava, major vessels leading away from and into the heart. Supine hypotension, a related condition, occurs when you lie down; it is alleviated or prevented by not sleeping or lying on your back.

Second, rising rapidly from a sitting, kneeling or squatting position causes postural hypotension. Your blood pressure drops when you get up rapidly, and gravity pulls blood toward your feet and away from your brain, making you lightheaded. You can avoid postural hypotension by rising slowly from a sitting or a recumbent position.

Incompetent Cervix

An incompetent cervix describes a condition in which a woman's cervix dilates (stretches) prematurely. Usually the woman doesn't notice it. Membranes may rupture without warning, and the baby is usually delivered prematurely.

The problem is not usually diagnosed until after one or more deliveries of a premature infant without any pain before delivery. If it's your first pregnancy, you cannot know if you have an incompetent cervix.

Some researchers believe the condition occurs because of previous trauma to the cervix, such as a miscarriage. It may occur if surgery has been performed on the cervix.

Treatment is usually surgical. A weak cervix can be reinforced by sewing the cervix shut, called a *cerclage*. At the end of the pregnancy or when the woman goes into labor, the surgical stitch is removed and the baby is born normally.

Rh-Compatibility

If you have Rh-negative blood, you may require additional attention during pregnancy and after your baby is born. Your blood type contains a factor that determines if it is positive or negative. When you are "Rh-negative," your blood contains the negative factor. Fifteen percent of all women have Rh-negative blood.

In the past, an Rh-negative woman who carried an Rh-positive baby faced complications in pregnancy that could result in a very sick newborn. Today, many of these problems can be prevented.

❧❧❧❧

When we did lab tests on Linda, we discovered she was Rh-negative. Her mother was Rh-negative and had told Linda stories about pregnancy problems she had had 30 years before. Understandably, Linda was scared. I told Linda that years ago, it *was* a serious problem to be Rh-negative, but it is a problem we have solved. We had checked Linda for Rh-antibodies, and she was negative for them. I told her we would check her again at 28 weeks and would give her RhoGAM®, a blood product, to help ensure that she would not form antibodies during the last part of her pregnancy. If the baby was Rh-positive, we would give her RhoGAM again after the birth. I reassured Linda it wasn't anything to worry about and explained this is one reason we do all the blood tests we do.

❧ How It Occurs

Rh-incompatibility occurs when a fetus inherits Rh-positive blood from its father; the mother, who is Rh-negative, develops antibodies to the fetus' antigens (substances that stimulate the body's immunities against antibodies). Antibodies are made only when the mother has Rh-negative blood and the fetus has Rh-positive blood. These antibodies circulate inside your system. They don't harm you, but they can cross the placenta and attack the blood cells of an Rh-positive fetus. This can lead to serious problems in the fetus, such as anemia; however, it is rare.

If you are Rh-negative, you need to know it. You could become Rh-sensitized, also called *isoimmunized*, under many other circumstances. ("Rh-sensitized" means that your antibodies will recognize and attack your baby's Rh-positive blood.) These circumstances include:

• if you have had a blood transfusion with Rh-positive blood
• if you received blood products of some kind
  ~ during a previous pregnancy
  ~ with a previous ectopic pregnancy
  ~ when a previous pregnancy ended in miscarriage
  ~ with a previous abortion

The problem doesn't usually occur with a first pregnancy. A woman does not develop antibodies until her immune system comes in direct contact with Rh-positive blood. This usually doesn't happen until delivery, when the placenta separates from the uterus.

❧ Treatment

Many problems can be prevented with the use of RhoGAM®, which is Rh-immune globulin. If you are Rh-negative and pregnant, you will be checked for antibodies at the beginning of pregnancy and at 28 weeks. An injection of RhoGAM is given at 28 weeks to prevent sensitization before delivery. It is also administered when you have amniocentesis, a miscarriage, an ectopic pregnancy, an abortion or bleeding during pregnancy.

Sometimes a baby needs a blood transfusion shortly after birth. In severe cases, transfusions are done *before* the baby is born.

RhoGAM is a blood product. If you have religious or ethical reasons for not using blood products, discuss the situation with your minister and your physician.

Some women have expressed concern about the risk of contracting hepatitis or HIV, but no such problems have been reported. Donors for Rh-immune globulin are screened carefully to eliminate those in high-risk groups for transmission of infectious diseases. Immune globulins have not been reported to transmit hepatitis, HIV/AIDS or any other infectious diseases. If you are concerned, talk with your healthcare provider.

If your baby is Rh-positive and you are Rh-negative, you will be given an injection of RhoGAM within 72 hours after delivery. If your baby is Rh-negative, like you, a RhoGAM injection isn't necessary.

Sexually Transmitted Diseases

A sexually transmitted disease can be a serious health problem. Sexually transmitted diseases (STDs) are contracted during sexual activity, whether sexual, oral or anal intercourse. An STD during pregnancy can be even more serious because it can harm a developing fetus. If you have an STD, you must be treated as soon as possible!

Today, the incidence of STDs appears to be on the increase. As many as 1 in 5 Americans is currently infected with an STD. One out of every 20 adults will contract an STD in the next 12 months.

Sexually transmitted diseases are more common in women than in men. A woman is more susceptible to sexually transmitted diseases because her reproductive organs are inside her body, a fertile environment in which infections can grow. This also makes diagnosis in women more difficult than in men.

Left untreated, STDs can harm an unborn baby. Every year, thousands of babies are born early or suffer from infection because of undetected STDs passed to them by their mothers. Effects include early rupture of membranes, miscarriage, stillbirth and preterm birth. Other serious effects include blindness, mental retardation, neurological problems, brain damage and even death. In some cases, effects are not evident until years after birth.

Some STDs are transmitted when the baby comes in contact with the virus during birth. Others are passed to the baby through the mother's blood and infect the baby during pregnancy or birth.

The most common sexually transmitted diseases include monilial vulvovaginitis, trichomonal vaginitis, condyloma acuminatum (venereal warts), genital herpes simplex infection, chlamydia, gonorrhea, syphilis and HIV/AIDS.

Some sexually transmitted diseases can be diagnosed and cured during pregnancy. With the exception of AIDS, those that can't be cured usually can be treated successfully. It's important to be tested for an STD if you believe you might have been exposed. Discuss this important subject with your healthcare professional.

Substance Use and Abuse

It's never too early to start thinking about how your every action will affect the baby growing inside you. Substance abuse is never healthy for you, but when you are pregnant, it can also harm your developing baby.

We usually cannot make exact statements about particular substances and their effects on the mother or developing baby. It's easier to identify substances that cause nutritional deficiencies and fetal-growth problems than those that cause birth defects. However, much circumstantial evidence associates substance abuse with fetal problems.

Many substances you normally use without adverse effects can adversely affect a developing fetus. Some substances readily cross the placenta and enter your baby's bloodstream, where they can cause problems. Alcohol, cigarette smoke and drugs are most dangerous for the fetus during the first trimester.

Cigarette Smoking

Cigarette smoke is the most common known harmful exposure in pregnancy, and it can have serious effects on a woman and her developing baby. Do stop smoking before or during pregnancy; fetal and infant mortality rates increase by more than 50% in first-time pregnant women who smoke more than a pack of cigarettes a day.

Tobacco smoke contains harmful substances, including nicotine, carbon monoxide, hydrogen cyanide, tars, resins and some cancer-causing agents. When you inhale cigarette smoke, it crosses the placenta to your baby with all the additional substances, which may harm the fetus.

The problem is so serious that warnings for pregnant women appear on every cigarette package:

SURGEON GENERAL'S WARNING: Smoking by pregnant women may result in fetal injury, premature birth and low birth weight.

Effects of smoking on the fetus. A pregnant woman who smokes reduces a fetus' oxygen supply by as much as half because carbon monoxide in cigarette smoke displaces oxygen in the mother's bloodstream, and toxins in cigarette smoke narrow blood vessels. Smoking can damage the placenta and hinder the baby's growth.

Infants born to mothers who smoke weigh less than other babies, which can cause problems. Increased incidents of reading disorders have been noted in children born to mothers who smoked during pregnancy. Hyperactivity (minimal-brain-dysfunction syndrome) is also more common in children born to women who smoke.

If a woman smokes during pregnancy, the substances she inhales interfere with her body's absorption of vitamins B and C and folic acid, and increase her risk of pregnancy-related complications. Smoking has been associated with specific birth defects, including cleft palate, heart defects and neural-tube defects, such as spina bifida.

Effects of smoking on the pregnant woman. Serious pregnancy complications are more common among pregnant women who smoke than among women who don't. The risk of developing placental abruption increases by 25% in moderate smokers and 65% in heavy smokers. Placenta previa occurs 25% more often in moderate smokers and 90% more often in heavy smokers. (For further information on these problems, see pages 246 and 247.)

Cigarette smoking increases the risk of miscarriage, premature rupture of membranes and fetal death or death of a baby soon after birth. Risk is directly related to the number of cigarettes a woman smokes each day. Risk can increase as much as 35% for a woman who smokes more than a pack of cigarettes a day.

The best thing to do is to quit smoking completely before and during pregnancy. If you can't quit totally, reduce the number of cigarettes you smoke to help reduce the risks.

Effects of secondary smoke. Exposure to secondary smoke increases a nonsmoker's risk of giving birth to a low-birth-weight baby. Researchers have found significant levels of nicotine in the hair of newborns exposed to passive smoke for at least 3 hours a day during pregnancy. Ask your husband, family members, friends and co-workers to stop smoking around you while you are pregnant.

ஃ Alcohol

When you drink, so does your baby—the more you drink, the more your baby "drinks".

Alcohol use by a pregnant woman carries considerable risk to her developing baby. Alcohol inhibits the transport of amino acids and glucose in the placenta. The fetus is especially vulnerable to the effects of alcohol in early pregnancy.

Your developing baby may be harmed by an alcohol level that has little apparent effect on you. A fetus cannot metabolize alcohol as quickly as an adult, so alcohol remains in the fetus's system longer. Moderate use of alcohol has been linked to a greater risk of miscarriage. Studies show that spina bifida is up to 60 times more common in babies exposed to alcohol before birth than in babies that were not exposed to alcohol.

ೂೀೂೀ

Before pregnancy, Ruth drank socially but she hadn't missed alcohol during her pregnancy. She felt that by abstaining from alcohol, she was doing something good for her baby. At a party, she was offered a glass of wine. The pregnancy was going well, and she hadn't had any problems; what would be the harm? She wasn't sure, so she decided to stay with fruit juice.

At her next visit with me, she wanted to know how much alcohol she could drink safely. I supported her in her decision not to drink during her pregnancy at all. I told her that no research has identified a "safe" amount of alcohol to consume during pregnancy. The more we learn, the more it appears that even a little alcohol may be harmful.

The word is spreading about alcohol use during pregnancy. Today in North America, nearly 80% of all pregnant women abstain from alcohol during pregnancy.

Excessive alcohol consumption during pregnancy often results in abnormalities in the baby. However, drinking as little as two drinks a day has been associated with fetal-alcohol effects. Chronic use of alcohol during pregnancy can lead to fetal-alcohol syndrome (FAS), which is characterized by abnormal fetal development.

Fetal-alcohol syndrome. Fetal-alcohol syndrome (FAS) is a collection of problems that affect children born to alcoholic women. The complete syndrome occurs in 1 or 2 of every 1000 births.

FAS is characterized by growth retardation before and after birth. Defects in the heart and limbs, and unusual facial characteristics, such as a short, upturned nose, a flat upper jawbone and "different" eyes, have also been seen in FAS children. These children may have behavioral problems, impaired speech and impaired gross-motor functions. FAS ranks with neural-tube defects and Down syndrome as a major cause of mental retardation in babies.

At this time, we don't know how much alcohol causes FAS, so I advise women that any amount of alcohol is too much. Most studies indicate four or five drinks a day cause FAS, but mild abnormalities have been associated with as little as two drinks a day (1 ounce of alcohol). It's best to avoid alcohol completely while you're pregnant.

Other facts about alcohol use. Taking drugs with alcohol increases the risk of damaging the fetus. Drugs that cause the greatest concern include analgesics, antidepressants and anticonvulsants.

Some researchers believe heavy alcohol consumption by a baby's father before or at the time of conception may also produce FAS in the baby. Alcohol consumption by the father has also been linked to intrauterine-growth retardation.

Be very careful about substances you use that may contain alcohol. Over-the-counter cough medicines and cold remedies often contain alcohol—as much as 25% of the preparation!

❧ Drug Use and Abuse

Drug abuse usually refers to drugs prohibited by law, but it can also include recreational use of legal substances, such as alcohol, caffeine and tobacco. Legal medications, such as benzodiazepine or barbiturates, may also have harmful effects, whether they are used for legitimate or illegal reasons.

Drug use can affect your pregnancy greatly. A woman who abuses drugs may have more pregnancy complications because of her lifestyle. Women who abuse certain substances commonly display nutritional deficiencies; anemia and fetal-growth retardation can occur as a result. A pregnant woman who abuses drugs may increase her risk of pre-eclampsia.

Marijuana. Marijuana contains tetrahydrocannabinol (THC), which crosses the placenta and enters the baby's system. Exposure can cause attention-deficit disorders, memory problems and impaired decision-making ability in children; these problems can appear in a child between 3 and 12 years of age.

Central-nervous-system drugs. Central-nervous-system stimulants, such as amphetamines, are associated with an increase in cardiovascular defects in babies when they are used during pregnancy. These babies frequently show signs of withdrawal, poor feeding, seizures and other problems.

Tranquilizing agents include benzodiazepines (Valium® and Librium®) and newer agents. These drugs are associated with an increase in congenital malformations. Heavy use in pregnancy is associated with infant withdrawal after birth.

Narcotics include morphine, Demerol®, heroin and codeine. Habitual use can lead to physical dependence.

A pregnant woman who uses narcotics is subject to pre-eclampsia, preterm labor, growth problems in the fetus and narcotic withdrawal in a baby following birth. The incidence of sudden-infant-death syndrome (SIDS) is 10 times higher among babies born to mothers who used narcotics during pregnancy than to babies whose mothers did not.

Intravenous drug use is frequently accompanied by health problems, such as AIDS, hepatitis and endocarditis. Any of these problems is considered extremely serious during pregnancy.

❧❧❧❧

One of the most difficult discussions I've had was with Sue. She came to see me for her yearly exam and Pap smear, and she was upset and discouraged. Adam, her 10-year-old pride and joy, was now in the fifth grade. He was having trouble in school and had been diagnosed with attention-deficit disorder. Her pregnancy had seemed to go OK 10 years ago. She hadn't been able to talk about it then, but she said she had continued using cocaine through the first part of her pregnancy. She was now contemplating another pregnancy. Sue realized that although there was nothing she could do now to change her pregnancy with Adam, she would do things differently for this baby.

Mind-altering drugs. Hallucinogens, such as LSD, mescaline, hashish and peyote, are still used by many people. Phencyclidine (PCP, angel dust) falls into this group. PCP is believed to cause abnormal development in human babies, although it has not been definitely proved.

Cocaine and crack. Cocaine use definitely complicates a pregnancy. Often a user consumes the drug over a period of time, such as several days. During this time, the user may eat or drink very little, with serious consequences for a developing fetus.

Among other problems, continual use of cocaine or its stronger form, crack, can affect maternal nutrition and temperature control, which can harm the fetus. Cocaine use has been linked with miscarriage, preterm labor, bleeding complications, placental abruption and congenital defects. A woman who uses cocaine during the first 12 weeks of pregnancy faces an increased risk of miscarriage. Cocaine can damage the developing baby as early as 3 days after conception.

Infants born to mothers who use cocaine during pregnancy often have long-term mental deficiencies. Sudden-infant-death syndrome (SIDS) is more common among these babies. Many babies are stillborn.

Urinary-tract Infections

A urinary-tract infection (UTI) refers to an infection anywhere along the urinary tract, which includes the bladder, the urethra, the ureters and the kidneys. Your doctor usually does a urinalysis and a urine culture for UTIs at your first visit. He or she may also check your urine for infections on subsequent visits.

UTIs are common during pregnancy because of the changes in a woman's urinary tract and increased pressure on the area. The uterus sits directly on top of the bladder and on the tubes, called *ureters,* that lead from the kidneys to the bladder. An enlarging uterus puts increasing pressure on the bladder and ureters.

Symptoms of a bladder infection include frequent or burning urination, blood in the urine (if the infection is severe) or the urge to urinate, though nothing comes out.

Pyelonephritis is an infection of the urinary tract that also involves the kidneys; it occurs in 1 to 2% of all pregnant women. Symptoms of pyelonephritis include many of those associated with a bladder infection. The infection may require hospitalization and treatment with intravenous antibiotics.

Kidney stones occur about once in every 1500 pregnancies. Symptoms usually include severe back pain and blood in the urine. In pregnancy, ultrasound is usually used to diagnose a kidney stone. A kidney stone in pregnancy is usually treated with pain medication and by drinking lots of fluid or receiving I.V.s to hydrate you so you can pass the stone.

Genetic Counseling May Be Recommended

If you are older than 35, your doctor may recommend genetic counseling for you and your partner. This is different from your medical history. With genetic counseling, your healthcare provider interprets information gathered from interviews, tests and health histories.

Genetic counseling seldom provides exact information. Instead, information is described in terms of percentages and odds. Most genetic counselors will not tell you what to do; they provide you with information and support so you can make your own decision.

Genetic counseling can help you understand your current situation, its diagnosis and prognosis. It can help you in family planning and provide support to your family. Counselors can help you explore options for now and the future.

Genetic counseling is advised in a number of situations. It is usually recommended:

- if there is a family history of birth defects, mental retardation, chromosome abnormality or neurologic disorders
- when the woman is 35 or older at the time of birth
- if a woman has had three or more miscarriages
- when a woman has been exposed to teratogens (environmental factors harmful to the fetus)
- with consanguinity (couple is related)
- for high-risk ethnic groups

Genetic counseling is complicated and requires input from several different healthcare professionals. These professionals can include a medical geneticist, genetic counselor, social worker, psychologist or psychiatrist, laboratory specialists, clergy, parent groups and others.

It's critical that you and your partner feel free to ask your genetic counselor questions about the information you are given. This person can help you use all the resources available and help you understand what is involved in making important decisions.

As information is gathered, it may be necessary to share it with other members of your family. If a gene abnormality is identified, your sister, for example, will probably want to know about it before she starts her own family.

◆ Incidence of Genetic Disease

The hoped-for and anticipated outcome for every pregnant couple and their healthcare provider is a normal, healthy infant. It is expected and taken for granted. However, that is not always the case—about 1% of all babies born have a chromosomal abnormality; 4 to 7% of perinatal deaths (death after birth) are attributed to chromosome problems. Almost half of all first-trimester miscarriages are caused by some type of chromosomal abnormality.

Among newborns, 3 to 5% are born with a major congenital malformation, such as a heart defect; many of these birth defects are found to have a genetic component. In the U.S., this represents more than 250,000 children each year.

Mental retardation is another area of concern; about 3% of the general population is mentally retarded. It is estimated that 70% of mental retardation is caused by genetic problems. Genetic counseling can offer an indication that some of these cases might occur.

⅋ Basic Genetics

Human cells contain 46 chromosomes each (diploid number); each sperm and each egg contain 23 chromosomes (haploid number). Chromosomes are composed of DNA and proteins that contain genes. Each cell contains 23 pairs of chromosomes—one chromosome of each pair is inherited from each parent.

Of the 23 pairs, 22 are autosomes (non-sex chromosomes), and one pair is the sex chromosomes, X and Y. In a normal woman, the sex chromosomes are represented by two X (XX) chromosomes, and in the normal man by X and Y (XY) chromosomes.

Blood cells are usually used for chromosome analysis. Chromosomes are viewed through a microscope, then photographed and enlarged. They are then arranged in pairs, called a *karyotype;* a karyotype is used to identify abnormalities in the number of chromosomes.

With recent advances, individual chromosomes can also be examined for abnormalities. We have learned that too much chromosome material or too little chromosome material can cause an abnormality.

Preconception Counseling

In the past, genetic counseling was offered only after the birth of a child with a defect. With increased awareness and advances in technology, today we can provide couples with information before conception. The three major areas we focus on to provide a couple with information before they conceive include reproductive history, family history and consanguinity (you and your partner are related).

✣ Reproductive History

When a genetic counselor asks questions about your reproductive history, he or she seeks information on any type of pregnancy loss, miscarriage, stillbirth or perinatal death (death of the baby at the end of pregnancy or after birth). Other important information can include fertility problems, the type and duration of contraception and environmental exposures (as from your job). The information is evaluated so recommendations can be made.

✣ Family History

Your family history can be important in determining a high-risk situation. Information essential to your genetic counselor includes a description of the health status of you, your partner and siblings, cause of death of any relatives, the age at death of these relatives and any birth defects in relatives. Your family history helps identify abnormalities that occurred in the past in those related to you and helps predict the likelihood of these defects occurring with your child.

Ethnic background can be an important aspect of family history. For example, if both partners are of Ashkenazi Jewish descent, there is an increased risk of giving birth to a baby with Tay-Sachs disease. Some people of African and Mediterranean descent are at an increased risk for having a baby with sickle-cell anemia.

If you are unsure of all the information a family history requires, ask your parents and other family members for help. By working together, you will be able to provide the data necessary for the most thorough evaluation.

✣ Consanguinity

Consanguinity (being related by birth to your partner, such as a cousin) can create problems. A related couple may have a very high risk of having a child with a genetic birth defect, especially if there is a family history of genetic defects. (First cousins have one-sixteenth of their genes in common.) If you are related to your partner, be sure to advise your genetic-counseling team of the fact.

✤ Prenatal Diagnosis

A couple should consider prenatal diagnosis in a variety of situations. These include:

• the mother is older than 35 at the time of delivery
• a couple has previously given birth to a child with a chromosome abnormality
• a family history of chromosomal abnormalities
• one parent has a chromosomal abnomormality
• the mother is a carrier of a sex-chromosome disorder
• either parent is a carrier of a chromosomal disorder
• there is a family history of neural-tube defects (such as spina bifida)

Amniocentesis, ultrasound, chorionic villus sampling, fetoscopy and X-ray are all techniques that help identify chromosomal abnormalities. The tests are discussed in chapter 9.

✤ How Prenatal Diagnosis Can Help You

Prenatal testing does not guarantee the birth of a normal baby. It only provides information about malformations or disorders that can be specifically tested for. Some malformations cannot be found or are difficult to find before a baby is born, such as phenylketonuria, cleft lip and cleft palate.

Testing for a fetal abnormality allows for termination of a pregnancy, if that is desired. Sometimes a prenatal diagnosis may call for prenatal surgery in utero (in the uterus) to correct various conditions, such as kidney blockage or omphalocele (congenital hernia of the navel).

Results learned from prenatal genetic counseling can be used to make special arrangements for care of the baby, if necessary, after it is born. Results may also influence which method of delivery is chosen.

Counseling and support of the couple or family can help prepare them for what lies ahead after the baby's birth. This support can include social services, mental-health counseling (psychiatrist, psychologist, social worker) and spiritual guidance.

For some couples, prenatal genetic counseling is the beginning of the grieving process over the loss of the "perfect baby." Counseling can help a couple begin to deal with the possible death of the fetus or baby, or the challenges associated with a child with special needs.

Postconception Counseling

Counseling may be provided to a couple after the couple achieves pregnancy or after their baby is born. Some couples expecting a child have a specific reason for a prenatal diagnosis, as in the case of an older mother. In this situation, diagnostic testing is done during pregnancy.

When a couple gives birth to a child with a birth defect or a genetic disorder, genetic testing of the couple may be recommended after the birth, especially if they desire more children. Testing may alert the couple to problems that could arise in subsequent pregnancies.

☞ Postnatal Diagnosis

Most infants with problems are identified at birth or shortly afterward. Babies born with genetic malformations or birth defects are usually grouped in one of three categories:

- babies with obvious malformations at the time of birth
- babies who are "sick" or have a difficult time immediately after birth
- babies who appear normal at birth but develop abnormalities later

An important goal with postnatal diagnosis is an accurate diagnosis. Sources of information that are helpful in making a diagnosis include family history, laboratory results, physical exam, pregnancy history (including medications, complications and environmental exposures), growth and development history during the pregnancy and after the birth, and photographs of the baby.

The information can provide guidance about what lies ahead and various treatments that might be available. Genetic counseling after a baby is born with a birth defect is most helpful in answering the question, "What are the chances of it happening again?"

If the risk of recurrence of a problem is low, some families choose to have more children. If the risk is high or if prenatal diagnosis is not available, a couple may decide not to have children or to choose sterilization.

In some cases, a couple may opt for donor insemination, if that might prevent a recurrence of a problem. This choice isn't for every couple. Donor insemination uses donor sperm to achieve pregnancy. The partner's sperm is not used if he has a chromosome disorder or is a carrier of a chromosome disorder.

Your Medical History

To give you and your baby the best care possible, your doctor will ask you for a lot of information at your first prenatal visit. You can help your doctor a great deal by gathering the information before you meet.

⅋ DES Use by Pregnant Woman's Mother

In the 1940s and 50s, a non-steroidal synthetic estrogen, diethylstilbestrol (DES), was given to some women to prevent miscarriage. The compound was even included in some prenatal vitamins. Research proved later that DES caused problems in some of the female offspring of women who used it. Daughters born to women given DES during the first trimester of their pregnancies have higher rates of vaginal cancer.

DES has been shown to cause other problems for female offspring, including an increased risk of miscarriage and premature labor when the women become pregnant. A higher rate of ectopic pregnancy is blamed on DES-related Fallopian-tube deformities and uterine deformities. DES affects uterine-muscle development, resulting in an abnormally shaped uterus.

Because DES was prescribed in the 1940s and 50s, most affected women have passed through their years of conception. However, as an older pregnant woman, it could be significant for you. Ask your mother if she knows if she received DES while she was pregnant with you. If you were exposed to DES through your mother's use of the drug, some researchers recommend prenatal counseling before pregnancy about the risks of miscarriage, premature delivery and ectopic pregnancy.

Preparing Your Medical History

Check family records, and ask family members if anyone in the family has suffered from problems listed on pages 90 and 91. Be sure your partner does the same with his family. This information may help your doctor address potential problems.

❧❧❧❧

Ella didn't fill out all of the forms at her first office visit; she left the family-history portion blank. She said she didn't realize it mattered. We discussed how her family history could affect her and her pregnancy. The next month, she told me she had spoken to her mother, and there was a family history of diabetes and twins, both important pieces of information for her pregnancy.

Medical History Chart

Directions: If a problem applies to you, your partner or another family member, make a check in the appropriate column.

Problem	You	Partner	Family
AIDS/HIV	☐	☐	☐
Alcohol abuse	☐	☐	☐
Allergies	☐	☐	☐
Anemia	☐	☐	☐
Cancer	☐	☐	☐
Cleft lip/palate	☐	☐	☐
Cystic fibrosis	☐	☐	☐
DES use by pregnant woman's mother	☐	☐	☐
Diabetes	☐	☐	☐
Down syndrome	☐	☐	☐
Drug abuse	☐	☐	☐
Epilepsy	☐	☐	☐
GBS infections	☐	☐	☐
Genital herpes	☐	☐	☐

Problem	You	Partner	Family
Heart disease	☐	☐	☐
Hemophilia	☐	☐	☐
Huntington's disease	☐	☐	☐
Hypertension	☐	☐	☐
Miscarriage	☐	☐	☐
Multiple pregnancies	☐	☐	☐
Muscular dystrophy	☐	☐	☐
Rubella (German measles)	☐	☐	☐
Sexually transmitted diseases	☐	☐	☐
Sickle-cell anemia	☐	☐	☐
Spina bifida	☐	☐	☐
Systemic lupus erythematosus	☐	☐	☐
Tay-Sachs disease	☐	☐	☐
Thyroid disease	☐	☐	☐
Urinary-tract infections	☐	☐	☐

Chapter 7

How Your Body Changes during Pregnancy

Pregnancy is exciting, and it may be a little unsettling, too. You will see yourself change—your abdomen will grow, your breasts will enlarge, and hands and feet may swell, among other changes. If you are aware of these changes before they occur, you may be more comfortable with the situation.

During the first trimester, you may notice little change in yourself, although your baby is growing and changing quite rapidly. You may not even realize you are pregnant until the middle or close to the end of this trimester. You gain little weight—probably no more than 5 pounds for the entire 13 weeks. Your abdomen grows a little; you may be able to feel your uterus about 3 inches below your bellybutton. You won't feel the fetus move during this time.

During the second trimester, others begin to notice you are pregnant. At the beginning of the second trimester, you will be able to feel your uterus about 3 inches below your bellybutton. By the end of the second trimester, you'll feel your uterus about 3 inches above your bellybutton. Average weight gain at the end of this trimester is 17 to 24 pounds (including weight gained in the first trimester). During this time you will begin to feel your baby move!

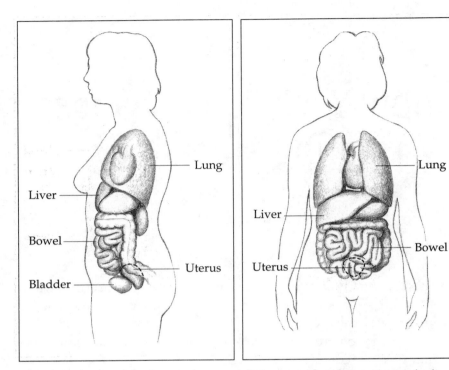

During the first trimester of pregnancy, you will notice very few changes in your body.

The greatest change during the third trimester is the growth of your baby. By delivery, you'll be able to feel the uterus 6-1/2 to 8 inches above your bellybutton. Your baby gains a great deal of weight during this time, although you may not. The average total weight gain for a normal-weight woman by delivery is between 25 and 35 pounds.

Your abdominal muscles are stretched and pushed apart as your baby grows. Muscles attached to the lower portion of your ribs may separate in the midline, called a *diastasis recti*. The condition isn't painful and does not harm the baby. Diastasis recti may still be present after the birth of your baby, but the separation won't be as noticeable. Exercising can strengthen the muscles, but a small bulge or gap may remain.

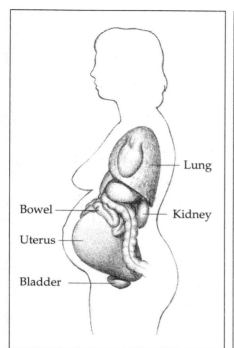 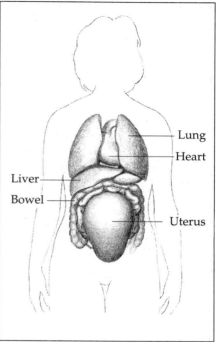

Your body undergoes fantastic changes later in pregnancy. Close to delivery, your uterus takes up a great deal of room and "rearranges" various organs.

Skin Changes

Most women experience some changes in their skin while pregnant. Some women find their skin becomes less oily and softer. Other women develop acne. Skin changes of this type are due to the hormones of pregnancy; skin usually returns to normal after your baby is born.

Many patients tell me they believe their skin becomes more alive and glowing while they are pregnant. While there is no medical fact to back this belief, I have seen women who do seem to "glow" during pregnancy.

❧ Surface Skin Changes

In some women, a vertical line appears along the midline of the abdomen, called the *linea nigra*. The linea nigra fades markedly after pregnancy but does not usually fully disappear.

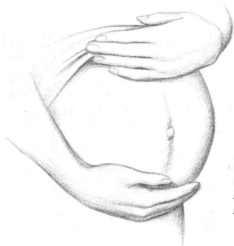

The linea nigra is a vertical line that appears along the abdominal midline in some pregnant women.

Occasionally irregular brown patches appear on the face and neck of a pregnant woman, called *chloasma* or *mask of pregnancy*. We believe this change is caused by the hormonal changes of pregnancy. Usually dark patches disappear completely or get lighter after your baby is born. (Oral contraceptives can cause similar pigmentation changes.)

During pregnancy, you may develop small red elevations with branches extending outward on your skin. These changes are called *vascular spiders*, *telangiectasias* or *angiomas*. They usually occur on the face, neck, upper chest and arms. After pregnancy they will fade, but may not disappear completely.

The palms of your hands may turn red during your pregnancy. The condition is called *palmar erythema* and is fairly common. Palmar erythema is probably caused by increased estrogen and has no other symptoms. It's fine to use lotions on your hands, but the redness may not disappear until after delivery. Vascular spiders and red palms often occur together.

⁕ Moles

Pregnancy can cause moles to appear for the first time or cause existing moles to grow larger and darken. If a mole changes, have a doctor check it.

✿ Itching Skin

Itching, also called *pruritis gravidarum,* is a common problem occurring later in pregnancy. About 20% of all pregnant women suffer from it. The itching is harmless but can be annoying. As your uterus grows and fills your pelvis, abdominal skin and muscles stretch to accommodate it. Stretching the skin can cause itching.

Scratching can make itching worse. Use lotions to help reduce itching; occasionally cortisone creams may be advisable. Discuss it with your healthcare provider if it continues to trouble you.

✿ Stretch Marks

Stretch marks, also called *striae distensae,* are areas of stretched skin that may become discolored. Marks usually occur as your uterus grows larger and stretches abdominal skin. They can also occur on the breasts, hips or buttocks.

Stretch marks usually fade and aren't as noticeable after your pregnancy, but they don't disappear completely. To date, no one has found a reliable way of avoiding stretch marks. Women have tried many kinds of lotions with little success. There is certainly no harm in using lotion products, but they probably won't help.

Cream and lotion can help soothe irritated skin, especially on the abdomen.

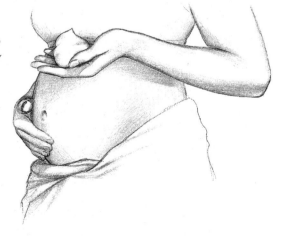

Dental Care

Be sure to have regular dental checkups and take very good care of your teeth during pregnancy. Good dental care at this time is important because the hormonal changes of pregnancy may cause dental problems.

If possible, avoid dental X-rays while you are pregnant. If you must have one, be sure your abdomen and pelvis are completely shielded by a lead apron. Tell your dentist you are pregnant when you check in at the office.

Pregnancy may cause sore, bleeding, swollen gums. Gums are more susceptible to irritation during pregnancy and may bleed more often when you brush your teeth. The condition usually clears up by itself after the baby is born. Talk to your dentist if the problem becomes uncomfortable.

You may develop small nodules on your gums that bleed when you brush your teeth or eat. This condition is called a *pyogenic granuloma* or *pregnancy tumor*. It usually clears up after pregnancy, but don't ignore it if it causes you problems.

Emotional Changes

Crying easily, mood swings, energy lows and fatigue can be normal aspects of pregnancy. During the first trimester of pregnancy, hormone production increases to support your body's pregnancy needs. Some women are more sensitive to these changes, especially those who are sensitive to similar hormonal shifts before menstruation. If you become weepy or edgy around your menstrual period, you may experience similar emotions as your body adjusts to pregnancy. Let your partner and other family members know that you may experience these mood swings.

Antidepressant medication is not usually prescribed during pregnancy because it is not considered safe. However, if it is necessary, most physicians prefer to use tricyclic antidepressants such as amitriptyline and desipramine. Treatment is always individualized to the patient. Your doctor and possibly a psychiatrist or psychologist will discuss the situation with you.

You may feel more emotional in your third trimester. Mood swings may occur more frequently, and you may be more irritable. You may be feeling anxious about the upcoming labor and delivery. Relax and let go of your feelings. Talk to your partner about how you are feeling and what you are experiencing, and ask for his help and understanding. This may be a good time to practice relaxation exercises (see page 21).

Feeling Your Baby Move

One of the greatest joys of pregnancy is feeling your baby move inside you. It's a positive sign! The first time you feel your baby move is different for every woman. It can be different from one pregnancy to another.

❧ When You First Feel Your Baby Move

Many women describe the first feelings of fetal movement as a gas bubble or fluttering in their abdomen. It may be something you notice for a few days before you realize what it is. Movements become more common and occur fairly frequently—that's how you'll know that what you're feeling is your baby moving. Movement can be felt below your bellybutton. If it's your first baby, it may be 19 or 20 weeks before you are sure you feel the baby move.

At first you probably won't feel your baby move every day; that's normal. As your baby grows, movements become stronger and probably more regular.

❧ Babies' Movements Are Different

The movement of every baby is different. One baby will move less than another. If your baby has been very active, then is very quiet for a long while, you may want to discuss it with your doctor. He or she will determine if there is cause for concern.

Some women complain their baby is extremely active during the night, and it keeps them awake. There really isn't much you can do about it, but you can try changing your position in bed.

Avoid exercising just before bed—it may cause your baby to move more. Taking acetaminophen or relaxing in a warm (not hot) bath may help. Between 20 and 32 weeks of pregnancy, the fetus can move between 200 and 500 times a day, kicking, rolling or wiggling!

ജ്യഞ്ജ

> When Veronica came in for her 28-week visit, she was tired and concerned. She had been up all night because the baby was kicking her. She wanted to know if this was OK. Was it a bad sign about the baby? Could it be moving too much? I reassured her that this wasn't bad and told her that I'd rather have a baby move a lot than not enough.

Occasionally you might feel pain or pressure from your baby's position in the uterus. For relief, rest on your opposite side for a while. For example, if you feel pressure under your right ribs, lie on your left side.

I've had women ask if some of the pressure they feel low in the uterus means the baby is falling out of the birth canal. Your baby can't "fall out" of the birth canal. If you experience this sensation, what you are probably feeling is the pressure of your baby as it moves lower in the birth canal. If this occurs, tell your doctor about it. He or she may want to do a pelvic exam to check how low the baby's head is.

A doctor may ask a pregnant woman to monitor the baby's movements if she has had a difficult pregnancy, if she had a previous stillbirth or if she has a medical condition, such as diabetes. Recording the movements at certain times each day may provide the doctor with additional information about the baby's status.

Some Discomforts of Pregnancy

Along with the many joys of pregnancy, there are some discomforts. Most of the them are minor (although it may not seem that way at the time!). At the beginning of pregnancy, you may have the urge to urinate frequently. As you progress through pregnancy, you may have to deal with constipation. Toward the end of pregnancy, swollen hands and feet may be a problem, along with more frequent heartburn. Let's look at some of these common complaints and see what you can do to relieve them.

✖ Uterine Tightening

Your uterus tightens and contracts throughout pregnancy. (If you don't feel this, don't worry.) As your uterus grows, you may feel slight cramping or even pain in the lower abdominal area, on your sides; this is normal. However, if contractions are accompanied by bleeding from the vagina, *call your healthcare provider immediately.*

Braxton-Hicks contractions during pregnancy are painless, nonrhythmical contractions you may feel when you place your hands on your abdomen. You may also feel them in the uterus itself. These contractions may begin early in pregnancy and are felt at irregular intervals throughout pregnancy. They are *not* signs of true labor.

Some women experience tingling, numbness or pressure in the uterine area or abdomen. These feelings are associated with increased pressure as the baby moves lower in the birth canal. To help decrease pressure in your pelvic area, lie on your left side. This position helps relieve pressure on pelvic nerves, veins and arteries.

✖ Round-ligament Pain

Round ligaments lie on either side of the uterus; as your uterus gets bigger, these ligaments stretch, becoming longer and thicker. Quick movements can overstretch the ligaments, causing round-ligament pain. This is not harmful to you or your baby, but it can be uncomfortable.

Be careful about making quick movements. If you feel pain, lie down and rest. Most doctors recommend acetaminophen (Tylenol®) if the pain bothers you. Tell your doctor if it gets worse.

❧ Urinary Discomfort

One of the first symptoms of early pregnancy is frequent urination. The problem continues off and on throughout pregnancy; you may have to go to the bathroom at night when you never did before. It usually lessens during the second trimester, then returns during the third trimester, when the growing baby puts pressure on the bladder.

Some women experience urinary-tract infections during pregnancy; they are also called *bladder infections, cystitis* and *UTIs*. See the discussion of urinary problems beginning on page 82.

You'll do yourself a favor by not "holding" your urine. Empty your bladder as soon as you feel the need. Drink plenty of fluids; cranberry juice helps kills bacteria and may help you avoid infections. For some women, urinating after having intercourse is helpful.

During pregnancy, urinary-tract infections may cause premature labor and low-birth-weight infants. If you think you have an infection, discuss it with your healthcare provider. If you do, take the entire course of antibiotics prescribed for you.

❧ Increased Vaginal Discharge

It's normal to notice an increase in vaginal discharge or vaginal secretion during pregnancy. It is called *leukorrhea.* The discharge is usually white or yellow and fairly thick; it is not an infection. We believe the discharge is caused by the increased blood flow to the skin and muscles around the vagina.

Do not douche if you have a heavy vaginal discharge during pregnancy. Wear sanitary pads if necessary. Avoid wearing pantyhose and nylon underwear—choose underwear with a cotton lining.

The discharge that accompanies a vaginal infection is often foul-smelling, has a greenish or yellowish color, and causes itching or irritation around or inside the vagina. If you have these symptoms, notify your healthcare provider. Treatment is often possible; many medicinal creams and ointments are safe to use during pregnancy.

Other Changes

Changes in your hair are often triggered by pregnancy hormones circulating through your body. You may notice less hair loss than usual. After your baby is born, the hair you retained during pregnancy falls out. If it happens to you, don't worry about it—you're not going bald!

The same hormones that encourage the growth of your hair also influence your nails. You may find during pregnancy that you have problems keeping your nails filed to a practical length. Enjoy them!

Some women find they experience increased facial hair during pregnancy. Usually it's not a problem, but check with your healthcare provider if it worries you. Facial hair will probably disappear or decrease after pregnancy, so wait before making any decisions about permanent hair removal.

Pregnancy hormones can elevate your body temperature slightly, which may lead to greater perspiration. If you perspire heavily, keep up your fluids to avoid dehydration.

✣ Breast Changes

Your breasts undergo many changes during pregnancy. After about 8 weeks, breasts normally start getting larger; you may notice they are lumpy or nodular. Tenderness, tingling and breast soreness early in pregnancy are common. These are all normal changes at this time.

Your breasts may change color slightly. Before pregnancy, the areola (the area surrounding the nipple) is usually pink, but it can turn brown or red-brown and may enlarge during pregnancy and lactation.

During the second trimester, a thin yellow fluid called *colostrum* is formed; it is the precursor to breast milk. Sometimes it leaks from the breasts or can be expressed by squeezing the nipples. This is normal. Leave your breasts alone; don't express the fluid.

๛ Inverted Nipples

Some women have inverted nipples, which are flat or retract (invert) into the breast. Women with inverted nipples may find it more difficult to breastfeed, but breast feeding is not impossible.

To determine if you have inverted nipples, place your thumb and index finger on the areola, the dark area surrounding the nipple. Gently compress the base of the nipple; if it flattens or retracts into the breast, you have inverted nipples.

Plastic breast shells worn under your bra during the last few weeks of pregnancy create a slight pressure at the base of the nipple that helps draw out the nipple. Ask your healthcare provider for further information.

๛ Lightening

Often a few weeks before labor begins or at the beginning of labor, the head of your baby begins to enter the birth canal, and your uterus seems to "drop" a bit. This is called *lightening*. Don't be concerned if it happens to you.

A benefit of lightening is it allows you more room to breathe. However, as your baby descends into the birth canal, you may notice more pressure in your pelvis, bladder and rectum, which can be uncomfortable.

๛ When Your Doctor Measures Your Abdomen

As you progress in your pregnancy, your doctor needs a point of reference from which to measure the growth of your uterus. Some doctors measure from the bellybutton. Some measure from the pubis symphysis, the place where pubic bones meet in the middle-lower part of your abdomen.

These measurements can reveal a great deal. A higher-than-expected measurement at 20 weeks, for example, may alert your doctor to the possibility of twins or an incorrect due date. A lower-than-expected measurement at this point may mean your due date is wrong or that there may be some other problem. In either case, your doctor would probably have you evaluated further by ultrasound.

Chapter 8

How Your Baby Grows and Develops

During the time your baby grows inside your uterus, it goes through the most incredible changes of its life. From a few small cells, it grows into a fully developed baby.

The first 13 weeks of pregnancy represents the most critical period of development for the fetus. During this time, the fetus is most susceptible to effects from outside influences, such as medications you may take or other substances you might ingest or be exposed to.

By the end of the first half of your pregnancy—20 weeks— your baby has developed nearly all of its organs. During the last half of pregnancy, these organs mature, and your baby grows and gains weight, until it is ready to be born.

Your baby goes through an early period of development, called *embryonic development,* which lasts from fertilization through week 8 of fetal development. The *fetal development* period lasts from week 9 of fetal development until your baby is born.

Normal Fetal Development

During the first 8 weeks of pregnancy, your baby is called an *embryo.* During the rest of your pregnancy, the developing baby is referred to as a *fetus.*

❧ Trimesters of Pregnancy

Your pregnancy is divided into 13-week periods called *trimesters*. The first trimester is the one of greatest change for the developing baby. During this time, your baby grows from a collection of cells the size of the head of a pin to a fetus the size of a grapefruit. Organs begin to develop, and your baby begins to look like a baby.

At the beginning of the second trimester, your baby weighs less than an ounce (25g) and is only about 4 inches (110cm) long. By the beginning of the third trimester, he or she is almost 16 inches (34cm) long and weighs more than 2 pounds (1000g). At delivery, your baby will weigh close to 7-1/2 pounds (3400g) and be about 21-1/2 inches (48cm) long.

Very few, if any, structures in the fetus are formed after the twelfth week of pregnancy. This means your baby has formed all of its major organ systems by the end of the first trimester. However, these structures continue to grow until your baby is born.

If a baby is born before the 38th week of pregnancy, it is called a *preterm baby*. A fetus born between the 38th and 42nd week of pregnancy is called a *term baby* or a *full-term infant*. A baby delivered after 42 weeks of pregnancy is called a *postdate baby* (see page 297).

❧ Your Baby's Sex

The sex of the baby is determined at conception. If a sperm carrying a Y chromosome fertilizes the egg, a male child is created. A sperm carrying an X chromosome results in a female child.

❧ The Baby's Size

Sometimes my patients express concern about giving birth to a large baby. Many factors affect how big your baby will be. If you are in good health, have no medical problems and take good care of yourself during pregnancy, you'll probably have an average-size baby. Although weight varies greatly from baby to baby, the average baby at term weighs 7 to 7-1/2 pounds (3280 to 3400g).

ભ્ભ્ભ્ભ

Sally said she weighed 9 pounds at birth, and all her brothers
and sisters were big, too. She was worried that her baby would
be too big, and she would need a C-section. I reassured her
that her pregnancy growth had been normal and told her it
was difficult to estimate the size of the baby. She laughed and
relaxed a little when I told her if 100 doctors tried to guess the
weight of her baby, the guesses would range from 6 to 8
pounds. When she delivered the baby, it weighed 8 pounds
and Sally did fine.

Some factors do affect the size of a baby at birth, including
hypertension and diabetes, which are more common in older
pregnant women. Hypertension during pregnancy causes IUGR
(intrauterine-growth retardation), which results in smaller babies.
Diabetes can influence the development of a larger or smaller
baby. Blood-sugar levels are higher in those with gestational diabetes or mild diabetes that is not controlled. Diabetes exposes the
baby to higher sugar levels, and larger babies are the result. In
cases of insulin-dependent diabetes, the result may be a smaller
baby. Women with insulin-dependent diabetes may have circulation problems, which can result in decreased blood flow to the
baby and IUGR.

ஃ Can a Baby Hear Inside the Womb?

A baby can hear inside the womb. It may be similar to living
near a busy airport—the developing baby hears a constant murmur
of digestive noises and the maternal heartbeat. The fetus hears its
mother's voice, too, but it may not hear higher-pitched tones.

There is evidence that by the third trimester the fetus responds
to the sounds it hears. Researchers have noted fetal heart rate
increases in response to tones heard through the mother's
abdomen.

Newborns have been found to prefer their mother's voice to a
stranger's, which suggests they recognize her voice. They have
also been found to prefer their mother's native language, and they
respond strongly to a recording of an intrauterine heartbeat.

Too much noise may be harmful to an unborn baby. A baby exposed in utero to noise levels between 85 and 95 decibels (common at rock concerts and dance clubs) is three times more likely to suffer from high-frequency hearing loss.

The Fetal Environment

Your baby is growing and developing inside a complex system within your body. There are three major parts to this system, and each relies upon the other to work together as a complete unit. Your baby's first home consists of the placenta, the umbilical cord and the amniotic sac. Together they provide nourishment, warmth and protection while your baby matures and prepares to live on its own, outside your uterus.

৵ The Placenta

The placenta is a soft, round or oval organ that grows with your baby. At 10 weeks, it weighs about 1/2 ounce (12g); by the time your baby is born, it weighs about 1-1/2 pounds (700g).

When the early pregnancy implants in your uterus, the placenta grows and sends blood vessels into the uterine wall. These blood vessels remove nourishment and oxygen from your blood for use by your baby. Your baby's waste products pass back into your bloodstream through these vessels for disposal by your body.

We once believed the placenta acted as a barrier to all outside substances, but we know this is not the case. In some instances, the placenta cannot keep your baby from being exposed to substances that you are exposed to or that you ingest. We know that alcohol, most medications, other substances (such as nicotine) and many vitamins and minerals cross the placenta to your baby. This is one reason women are warned to avoid various substances during pregnancy.

The placenta is important to your pregnancy and remains so until the birth of your baby. At that time, when your uterus begins to shrink after your baby is born, the placenta detaches from it and is delivered on its own.

❧ The Umbilical Cord

The umbilical cord is the connection between your baby and the placenta. It is usually about 24 inches long. The cord is gray or white, coiled or lumpy, and contains two arteries that carry the baby's blood to the placenta, where it absorbs oxygen and nutrients. A vein in the umbilical cord carries blood and nutrients back to the baby.

Occasionally knots form in an umbilical cord, but it is unusual. Doctors believe knots form as the baby moves around early in pregnancy. A loop forms in the umbilical cord, and when the baby moves through the loop, a knot is completed. You can't do anything to prevent it.

You may have heard about saving blood from your baby's umbilical cord for future use. Umbilical-cord blood banking is a fairly new technology that is not available everywhere. Since 1989, cord blood has been used as an alternative to bone-marrow transplants. Cord blood has been used to treat some forms of anemia (such as Fanconi's anemia), Wiskott-Aldrich syndrome, Hunter's syndrome, some forms of leukemia, neuroblastoma and breast cancer. Talk with your doctor about cord-blood banking if you are interested in learning more.

❧ The Amniotic Sac

The amniotic sac is a bag inside your uterus that contains your baby and the amniotic fluid that surrounds it. Early in pregnancy, amniotic fluid comes from the amniotic membrane that covers the placenta and cord. Later in pregnancy, the fluid is mainly composed of fetal urine and fluid excreted by fetal lungs.

As your pregnancy progresses, the amount of amniotic fluid produced increases. This continues until close to the time of delivery, when it begins to decrease.

Amniotic fluid keeps the sac from collapsing and enables the baby to move around so muscles and joints can develop. Fluid regulates temperature and cushions the fetus from injury. It also helps a baby's lungs to mature as fluid passes into and out of fetal lungs when the baby's chest moves in and out.

By 21 weeks, the fetal digestive system has developed enough to enable the fetus to swallow the fluid. The fetus absorbs much of the water contained in the swallowed fluid.

Swallowing amniotic fluid may encourage development of the fetal digestive system. It may condition the digestive system to function after birth. By term, a baby may swallow large amounts of amniotic fluid, as much as 17 ounces (500ml) of amniotic fluid in a 24-hour period.

Amniotic fluid is an important gauge of fetal well-being. If you have amniocentesis, amniotic fluid is removed from your uterus for study. The amount of fluid can also be an indication of fetal health; ultrasound is used to evaluate the amount of fluid in the sac. Too much fluid may indicate a malformation in the spinal cord or digestive system. Too little may signal fetal bladder or kidney problems.

The Presence of Meconium

The term *meconium* refers to undigested debris from swallowed amniotic fluid in the fetal digestive system. Meconium is a greenish-black to light-brown substance that your baby may pass from its bowels into the amniotic fluid. This can happen before or at the time of delivery.

The presence of meconium in amniotic fluid may be caused by fetal distress. When meconium is present, it doesn't always mean distress, but the possibility must be considered. Meconium in the amniotic fluid can be swallowed by the baby just before birth or at the time of birth. If inhaled into the lungs, meconium may cause pneumonia or pneumonitis.

Meconium can be detected when your water breaks. Before then, the only way to know about it is by amniocentesis. If meconium is present at the time of delivery, an attempt is made to remove it from the baby's mouth and throat with a small suction tube so the baby won't swallow it.

Problems for the Developing Fetus

The embryonic period (the first 8 weeks of the baby's growth) is a time of extremely important development for your baby. During this time, the embryo is most susceptible to factors that can interfere with its development. Most malformations originate during this period.

⚘ Teratogenic Effects on a Fetus

Teratology is the study of abnormal fetal development. When a birth defect occurs, we want to know why it happened. This can be frustrating because in most instances we are unable to determine a cause. A substance that has been identified as causing birth defects is called a *teratogen* or is said to be *teratogenic*.

Some things that have a bad effect (are teratogenic) at one point in pregnancy are safe at other times. The most critical period appears to be early in pregnancy, during the first trimester or first 13 weeks. Rubella is an example. If the fetus is infected during the first trimester, abnormalities such as heart defects can occur. Infection later can be less serious for the fetus. The box below shows critical periods of fetal development.

Critical Periods of Fetal Development	
Time Period	*Fetal Development Affected*
3 to 5-1/2 weeks	Central nervous system
3-1/2 to 5-1/2 weeks	Heart
3-1/2 to 7 weeks	Upper and lower limbs
3-1/2 to 7-1/2 weeks	Eyes
3-1/2 to 8-1/2 weeks	Ears
5-1/2 to 8 weeks	Teeth
5-1/2 to 8-1/2 weeks	Palate
6-1/2 to 9 weeks	External genitalia
20 to 36 weeks	Brain

✄ Maternal Medication Use

Some medications a pregnant woman takes can harm a developing fetus; others are safe at any time during pregnancy. Still others are safe for one part of pregnancy but not advised for another. It's best to avoid medications during pregnancy unless you discuss them with your doctor first. See the discussion of medication use during pregnancy that begins on page 209.

Premature Birth

It is hard to believe, but today a baby born at only 25 weeks gestation may survive. Some of the greatest advances in medicine have been in the care of premature babies. Because of advances in technology, fewer than 10 deaths per 1000 are reported in premature births.

However, babies born extremely early are in the hospital a long time and often have serious problems. Physical and mental handicaps are more common in babies born too prematurely. The average hospital stay for a premature baby in 1996 ranges from 50 days to more than 100 days. The cost is extremely high; a stay of 100 days can cost $200,000 or more.

Intrauterine-growth Retardation

Intrauterine-growth retardation (IUGR) means a newborn baby is small for its age. By medical definition, the baby's weight is "below the 10th percentile" for the baby's gestational age. This means that 9 out of 10 babies of the same gestational age are larger.

The word "retardation" frequently causes prospective parents some concern. Retardation in this sense does not apply to the development or function of the baby's brain. It means the growth is slow ("retarded"), and the fetus is inappropriately small.

✿ Causes of Intrauterine-growth Retardation

Conditions that increase the chance of IUGR include:
• maternal anemia
• maternal smoking during pregnancy
• poor weight gain by the mother
• maternal vascular disease, including high blood pressure
• maternal kidney disease
• alcoholism or drug abuse by the pregnant woman
• multiple fetuses
• fetal infections
• abnormalities in the umbilical cord or the placenta

A small woman is more likely to have a small baby, but this would probably not be a cause for alarm. A woman who has previously delivered a very small baby is more likely to do so in subsequent pregnancies.

IUGR is usually suspected when the size of the uterus does not change over a period of time. If you measure 10.8 inches (27cm) at 27 weeks of pregnancy and at 31 weeks you measure 11 inches (28cm), your doctor might want to look into the situation. Checking for IUGR is one important reason to keep all your prenatal appointments.

✿ Risks with IUGR

The greatest risk associated with IUGR is stillbirth (the baby dies before delivery). Delivery of the baby before full term may be required to avoid this serious problem. The baby may be safer outside the uterus than inside. Because infants with IUGR often do not tolerate labor well, a Cesarean delivery is more likely.

Hydrocephalus

Hydrocephalus causes an enlargement of the fetus' head. It occurs in about 1 in 2000 babies and is responsible for about 12% of all severe fetal malformations found at birth.

The organization and development of the brain and central nervous system of the baby begin early. Cerebral spinal fluid circulates around the brain and spinal cord, and must be able to flow without restriction. If openings are blocked and the flow of fluid is restricted, it can cause hydrocephalus (sometimes called *water on the brain*). Fluid accumulates and the baby's head becomes enlarged.

Hydrocephalus is only a symptom, and it can have several causes. Once hydrocephalus is diagnosed, a cause is sought; these causes include spina bifida, meningomyelocele and omphalocele. Sometimes intrauterine therapy—therapy performed while the fetus is still in the uterus—is possible. See the discussion in the following section.

Prenatal Treatment

In this discussion, "prenatal treatment" refers to treatment of the baby, not treatment of the pregnant woman. Today, physicians can treat many fetal problems before a baby is born. Some procedures available today were unknown even a few years ago.

Treatment of a fetus in utero has proved to be a valuable tool in saving the lives of some babies. Today, about 10 specific problems can be dealt with by treatment of the fetus in utero or with fetal surgery.

Transfusions before Birth

The earliest form of in-utero treatment was done in 1963 and involved blood transfusions to fetuses with a life-threatening form of anemia. Today we have developed more refined blood transfusion techniques. Cordocentesis is a transfusion procedure by which blood is introduced directly into the fetal bloodstream, through the umbilical cord. See page 130 for a detailed discussion.

Prenatal Medications in Utero

The greatest use of medication in utero is to hasten development of fetal lungs. If you are at high risk for a preterm birth, your healthcare provider may recommend this treatment to ensure that your baby's lungs are adequately developed before birth. If a baby is born before its lungs are mature, it can develop respiratory-distress syndrome.

If your healthcare provider believes you are at risk of delivering your baby before 34 weeks' gestation, you may be advised to receive injections of corticosteroids. This medication passes from your bloodstream into the fetus' bloodstream, reducing the risk of infant death or the risk of complications, such as breathing problems. It appears safe for both mother and fetus.

A less-common problem that can be treated before birth with medication is a heart-rhythm disturbance. One of a number of medications is given to the mother to treat her baby. In some cases, doctors deliver medication directly to the fetus via cordocentesis.

Other problems for which cordocentesis is used include inherited inborn errors of body chemistry. Treatment of these problems with medication given to the mother has been very successful.

☞ Fetal Surgery

Fetal surgery can treat various problems while the baby is still growing inside the mother. Open surgery or closed-uterus surgery may be performed.

Most surgeries, whether open or closed-uterus, are not performed until around 28 weeks of pregnancy. Surgeries treat a variety of problems, including urinary-tract blockages, tumors and fluid in the lungs.

Open surgery. With open surgery, the surgeon makes a Cesareanlike incision in the mother's abdomen and partially removes the fetus. The fetus is operated upon and returned to the uterus. The surgery carries risks for mother and baby, and only about 50 have been performed since the first one was done in 1981. One problem with open surgery is that it may stimulate uterine contractions, which can lead to premature birth. The surgery exposes the mother to all the risks of surgery, including anesthesia problems and infections. After open surgery, the mother must have a Cesarean delivery.

Closed-uterus surgery. Closed-uterus procedures are more common than open surgeries today. With this surgery, a needle-thin, fiberoptic instrument is guided by miniature cameras into the fetus' body. The fetus remains inside the uterus. The most successful closed-uterus surgeries are associated with the opening of urinary-tract blockages.

Chapter 9

Tests for You and Your Baby

Tests for you and your baby during pregnancy are an important part of prenatal care. From weighing you to amniocentesis, every test provides your healthcare provider with information. Doctors use the information to plan the best course of treatment for you and your developing baby. Tests described in this chapter can help reassure you that your baby is doing well as it develops and that anything that might need to be done, can be done.

Pregnancy Tests

The first challenge of pregnancy may be figuring out if you really are pregnant! Before you invest in a home pregnancy test or go to your doctor's office to have a pregnancy test, look for the signs and symptoms of pregnancy, which include:

- missed menstrual period
- nausea, with or without vomiting
- fatigue
- breast changes and breast tenderness
- frequent urination

If you think you are pregnant, then take an at-home pregnancy test. If the test is positive, contact your healthcare provider to make your first prenatal appointment. Pregnancy tests have become increasingly sensitive and can show positive results even before you miss a menstrual period. Most tests are positive 7 to 10 days after you conceive. Most doctors recommend you wait until you miss your period before having a test to save you money and emotional energy.

A special type of pregnancy test, called a *quantitative HCG test,* is a blood test done in the first trimester; it is ordered when there is concern about miscarriage or ectopic pregnancy. The test measures the hormone HCG (human chorionic gonadotropin), which the pregnancy produces early in pregnancy in rapidly increasing amounts. Two or more tests done a few days apart identify the change in the amount of the hormone. An ultrasound may also be done.

Tests at Your First Prenatal Visit

Your healthcare provider will probably order a battery of tests during your first or second visit. These may include:

- a complete blood count (CBC) to check iron stores and for infections
- urinalysis and urine culture
- a test for syphilis
- cervical cultures, as indicated
- rubella titers, for immunity against rubella
- blood type
- Rh-factor
- a test for hepatitis-B antibodies
- alpha-fetoprotein
- Pap smear

The results of these tests give your healthcare provider information he or she needs to provide the best care for you. For example, if testing shows you have never had rubella or rubella vaccine (German measles), you know you need to avoid exposure during this pregnancy and receive the vaccine before your next pregnancy. See the discussion about rubella starting on page 66.

Later in pregnancy, your doctor may repeat some tests or order new tests. For example, the 28th week of pregnancy is the best time to pick up blood-sugar problems.

Routine Tests

Every time you visit your healthcare provider during your pregnancy, you are weighed and your blood pressure is checked. Simple as they are, these two tests provide your healthcare provider with a great deal of information. Checking your weight is an easy way to check your well-being. Not gaining enough weight, or gaining too much, can indicate problems. High blood pressure, discussed on pages 242 to 243, can be very significant during pregnancy, especially as you near your due date. By taking your blood pressure throughout the pregnancy, your physician establishes what is normal for you. Changes in blood pressure readings alert him or her to potential problems.

As your baby grows, you are checked to see how much your uterus has grown since your last visit. Your healthcare provider also listens to the fetal heartbeat.

Third-trimester Tests

If you are like most women, your pregnancy progresses normally and you are in good health in your third trimester. You continue to have your weight and blood pressure checked at each prenatal visit. You may undergo urine analyses as well. Checking your blood pressure and urine are important during the last trimester to help detect *pre-eclampsia,* a condition more common in first-time pregnancies and in older pregnant women. See the discussion of pre-eclampsia that begins on page 248.

In this last trimester, your physician may do an internal examination to see whether your cervix has begun to thin and dilate, to evaluate the size of your pelvis and to see if your baby is in the head-down position. This examination is usually done in the last few weeks of pregnancy. It *cannot* predict when you will go into labor.

Other tests may be ordered by your healthcare provider if your baby is postterm (overdue), your pregnancy is considered high risk or your physician believes your baby might have a problem. Possible tests include a nonstress test (NST), stress test (CST; contraction stress test), ultrasound and a biophysical profile. These tests help determine the well-being of mother and baby or the kind of problem you or your baby may be experiencing.

Tests for the Mother Expecting Multiples

If you are carrying more than one baby, your pregnancy is different. Even the number of tests you receive, and when you receive them, is different.

Some researchers recommend that if you are at least 32 years old and your doctor determines you are carrying more than one baby, you should be offered chromosome testing, such as amniocentesis or chorionic villus sampling. Research indicates that there is a slightly greater chance of an abnormality when a woman is carrying two babies or more.

In many cases, screening tests are the first indication a woman is carrying more than one baby. Sometimes these tests give an "abnormal" result. Be assured that an abnormal test result does not necessarily indicate the babies have a problem; it alerts the doctor to perform follow-up tests.

Often with a multiple pregnancy, blood tests are repeated around week 28 to check for gestational diabetes. Tests can also reveal if the mother-to-be is anemic, which is more common in women carrying multiples.

Tests may be performed if other problems develop. Amniocentesis may be done to check lung maturity in the babies if there is indication of preterm labor or pre-eclampsia in the mother. Premature lung disease is a serious complication for multiples who are delivered too early.

Ultrasound

An ultrasound exam may be one of the most exciting tests you have during pregnancy! You and your partner can actually see your growing baby inside your uterus. The test is also a valuable tool for your healthcare provider because it enables him or her to check for many details of fetal development. (*Ultrasound, sonogram* and *sonography* refer to the same test.)

Many doctors routinely perform ultrasound exams on their pregnant patients, but not every doctor does them with every patient. Some doctors perform ultrasounds only when there is a problem.

⅋⅋⅋⅋

Katie had done most of the talking at her prenatal visits. I mainly listened to this bubbly, excited first-time mom-to-be. I don't think her husband, Ron, had said a word. They both came for her 18-week visit, when we were doing an ultrasound. Katie had been a little unsure about her last period, and I thought her uterus was larger than expected, so we hoped her ultrasound would help us determine if we had the right due date. The ultrasound told us a lot—her due date was right, but she was carrying twins! Katie was in shock; all she could do was gasp. Ron was ecstactic—he whooped with joy. They left with Katie shaking her head and Ron grinning from ear to ear. At her next visit, Katie and I talked about twins and twin pregnancies.

Ultrasound exams pose no threat to you or to your baby. The possibility of adverse effects has been studied many times without any evidence of problems.

✒ How the Test Is Performed

Ultrasound is a test that gives a two-dimensional picture of the developing embryo or fetus. It involves use of high-frequency soundwaves made by applying an alternating current to a device called a *transducer*. The transducer sends and receives soundwaves. While this happens, you lie on your back. The transducer moves over gel that has been spread over your abdomen. The transducer picks up echoes of soundwaves as they bounce off the baby, then a computer translates them into a picture. This can be compared to "radar" used by airplanes or ships to create a picture of the terrain under a night sky or the ocean floor.

Before the test, you may be asked to consume 32 ounces of water. Drinking all that water makes it easier for the technician to see your uterus. The bladder lies in front of the uterus; when it is full, the uterus is pushed up and out of the pelvis area and can be seen more easily by the ultrasound. When your bladder is empty, your uterus lies farther down in the pelvis and is harder to see.

✵ Reasons for an Ultrasound

An ultrasound can help confirm or determine your due date, determine if there is one baby, not multiples, and determine if major physical characteristics of the fetus are normal. An ultrasound can be done just about any time during pregnancy.

Whether you have an ultrasound during your pregnancy depends on several factors, including problems such as bleeding, previous problem pregnancies and your insurance coverage. Many doctors like to do at least one ultrasound during pregnancy. If your pregnancy is "high risk," you may have several.

A doctor may order an ultrasound to learn vital information about a fetus' brain, spine, face, major organs, limbs or sex. An ultrasound can show where the placenta is, so it is used with other tests, such as amniocentesis. The test can also provide information on fetal growth, the condition of the umbilical cord and the amount of amniotic fluid in the uterus.

Healthcare providers generally perform an ultrasound for the following reasons:

• to identify an early pregnancy
• to show the size and rate of growth of the embryo or fetus
• to measure the fetal head, abdomen or femur to determine the duration of pregnancy
• to identify some fetuses with Down syndrome
• to identify fetal abnormalities, such as hydrocephalus
• to identify the location, the size and the maturity of the placenta or placental abnormalities

- to detect an IUD
- to differentiate between miscarriage, ectopic pregnancy and normal pregnancy

If you are 18 weeks or more when you have an ultrasound, you may be able to determine the sex of your baby, but don't count on it. It isn't always possible to tell the sex if the baby has its legs crossed or is in a breech presentation. Even if your doctor makes a prediction as to the sex of your baby, keep in mind that ultrasound is only a test, and tests can sometimes be wrong.

Vaginal Ultrasound

A lesser-used type of ultrasound is called *vaginal probe ultrasound* or *transvaginal sonography;* it can be very helpful in evaluating problems early in pregnancy, such as possible miscarriage or ectopic pregnancy. The instrument (probe transducer or other device) is placed just inside the opening of the vagina; it does not touch the cervix and will not cause bleeding or miscarriage. This type of ultrasound sometimes gives better information earlier in pregnancy than an abdominal ultrasound.

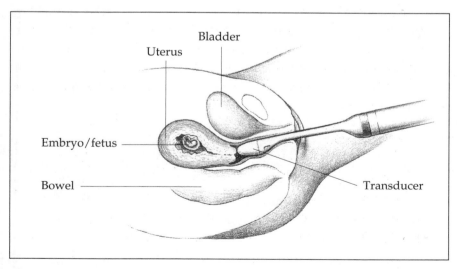

Vaginal probe ultrasound

❧ Ultrasound in Late Pregnancy

If your healthcare provider orders an ultrasound exam in the third trimester, he or she is looking for particular information. Performed later in pregnancy, this test can:

• evaluate the baby's size and growth
• determine the cause of vaginal bleeding
• determine the cause of vaginal or abdominal pain
• detect some fetal malformations
• monitor a high-risk pregnancy
• measure the amount of amniotic fluid
• determine which delivery method to use
• determine maturity of the placenta

The test can also be used to evaluate the fetus, including its size. Breathing movements, body movements and muscle tone can be checked. If the baby is too big, it may need to be delivered by Cesarean section. If the baby is very small, other decisions can be made.

❧ Other Facts about Ultrasound

You may be able to get a videotape of your ultrasound; ask about it when your ultrasound is scheduled to find out if you need to bring a videotape cassette. Most ultrasounds do include black-and-white photos you may keep.

The cost of an ultrasound varies. An average cost is about $150 but can range from $100 to $300. With many insurance plans, ultrasound is an "extra," not part of the normal fee for prenatal care. Ask about cost and coverage before having an ultrasound. Some insurance plans require preapproval for the test.

You can usually take your partner with you to the exam, so arrange to have the ultrasound when he can join you. You may want to have others come, such as your mother or older children. Ask if that is possible when you schedule your ultrasound.

Amniocentesis

Amniocentesis is a test done on fetal cells and is usually offered to women over 35. However, this guideline is currently being challenged. The age threshold for amniocentesis is discussed beginning on page 5.

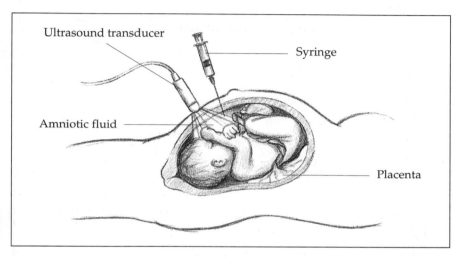

Amniocentesis performed near the end of pregnancy can determine if your baby's lungs are mature.

✺ What the Test Can Predict

Most women who have amniocentesis are being screened for chromosomal defects, such as Down syndrome, Turner's syndrome or neural-tube defects (spina bifida). The test can pick up some specific gene defects, including cystic fibrosis and sickle-cell disease. Other problems a physician can identify include:

- skeletal diseases, such as osteogenesis imperfecta
- fetal infections, such as herpes or rubella
- central-nervous-system disease, such as anencephaly
- blood diseases, such as erythroblastosis fetalis
- chemical problems or deficiencies, such as cystinuria or maple-syrup-urine disease

Amniocentesis can determine the baby's sex. However, the test is not used for this purpose, except in cases in which the sex of the baby could predict a problem, such as hemophilia. Amniocentesis may be performed to see if the baby of an Rh-negative woman is having problems, and it may be done to determine fetal lung maturity before delivery.

Who Receives Amniocentesis?

Amniocentesis does not need to be performed on every pregnant woman. It is often performed on women:

- who will deliver after their 35th birthday
- who have had a previous baby with a birth defect
- with a family history of birth defects
- who have a birth defect themselves
- whose partners have a birth defect

How the Test Is Performed

Ultrasound is used to locate a pocket of fluid where the fetus and placenta are not in the way. Skin over the mother's abdomen is cleaned and numbed with a local anesthetic. A needle passes through the abdomen into the uterus, and fluid is withdrawn with a syringe. About 1 ounce of amniotic fluid is needed to perform the tests. The test can identify about 40 fetal abnormalities.

Risks with Amniocentesis

Risks of amniocentesis include trauma to the fetus, to the placenta or to the umbilical cord, infection, miscarriage or premature labor. Although risks are relatively small, there is some risk associated with the procedure. Fetal loss from complications is estimated to be between 0.3 and 3%.

Discuss the risks with your doctor before the test. Only someone with experience, such as a physician at a medical center, should perform amniocentesis.

In a multiple pregnancy, genetic testing can be a complicated procedure. In most multiple pregnancies, for example, each baby lies in its own sac. Double abdominal punctures are required to withdraw fluids in each of these sacs, which can increase the risk of complications. In the case of one sac shared by the two babies, only one amniocentesis is performed.

❧ Disadvantages of the Test

The greatest disadvantage of the test is the time at which it is performed. Amniocentesis is usually performed for prenatal evaluation at around 16 weeks of pregnancy, making termination of a pregnancy (if that is what the woman chooses) more difficult. Some doctors are now performing the test at around 11 or 12 weeks. However, this is considered experimental.

Alpha-fetoprotein Testing

The alpha-fetoprotein (AFP) test is a blood test done on the mother-to-be. Alpha-fetoprotein is produced in the baby's liver, and it passes in small quantities into your bloodstream. Measurement of the amount of alpha-fetoprotein in your blood can help your healthcare provider predict problems in your baby, such as spina bifida or Down syndrome. (AFP detects only about 25% of Down-syndrome cases. If Down syndrome is indicated, additional detailed diagnostic tests will probably be ordered.)

At this time, AFP is not performed on all pregnant women but is required in some states, including California and New York. If the test is not offered to you, discuss it with your healthcare provider.

The test is usually performed between 16 and 20 weeks of pregnancy. Test results must be correlated with the mother's age and weight, and the gestational age of the fetus. If AFP detects a possible problem, more-definitive testing is usually ordered.

❧ What the Test Can Predict

AFP can detect neural-tube defects, severe kidney or liver disease, esophageal or intestinal blockage, Down syndrome, urinary obstruction, and osteogenesis imperfecta (fragility of the baby's bones).

❧ False-positive Results

One problem with the AFP test is a very high number of false-positive results; that is, the results say there is a problem when there isn't one. Currently, if 1000 women take the AFP test, 40 test results come back as "abnormal." Of those 40, only one or two women actually have a problem.

If you have an AFP and your test result is abnormal, don't panic. You'll take another AFP test, and an ultrasound will be performed. Results from these second tests should give you a clearer answer.

The Triple-screen and Quad-screen Tests

Tests that go beyond alpha-fetoprotein testing are available now to help your healthcare provider determine if your child might have Down syndrome and to rule out other problems in your pregnancy.

❧ The Triple-screen Test

The triple-screen test helps identify problems using three blood components: alpha-fetoprotein, a pregnancy hormone called *human chorionic gonadotropin (HCG)* and a form of estrogen produced by the placenta called *unconjugated estriol.*

Abnormal levels of these three blood chemicals can indicate Down syndrome. For older mothers, the detection rate is higher than 60%, with a false-positive rate of nearly 25%. Abnormal results of a triple-screen test are usually double-checked with ultrasound and amniocentesis.

❧ The Quad-screen Test

The quad-screen test is similar to the triple-screen but adds a fourth measurement—the blood level of inhibin-A, a chemical produced by the ovaries and the placenta. This fourth measurement raises the sensitivity of the standard triple-screen test by 20% in determining if a fetus has Down syndrome. The quad-screen test identifies almost 80% of fetuses with Down syndrome. It has a false-positive rate of 5%.

Chorionic Villus Sampling

Chorionic villus sampling (CVS) analyzes chorionic villus cells, which become the placenta. The test detects genetic abnormalities; sampling is taken early in pregnancy.

The advantage of CVS is that a doctor can diagnose a problem earlier in pregnancy with it. The test can be done at 9 to 11 weeks instead of 16 to 18 weeks, as with amniocentesis. Some women choose CVS so they can make a decision about their pregnancy earlier. If a woman decides to terminate her pregnancy, the procedure may carry fewer risks when performed earlier in the pregnancy.

⚘ How the Test Is Performed

An instrument is placed through the cervix or through the abdomen to remove a small piece of tissue from the placenta. The procedure carries a small risk of miscarriage; it should be performed only by someone who is experienced in doing the test.

Fetoscopy

Because of advances in fiber optics, today we can look at a fetus or placenta as early as 10 weeks into its development. Ultrasound cannot provide the same degree of detail. Fetoscopy enables the doctor to look through a fetoscope to detect even very subtle abnormalities and problems.

⚘ How the Test Is Performed

A small incision is made in the mother's abdomen, and a scope similar to the one used in laparoscopy is placed through the abdomen. The doctor uses the fetoscope to examine the fetus and the placenta.

The test is specialized and is not done very often. It is usually recommended if you have given birth to a child with a birth defect that cannot be detected by any other test. If your doctor suggests fetoscopy to you, discuss it with him or her. The risk of miscarriage is 3 to 4%. The procedure should be done *only* by someone experienced at it.

Percutaneous Umbilical Blood Sampling

Percutaneous umbilical blood sampling (PUBS), also called *cordocentesis,* is a fairly new test that is done on the fetus. The test has improved the diagnosis and treatment of Rh-incompatability and other blood disorders. The advantage of the test is that results can be available within a few days. The disadvantage is it carries a slightly higher risk of miscarriage than amniocentesis.

๛ How the Test Is Performed

Guided by ultrasound, a fine needle is inserted through the mother's abdomen into a tiny vein in the umbilical cord of the fetus. A small sample of the baby's blood is removed for analysis. Blood disorders, infections and Rh-incompatability are detectable with PUBS.

If the fetus is found to be Rh-positive and its mother is Rh-negative, doctors have time to give it a blood transfusion, if necessary. This procedure can help prevent life-threatening anemia that can develop if the mother is isoimmunized (she has antibodies that attack her baby's blood). See the discussion of Rh-compatibility on page 72.

Other Tests for the Mother-to-be

๛ Listening to the Baby's Heartbeat

A special listening machine, called a *doppler,* magnifies the sound of the baby's heartbeat so it can be heard. It is possible to hear the baby's heartbeat around your 12-week visit.

๛ Radiation Tests

There is no known safe amount of radiation from X-ray tests for a developing fetus. The baby may be harmed by exposure. Avoid exposure to X-rays during pregnancy, unless it is an emergency. The medical need for the X-ray must always be weighed against its risk to your pregnancy. Discuss the procedure with your physician before *any* X-ray is taken when you are pregnant. This warning also applies to dental X-rays.

Computerized tomographic scans, also called *CT scans* or *CAT scans,* are a very specialized X-ray. The test involves the use of X-ray with computer analysis. Many researchers believe the amount of radiation received from a CT scan is far lower than that from a regular X-ray. However, it is probably wise to avoid even this amount of exposure, if possible.

If you are over 35, you may have had a baseline mammogram, or breast X-ray, which is usually repeated every 2 years after the age of 40. If you had a mammogram before pregnancy, you're ahead of the game. If not, don't have one until after your baby is born. Unless you have a good reason for undergoing the test, such as a breast lump, don't expose your developing baby to this type of radiation.

With radiation exams, risk to the fetus appears to be the greatest between 8 and 15 weeks of gestation (between the fetal age of 6 weeks and 13 weeks). Some physicians believe the only safe amount of radiation exposure for a fetus is *no* exposure.

Magnetic resonance imaging, also called *MRI,* is a diagnostic tool widely in use today. No harmful effects have been reported from its use in pregnancy, but pregnant women are advised to avoid MRI during the first trimester of pregnancy.

❧ Pap Smear

Often on your first prenatal visit, you will have a Pap smear if it has been a year or more since your last test. If you have had a normal Pap smear in the last few months, you won't need another one.

A Pap smear is done to look for abnormal cells, called *precancerous, dysplastic* or *cancerous* cells, in the cervical area. The goal of a Pap smear is to discover problems early so they can be dealt with more easily. If you have an abnormal Pap smear, it usually identifies the presence of an infection, a precancerous condition or some other condition, such as hyperkeratosis.

If your test reveals an infection, it is treated immediately. If the first test reveals a precancerous condition, called *dysplasia,* the next step is usually a *colposcopy.*

In a colposcopy, a microscope is used to examine your cervix and to look for abnormal areas. If any are found, a sample of the tissue is removed, called a *biopsy*. Usually a biopsy is not done while you're pregnant; your doctor will usually wait until after your pregnancy for further testing. An abnormal Pap smear during pregnancy is a special situation and must be handled carefully.

✤ Home Uterine Monitoring

Some women are monitored during pregnancy with home uterine monitoring. Contractions of a pregnant woman's uterus are recorded while she is at home and are transmitted by telephone to her healthcare provider. This type of testing or monitoring is used to identify women at risk of premature labor. With it, labor can be stopped to prevent premature delivery. Costs vary but run between $80 and $100 a day.

✤ Pelvic Exam

A pelvic examination is usually done at the first or second prenatal visit and again in late pregnancy. It is done early in pregnancy to evaluate the size of the uterus and to help your healthcare provider determine how far along you are in pregnancy. It is needed late in pregnancy because it tells your doctor many things, including:

• the presentation of the baby—whether the baby is head first or breech
• the dilatation of the cervix—how much the cervix has opened (if at all)
• effacement—how much the cervix has thinned
• station—how low the baby is in your birth canal
• shape and size of your birth canal or pelvic bones

After a pelvic exam late in pregnancy, your doctor may tell you some numbers, such as "2 and 50%." This means your cervix has dilated 2 centimeters and is halfway thinned out. (See the illustration on page 275.)

The information collected during the exam is helpful if you go to the hospital thinking you're in labor. At the hospital, you'll be checked again. Knowing the measurements from your last pelvic exam can help your doctor determine if you are in labor.

A pelvic exam does not tell your doctor when you will go into labor. Labor can start at any time, regardless of the condition of your cervix.

Nonstress Test on the Baby

A nonstress test is a simple, noninvasive procedure done at 32 weeks' gestation or later; it is performed in the doctor's office or in the labor-and-delivery department at the hospital. This test measures how the fetal heart responds to the fetus' own movements. The test evaluates fetal well-being in late pregnancy and is commonly used in postterm and high-risk pregnancies. The information gained from a nonstress test gives reassurance that your baby is doing OK.

ஃ How the Test Is Performed

While you are lying down, a nurse attaches a monitor to your abdomen. Every time you feel the baby move, you push a button to make a mark on the monitor paper. At the same time, the fetal monitor records the baby's heartbeat on the same paper.

ஃ Test results

Each time the baby moves, the heart rate should accelerate by about 15 beats a minute for about 15 seconds. When this occurs twice in a 20-minute period, the test is considered normal or *reactive*. If the baby doesn't move or if the heart rate does not react to movement, the test is called *nonreactive*. This doesn't necessarily mean there is a problem—the baby may be sleeping. In more than 75% of nonreactive tests, the baby is healthy.

If the test is nonreactive, it could be a sign the baby is not receiving enough oxygen or is experiencing some other problem. In this case, you will probably have to repeat the test in 24 hours or have additional tests, including a contraction stress test or a biophysical profile.

Contraction-stress Test

If the nonstress test is nonreactive (see the discussion above), you may need to take a contraction-stress test. A contraction-stress test (CST), also called a *stress test*, evaluates the baby's well-being. It measures the response of the fetal heart to mild uterine contractions that mimic labor.

If you have had a problem pregnancy in the past or experienced medical problems during this pregnancy, your doctor may order this test in the last few weeks of pregnancy. If you have diabetes and take insulin, your baby may be at some increased risk of problems. Your healthcare provider may order this test on a weekly basis, beginning at around 32 weeks.

In some cases, the doctor may order the nonstress test alone or order both the nonstress test and the contraction-stress test. The contraction-stress test is considered somewhat more accurate than the nonstress test.

⁓ How the Test Is Performed

This test is usually done in the hospital because it can take an hour or more and occasionally triggers labor. A nurse places a monitor on the abdomen to record the fetal heart rate. In some hospitals, nipple stimulation is used to make the woman's uterus contract. In other hospitals, the drug oxytocin is given intravenously in small amounts to make the uterus contract. Results indicate how well a baby will tolerate contractions and labor.

⁓ Test results

A slowed heart rate after a contraction may be a sign of fetal distress. The baby may not be receiving enough oxygen or may be experiencing another difficulty. The doctor may recommend delivery of the baby. In other cases, the doctor may repeat the test the next day or order a biophysical profile. (A discussion follows.) If the test shows no sign of a slowed fetal heart rate, the test result is reassuring.

Biophysical Profile of the Baby

A biophysical profile is a comprehensive test that helps determine the fetus' health status. The test is commonly performed in high-risk situations, overdue pregnancies or pregnancies in which the baby doesn't move very much. It's useful in evaluating an infant with intrauterine-growth retardation.

A biophysical profile measures five areas, which are identified and scored: fetal breathing movements, gross body movements, fetal tone, reactive fetal heart rate and amount of amniotic fluid.

✦ How the Test Is Performed

Ultrasound, external monitors and direct observation are all used to take the various measurements. Each area is given a score between 0 and 2. A score of 1 in any test is a middle score; a total is obtained by adding the five scores. The higher the score, the better the baby's condition.

A baby with a low score may need to be delivered immediately. Your doctor will evaluate the scores, your health and your pregnancy before any decisions are made. If the score is reassuring, the test may be repeated at intervals. Sometimes a doctor will repeat the test the following day.

Fetal Monitoring during Labor

In many hospitals, a baby's heartbeat is monitored throughout labor with external fetal monitoring and internal fetal monitoring. Fetal monitoring enables doctors to detect problems early.

External fetal monitoring can be done before your membranes rupture. A belt with a recorder is strapped to your abdomen to pick up the baby's heartbeat. Internal fetal monitoring monitors the baby more precisely. An electrode is placed on the fetal scalp to measure the fetal heart rate.

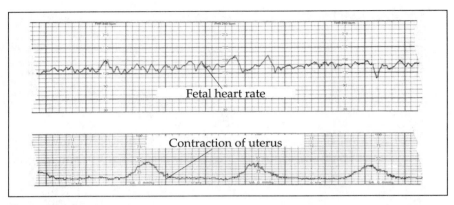

External fetal monitoring

Fetal Blood Sampling during Labor

Fetal blood sampling is another way of evaluating how well a baby is tolerating the stress of labor. Before the test can be performed, membranes must be ruptured, and the cervix must be dilated at least 2 centimeters (about an inch). An instrument is passed into the vagina and through the dilated cervix to the top of the baby's head, where it is used to make a small nick in the baby's scalp. The baby's blood is collected in a small tube, and its pH (acidity) is checked.

Knowing the baby's pH level helps doctors determine if the baby is having trouble during labor and is under stress. The test helps the physician decide whether labor can continue or if a Cesarean delivery is needed.

Evaluating Fetal Lung Maturity

The respiratory system is the last fetal system to mature. Premature infants commonly experience respiratory difficulties because their lungs are not yet mature. Knowing how mature the baby's lungs are helps your doctor make a decision about early delivery, if that must be considered.

If there are reasons the baby needs to be delivered early, fetal lung maturity tests can determine whether the baby will be able to breathe without assistance. The two tests used most often to evaluate a baby's lungs before birth are the L-S ratio and the phosphatidyl glycerol (PG) tests. Fluid for the tests is obtained by amniocentesis.

Chapter 10

When You're Expecting More Than One Baby

A multiple pregnancy almost always surprises expectant parents. However, because of today's advanced testing techniques, especially ultrasound, most parents know about it early enough to prepare for their new arrivals.

The rate of multiple births increased between 1980 and 1992; today 1.5% of all births are multiple births. This increase is due to the use of fertility drugs and because more women are having babies at an older age.

A multiple pregnancy occurs when a single egg divides after fertilization or when more than one egg is fertilized. Twins from one egg, called *identical* or *monozygotic twins*, occur about once in every 250 births around the world. Twins from two eggs, called *fraternal* or *dizygotic twins*, occur in 1 out of every 100 births in white women and 1 out of 79 births in black women. In certain areas in Africa, twins occur once in every 20 births! Hispanic women also have a higher incidence of twins. The occurrence of twins in Asian populations is less common—about 1 in every 150 births.

Today, we are also experiencing more triplet births. However, a triplet birth is not common. It happens about once in every 8000 deliveries.

Causes of Multiple Births

The increase in multiple births among older women has been attributed to higher levels of gonadotropin, the hormone that stimulates the ovaries to develop and release eggs. As a woman ages, the level of gonadotropin increases, and she is more likely to produce two eggs during one menstrual cycle. Most twin births in older women are fraternal twins (babies are born from two different eggs).

The incidence of twin births can run in families, on the mother's side. One study showed that if a woman is a twin, her chance of giving birth to twins is about 1 in 58. If a woman is the daughter of a twin, she also has a higher chance of having twins. Another study reported that 1 out of 24 (4%) of twins' mothers was also a twin, but only 1 out of 60 (1.7%; about the national average) of the fathers was a twin.

Multiple births are also more common with in-vitro fertilization. This may be due to the frequent use of fertility drugs to increase the chance of pregnancy or the introduction of several fertilized eggs in hopes at least one will implant.

Signs of a Multiple Pregnancy

Most multiple pregnancies are discovered well before delivery.

A healthcare provider usually finds out a woman is carrying more than one baby because of various signs, including a larger-than-expected uterus, more severe nausea and vomiting, and more than one fetal heartbeat.

When a healthcare provider suspects a woman is carrying more than one baby, an ultrasound is usually ordered. An ultrasound exam almost always detects a multiple pregnancy.

Increased Risks Associated with a Multiple Pregnancy

If a woman is pregnant with more than one baby, her risk of problems during pregnancy increases. Risks can be minimized and possibly avoided with good prenatal care and careful attention to the woman's health. Possible pregnancy problems include:

- increased miscarriage
- fetal death
- fetal malformations
- low birth weight or growth retardation
- pre-eclampsia
- maternal anemia
- problems with the placenta
- maternal bleeding or hemorrhage
- problems with the umbilical cords
- hydramnios or polyhydramnios
- labor complicated by breech or transverse presentation
- premature labor

If you're pregnant with more than one baby, take very good care of yourself during pregnancy. Pay strict attention to your eating plan; eat wisely and nutritiously for all of you. Extra rest is essential. Most pregnant women need at least 2 hours of rest during each day.

When you are pregnant with more than one baby, you are monitored more closely during pregnancy. You will probably have more frequent checkups, and more tests may be ordered for you.

Beginning in your 20th week, you will probably visit your healthcare provider every other week until the 30th week. Then you may be seen once a week until delivery. You may have an ultrasound more frequently to monitor the babies' growth. Your blood pressure is monitored very closely because of pre-eclampsia, which is twice as common in multiple pregnancies.

Take Care of Yourself during Pregnancy

One of the most important things to remember with a multiple pregnancy is to take things more slowly, from the beginning of your pregnancy until delivery. Taking care of yourself is the best way to take care of your developing babies.

Eat more—a woman carrying more than one baby needs to eat at least 300 more calories per baby each day than she would if carrying one baby. That means she must consume more protein, minerals, vitamins and essential fatty acids. For a normal-weight woman, a weight gain between 35 and 45 pounds for a twin birth is recommended.

A multiple pregnancy is more stressful for your body than a single pregnancy, and your needs increase in many areas. Often women pregnant with more than one baby have iron-deficiency anemia. Iron supplementation is often necessary.

You may need bed rest in your second trimester, even hospitalization, if you experience complications. With some multiple pregnancies, planned hospitalization at 28 to 30 weeks may be recommended. Bed rest at home or in the hospital can help prevent or stop premature labor. It gives the babies the best chance to grow because bed rest increases blood flow to the uterus.

Coping with Discomfort

When you are expecting more than one baby, your discomfort may be more pronounced; you may experience more problems, or problems may last longer. When you are carrying twins, you get "big" earlier, and you are larger than with a single pregnancy. This can cause you more problems, such as difficulty breathing, back pain, hemorrhoids, varicose veins, pelvic pressure and pelvic pain.

Treatment, however, is often the same for you as for a woman with a single-fetus pregnancy. Refer to those discussions appearing elsewhere in this book, including morning sickness, page 155; backaches, page 149; digestion changes, page 153; heartburn, page 151; and sleep problems, page 12.

Exercising with a Multiple Pregnancy

As a general rule, I advise women who are carrying more than one baby *not* to exercise during pregnancy because of the extra stress their bodies must deal with. Walking and swimming may be permissible for you, but check with your healthcare provider first.

If you do get the OK to do mild exercises, don't do anything that is strenuous—stop immediately if you feel overexerted. As much as you want to stay in shape, you may have to forgo all exercise programs until after your babies are safely delivered.

Other Pregnancy Considerations

✺ Working during Pregnancy

Often a physician advises a woman expecting twins to stop working at least 8 weeks before her due date. Ideally, you should stop working at 28 weeks with a twin pregnancy—24 weeks if your job requires standing or other physical exertion. Your doctor may recommend full or partial bed rest. These are general suggestions and may not apply in every case.

✺ Childbirth-education Classes

It's a great idea to take childbirth-education classes for any pregnancy. If you are expecting twins, triplets or more, schedule your classes to begin at least 3 months before your due date. If you have time, a brief course in Cesarean birth might also be worthwhile, if you can find a class in your area. Also see the discussion on childbirth-education classes that begins on page 41.

A Special Concern during Pregnancy

Some women are told early in pregnancy they will give birth to twins, only to discover later that they are carrying one baby. Early ultrasound exams reveal two babies; later ultrasounds of the same woman show one baby disappeared, but the other baby is OK. We believe one of the pregnancies dies and is then absorbed by the mother's body. This is one reason many healthcare providers prefer not to predict a twin birth before 10 weeks of pregnancy.

Delivering More Than One Baby

Multiple fetuses are often delivered early. Most doctors try to delay delivery of twins until about the 37th week, but the average twin pregnancy is delivered at 35 weeks. Although the ideal time for delivery of triplets is 35 weeks, the average length of pregnancy for triplets is 33 weeks. Quadruplets are delivered, on the average, at 29 weeks.

How multiple fetuses are delivered often depends on how the babies are lying in the uterus. All possible combinations of fetal positions can occur. When both twins are head first, a vaginal delivery is usually attempted. One baby may be delivered vaginally, with the second requiring a C-section if it turns, if the cord comes out first or if the second baby is distressed after the first one is born. Some doctors believe two or more babies should always be delivered by Cesarean section.

Breastfeeding More Than One Baby

It is possible to breastfeed twins or triplets. It may be more difficult and more demanding, but many women successfully breastfeed more than one baby. We know breast milk is especially valuable for small or premature infants; often twins or triplets are both. If you want to breastfeed, do it! See the discussion of breastfeeding that begins on page 52.

Extra Help after the Babies Are Born

Even the most efficient woman discovers having more than one baby can be exhausting. Extra help can make a tremendous difference in everyone's life. Your time of greatest need is immediately after your babies are born. Ask for help from family, neighbors and friends for the first 4 to 6 weeks after you bring your babies home. You may be fairly exhausted yourself, so it's very helpful to have extra pairs of hands available until you all settle into a routine.

Resources for Parents of Multiples

There are some wonderful resource groups for parents and families of multiples. Consult the resource list that begins on page 333.

Part 3

While You're Pregnant

Chapter 11

Coping with Common Discomforts

In this chapter, let's look at how you can more easily cope with minor discomforts to which age contributes during pregnancy. Being pregnant causes changes in your body; some of them are uncomfortable. Being aware of what they are before you experience them (if you do) may help relieve anxiety.

Backaches

Nearly every woman experiences backaches and back pain at some time during pregnancy, especially as her abdomen gets bigger. You may experience backache after walking, bending, lifting, standing or excessive exercise. Be careful about lifting—do it correctly, with knees bent and back straight.

Backache is treated with heat, rest and analgesics, such as acetaminophen (Tylenol). Some maternity girdles may provide support. Keep your weight under control, and participate in mild exercise, such as swimming, walking and stationary-bike riding. Lie on your left side when resting or sleeping.

Lower-back pain is common during pregnancy, but occasionally it indicates a serious problem, such as a kidney stone. If pain is constant or severe, discuss it with your healthcare provider.

Constipation

Your bowel habits may change during pregnancy. Many women notice constipation, often accompanied by irregular bowel habits and hemorrhoids. These problems are usually the result of a slowdown in the movement of food through the gastrointestinal system and the ingestion of iron as supplements or in prenatal vitamins.

You can take steps to help relieve the problem. Increase your fluid intake, and exercise 3 or 4 times a week. Many doctors suggest prune juice or a mild laxative, such as milk of magnesia, Metamucil® and Calace®. However, avoid excessive use of *any* preparation that contains magnesium. Certain foods that are high in fiber, such as bran and prunes, increase the bulk in your diet and may help relieve constipation.

Do not use laxatives, other than those mentioned above, without consulting your doctor. If constipation is a continuing problem, discuss it at your next office visit.

Headaches

Some women experience more headaches during pregnancy but hesitate to take medication for them. You can do a few things that are medicine-free to relieve headaches.

- Use deep-breathing exercises and relaxation techniques to help you relax.
- Drink plenty of fluids so you don't become dehydrated.
- Close your eyes and rest in a quiet place.
- Eat regularly.
- Avoid foods or substances, such as cheese, chocolate and caffeine, that sometimes cause headaches.
- Apply an ice pack to the back of your head.
- Get enough sleep.

If your headache doesn't go away using these techniques, you may take regular or extra-strength acetaminophen (Tylenol). If this doesn't help, call your healthcare provider.

✿ Migraine Headaches

A migraine headache is characterized by severe throbbing pain and is aggravated by physical activity, such as walking. Some women experience nausea, vomiting or diarrhea with a migraine headache.

Some women who experience migraines regularly do not suffer from them during pregnancy; others have worse migraine headaches, especially in the first trimester. For some, the second and third trimesters are migraine-free.

Try the techniques described above for headaches to deal with migraines. If they don't help, talk with your physician; he or she will prescribe the safest medication available. Do not take any medication, other than acetaminophen, for a migraine headache without discussing it first with your physician.

Heartburn

One of the most frequent discomforts of pregnancy, especially among older pregnant women, is heartburn. Heartburn may begin early in pregnancy and often becomes more severe as pregnancy progresses.

Heartburn during pregnancy is caused by two things—a reflux (backing up) of stomach acids into the esophagus and the hormonal changes of pregnancy. During pregnancy, your body produces hormones that relax involuntary muscles; one such muscle normally prevents stomach acids from backing up into the esophagus. Because the muscle isn't doing its usual job, you experience heartburn. You may notice heartburn during the third trimester especially, when the expanding uterus crowds the stomach and the intestines somewhat. This can cause some stomach contents to back up into the esophagus.

ఞఞఞఞఞ

Gina was having a hard time with heartburn. She loved to eat Italian food, Mexican food and other spicy foods, but she paid for it. She found that with a few modifications, she could eat

the things she liked and not suffer from heartburn afterward.
She ate earlier in the evening, at least 2 hours before retiring.
She ate smaller amounts, and she always carried antacids,
such as Tums® or Mylanta®. She started to call her Tums "my
after-dinner mints"!

Antacids may provide considerable relief. Follow your health-care provider's instructions or package directions relating to pregnancy. Don't overdo it and take too much in an effort to find relief. You can use some antacids, such as Amphojel®, Gelusil®, milk of magnesia and Maalox®, without too much concern. However, avoid excessive use of any product that contains sodium or magnesium. Sodium can contribute to water retention. Excessive use of magnesium antacids has been linked to magnesium poisoning.

In addition to taking antacids, try the following suggestions. (Also see the discussion of indigestion starting on page 153.)

- Eat smaller meals more frequently.
- Avoid carbonated beverages.
- Don't eat foods that you know give you heartburn, such as rich or spicy foods.
- Avoid eating before bedtime.
- When lying down, elevate your head and shoulders.

Hemorrhoids

Hemorrhoids are an annoying problem for many women during pregnancy. Hemorrhoids are dilated blood vessels (varicose veins) of the rectum that can itch, bleed and be painful. They appear around the area of the anus or inside the anus. Older women are especially vulnerable to developing hemorrhoids; they may have some dilated blood vessels around the rectum even before pregnancy.

Many patients ask me why they only have the problem during pregnancy. During pregnancy, your body tissue changes, with some loss of elasticity. Pressure from your enlarging uterus blocks blood flow in the pelvic area. These conditions encourage hemorrhoid formation.

❧ Relieving the Discomfort of Hemorrhoids

If hemorrhoids are a problem, try any or all of the following suggestions for relief.

- Rest at least 1 hour every day with your feet and hips elevated.
- Lie with your legs elevated and knees bent *(Sims position)* when you sleep at night.
- Eat adequate amounts of fiber, and drink lots of fluid.
- Take warm baths for relief.
- Suppository medications, available without a prescription, may help.
- Stool softeners can prevent hard stools from forming, which can aggravate delicate tissues.
- At work, try to arrange a time every day to take off your shoes and put up your feet.
- Apply ice packs or cotton balls soaked in witch hazel to the affected area.
- Don't sit for long periods.

Discuss the situation with your healthcare provider if hemorrhoids become a major problem. In rare cases, the problem is relieved with surgery.

Indigestion

My patients often ask me if there is a difference between heartburn and indigestion. There is. *Heartburn* is a burning discomfort related to the lower end of the esophagus and is felt behind the lower part of the sternum. *Indigestion* refers to an inability to digest food or to difficulty in digesting food. (Heartburn is discussed starting on page 151.)

If you have indigestion, you can take steps to relieve it. Eat foods that agree with you; avoid spicy foods. Eat small meals frequently. If you need antacids after meals, use them but don't overmedicate yourself.

New medications now available over the counter are advertised as being good to aid in indigestion and heartburn. Two popular medications are Pepcid AC® (for acid control) and Tagamet HB® (for heartburn relief). The data we have advises women *not* to use these products during pregnancy unless there is clear indication they are needed. Do not take these or any other medication without first discussing the situation with your healthcare provider.

Leg Cramps

Leg cramps, also called *charley horses,* can be bothersome during pregnancy, especially if you experience them at night. Cramps are characterized by a sharp, grabbing pain in the calf. A cramp is a spasm in two sets of muscles that forces your foot to point involuntarily.

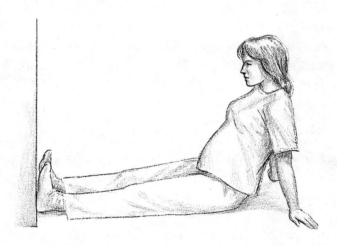

Stretching your legs can help relieve leg cramps. Sit on the floor, and place your feet flat against the wall. Pull toes away from the wall, keeping heels on the floor. Repeat 6 to 8 times when you experience leg cramps.

The best way to relieve a leg cramp is to stretch your muscles. Flex or bend your foot to stretch leg muscles in the opposite direction. You can do this by standing up or by gently pressing the knee down with one hand while you gently pull the upper part of the foot toward you with the other. Stretching exercises before you go to bed at night may help. Don't point your toes or stretch your legs before getting out of bed.

Some medical experts believe leg cramps occur more frequently if there is an imbalance of calcium and phosphorous in the body. Do not consume more calcium than you need—1200mg is the recommended daily dose. That's about four cups of milk. (Also see the chart on page 182 for the calcium content of some foods.) Soft drinks, snack foods and processed foods are all high in phosphates; you may need to cut down on them or eliminate them from your diet.

❧ How to Cope with Leg Cramps

These suggestions may help you relieve leg cramps.

- Wear maternity support hose during the day.
- Take warm baths.
- Have your partner massage your legs at the end of the day or whenever you feel like it.
- Take acetaminophen (Tylenol) for pain.
- Rest on your left side.
- Use a heating pad set on low for up to 15 minutes (no longer) on the cramp.

Your activities can also contribute to cramping. Avoid standing for long periods of time. Don't wear tight or restrictive clothing.

Morning Sickness

An early symptom of pregnancy for many women is nausea, sometimes with vomiting, often called *morning sickness*. Morning sickness is typically present at the beginning of pregnancy and is usually worse in the morning (it improves during the day).

Morning sickness usually begins around week 6 and lasts until week 12 or 13, when it starts to subside.

Try the suggestions below to help you deal with the nausea and vomiting related to morning sickness.

- Eat small portions of nutritious food throughout the day, instead of three larger meals.
- Eat a snack, such as dry crackers or rice cakes, *before* you get out of bed in the morning. Or ask your partner to make you some dry toast.
- Avoid heavy, fatty foods.
- Keep up your fluid intake—fluids may be easier to handle than solids and will help you avoid dehydration.
- Alternate wet foods with dry foods. Eat only dry foods at one meal, then wet foods or liquids at the next.
- Try ginger—it's a natural remedy for nausea. Grate it onto vegetables and other foods.
- Avoid things that trigger your nausea, such as odors, movement or noise.
- Suck on a fresh-cut lemon when you feel nauseous.
- Get enough rest.
- Avoid getting sweaty or overheated, which can contribute to nausea.
- Apply pressure to pressure points on your wrists. See the illustration and instructions below.

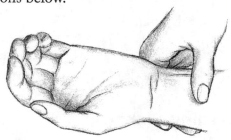

To help relieve nausea, find the pressure point that is three fingers above your wrist fold. Press on the point on each wrist at the same time—you'll probably need help doing this. Hold for 1 minute; repeat 3 times.

❧ Hyperemesis Gravidarum

A woman who experiences severe vomiting and can't eat or drink suffers from *hyperemesis gravidarum*. She may be treated for several days in the hospital if she becomes dehydrated and loses weight. In the hospital, she is fed intravenously. Usually the woman can resume eating solid foods after a couple of days in the hospital. Sometimes hypnosis treats the problem successfully.

Normal Swelling in Pregnancy

During the last few weeks of pregnancy, your ankles and feet may swell; some women also observe swelling in their hands and fingers. Swelling is caused by increased fluid in your bloodstream. It is more noticeable in your ankles and feet because the baby's weight puts pressure on the veins in your pelvis and slows the flow of blood from your legs back to your heart.

The best way to deal with the swelling is to improve your circulation through exercise and position changes. When possible, walk short distances. Do ankle circles while standing in line or sitting in a chair.

To deal with normal swelling in legs and feet, wear sneakers, flats or shoes with low heels (no higher than 2 inches) that fit comfortably. Choose the right kind of shoe for you. An ideal shoe has a 1-inch heel, good arch support, a roomy, box-shaped toe and adjustable straps or laces.

If swelling becomes extreme, especially during the last trimester, consult your physician; it could be a sign of problems. Rest lying on your left side as frequently as possible. You can also try the following.

- Take off shoes when possible, and wiggle toes to increase circulation.
- Don't stand for long periods.
- Don't wear stirrup pants.

Varicose Veins

Varicose veins, also called *varicosities* or *varices,* are dilated blood vessels that fill with blood. They occur to some degree in most pregnant women; however, varicose veins develop more often in older women.

There seems to be an inherited predisposition to varicose veins that can become more severe during pregnancy. If your mother had varicose veins, you are more likely to develop them.

Problems with varicose veins usually occur in the legs but also may be seen as hemorrhoids or appear in the birth canal and in the vulva. Pressure from the uterus and the change in blood flow during pregnancy can make varices worse. Varicose veins in the legs or varicose veins in the rectum (hemorrhoids) can cause great pain and discomfort.

Symptoms vary; for some women varicose veins are only a blemish or purple-blue spot on the legs that causes little or no discomfort, except in the evening. For other women, varices are bulging veins that require elevation at the end of the day or other measures.

Varicose veins may worsen during pregnancy. Increasing weight (from the growing baby, uterus and placenta), tight clothing that constricts at the waist or legs, and standing a great deal worsen varicose veins. If you continue to have problems with varicose veins after pregnancy, you may need surgery.

✦ Preventing and Treating Varicose Veins during Pregnancy

The most effective way to prevent varicose veins is to improve circulation in your legs, especially through exercise and changes in position. Walk when possible, and do ankle circles while sitting and standing. Even sitting and rocking in a rocking chair can help—rocking contracts and relaxes leg muscles, which moves blood from your feet to your heart. Lie on your left side when you lie down to improve blood flow. Elevate your hips and legs when resting or lying down. Keep your total pregnancy weight gain within normal range—between 25 and 35 pounds for a normal-weight woman.

If you get varicose veins while you are pregnant, you can take steps to feel better. Many women wear support hose to reduce swelling and ease leg pains. Many types of maternity support hose or graduated-compression stockings are available. Quite a few of my patients have told me how much maternity support hose have helped them, but the hose can be very difficult to get on. The following tricks can help.

First, turn the stockings inside out. Starting at the toe, unroll the stockings up your leg. Second, put on your support hose before you get out of bed in the morning—your legs may tend to swell as soon as you get up. (You may need to change your habits and bathe before you go to bed.)

Clothes that don't restrict circulation at the knee or groin may be your best choices. Wear loose panties to help prevent vulvar varicosities (varicose veins in the vulva area) from causing greater discomfort.

Spend as little time as possible on your feet. Wear flat shoes. Don't cross your legs at the knee, and don't stand for long periods. If you must stand, bounce gently on the balls of your feet every few minutes.

Sciatic-nerve Pain

Some women occasionally experience a servere pain in their buttocks and down the back or side of either leg. This pain is called *sciatic-nerve pain;* it may occur more frequently as pregnancy progresses.

The sciatic nerve is located behind the uterus, in the pelvic area, and it runs down into the leg. We believe pain is caused when the enlarging uterus puts pressure on the nerve.

The best way to deal with the pain is to lie on your opposite side. This helps relieve pressure on the nerve.

Chapter 12

Nutrition and Weight Management

The fetus growing inside you has many nutritional needs—needs that you must fulfill through the foods you choose to eat. A pregnant woman who eats a healthful diet during pregnancy is much more likely to give birth to a healthy baby. Eating well reduces the risk of complications and limits some pregnancy side effects.

You can meet most nutritional needs by eating a well-balanced, varied diet. The *quality* of your calories is extremely important—if a food grows in the ground or on trees, it's better for you nutritionally than if it comes from a can or a box.

I'm sure you've heard the adage "a pregnant woman is eating for two." Many women take this to mean they can eat twice as much. Not true! The saying really means that you must be concerned about getting the best nutrition for yourself and for your growing baby.

Some women have the false idea they can eat all they want during pregnancy. Don't fall into this trap. Don't gain more weight than your doctor recommends during your pregnancy—it can make you uncomfortable and it may be harder to lose the extra pounds after your baby is born.

A diet based on the recommended servings in the food-guide pyramid ensures good nutrition. See the illustration of the pyramid on page 163.

Your Caloric Needs in Pregnancy

If you are normal weight before pregnancy, your caloric intake should average about 2200 calories a day during the first trimester of pregnancy. You need to add up to 300 calories to that number during the remainder of your pregnancy, depending on your prepregnancy weight. See the discussion of weight management during pregnancy that begins on page 187.

These extra calories are the foundation of tissue growth in you and your baby. Your baby uses the energy from your calories to create and to store protein, fat and carbohydrates, and to provide energy for its body processes to function. You use the extra calories to support the changes your body goes through during pregnancy. Your uterus increases in size many times, your breasts increase in size and your blood volume increases by 50%, among other changes.

Calories aren't interchangeable. You can't eat whatever you want and expect to get the best nutrition for your baby and you; eating right takes care and attention. Where the calories come from is as important as the number you consume. You need to eat foods high in vitamins and minerals, especially iron, calcium, magnesium, folic acid and zinc. Fiber and fluids are also essential because constipation problems can be associated with pregnancy. Eating a wide variety of foods each day can supply you with the nutrients you need. Choose from dairy products, protein foods, fruits and vegetables, and breads and cereals.

During pregnancy, you will need to consume 6 to 7 ounces of protein every day to cover the growth or repair of the embryo/fetus, placenta, uterus and breasts. Carbohydrates are also important to your diet. There is no recommended dietary allowance (RDA) for daily carbohydrate intake during pregnancy. Most physicians believe carbohydrates should make up about 60% of the total number of calories in your diet. If you are eating 2000 calories a day, you would consume about 1200 carbohydrate calories.

You probably don't need to worry about an inadequate fat intake; in the North American diet, fat intake is usually excessive.

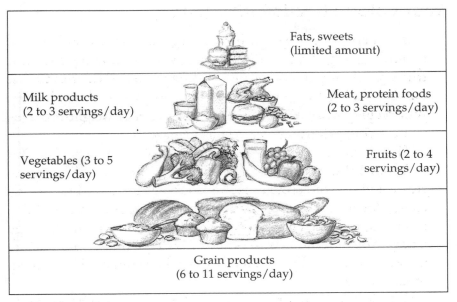

The food pyramid

There is no recommended daily amount for fat intake during pregnancy. Don't avoid all fats, but use them sparingly; measure how much you use of each, and read labels.

Eat a variety of foods throughout pregnancy. Suggested daily servings from each of the six food groups are listed in the box on page 164. Serving sizes are described for each food group in the sections that follow.

Food-group Recommendations

Be good to you and your baby, and eat the recommended number of servings from each food group every day. If you are carrying multiples, you will need to eat at least one more serving each of dairy products and protein each day. Discuss your nutrition plan with your doctor or a registered dietitian.

Daily Food-group Servings	
Food group	*Servings per day*
Dairy products	3 to 4
Meats, protein sources	2 to 3
Vegetables	at least 4
Fruits	3 to 4
Breads, cereal, pasta and rice	6 to 11
Fats and sweets	2 to 3

✠ Dairy Products

Dairy products contain calcium, a mineral that is important for you and your growing baby. The calcium content of many packaged foods is found on the nutrition label. Representative foods from this group, and their serving sizes, include:

3/4 cup cottage cheese
2 ounces processed cheese (such as American cheese)
1 ounce hard cheese (such as Parmesan or Romano)
1 cup pudding or custard
1 8-ounce glass of milk
1-1/2 ounces natural cheese (such as cheddar)
1 cup yogurt

If you must keep the fat content low of the dairy products you choose, select skim milk, lowfat yogurt and lowfat cheese instead of whole milk and ice cream. The calcium content is unaffected in lowfat dairy products. Refer to the box on page 182 for other common foods with calcium.

✠ Protein

Amino acids in protein are critical to the growth and repair of the embryo/fetus, placenta, uterus and breasts. The recommended amount of protein in pregnancy is 6 to 7 ounces a day, about twice the amount normally recommended. Foods you might choose from this group, and their serving sizes, include:

2 tablespoons peanut butter

1/2 cup cooked dried beans

2 to 3 ounces cooked meat

1 egg

Poultry, fish, lean cuts of red meat, dry beans, eggs, nuts and seeds are all good protein sources. If you need to watch your caloric intake, skinless chicken and fish are better choices than beef or pork.

❧ Vegetables

Vegetables are important in your nutritional plan. Because they change with the seasons, vegetables are also a great way to add variety to your everyday menu plans. Some vegetables are good sources of iron, folic acid, calcium and fiber; check a nutritional guide for particular information about vegetables you select. (Your produce grocer may be able to answer your questions.) Foods you might choose from this group, and their serving sizes, include:

3/4 cup vegetable juice

1/2 cup broccoli, carrots or other vegetable,
   cooked or raw

1 medium baked potato

1 cup raw, leafy vegetables (greens)

Eat a variety of vegetables for good nutritional balance in your diet. Eat at least one leafy, green or deep-yellow vegetable a day for extra iron, fiber and folic acid.

❧ Fruits

Fruit is good for you, and tastes good, too. It is an excellent source of many important vitamins and minerals, so enjoy many types of fruit. Foods you might choose from this group, and their serving sizes, include:

3/4 cup grapes
1/2 cup fruit juice
1 medium banana, orange or apple
1/4 cup dried fruit
1/2 cup canned or cooked fruit

In your daily diet, be sure to include one or two servings of a fruit rich in vitamin C, such as orange juice or orange slices. Fresh fruits are also a good source of fiber, which can help relieve symptoms of constipation.

❧ Breads, Cereal, Pasta and Rice

Foods from this group are nearly interchangeable, so you shouldn't find it hard to get all the carbohydrates you need. If you don't like pasta, choose rice. If cereal isn't appealing, choose bread. Foods you might choose from this group, and their serving sizes, include:

1 large tortilla, corn or flour
1/2 cup cooked pasta, cereal or rice
1 ounce ready-to-eat cereal
1/2 bagel
1 slice bread
1 medium roll

✣ Fats and Sweets

Be careful with fats and sweets, unless you are underweight and need to add a few pounds. Current guidelines suggest that fat make up no more than 30% of your total daily calories. While sugar adds flavor to food, it has little nutritional value. Use it sparingly.

Be careful with butter, margarine, oils, salad dressing, nuts, chocolate and sweets. Foods in this group are often high in calories but low in nutritional value. Use them sparingly. Foods from this group, and their serving sizes, include:

1 tablespoon sugar or honey

1 tablespoon olive oil or other type of oil

1 pat of margarine or butter

1 tablespoon jelly or jam

1 tablespoon prepared salad dressing

Eat sweets in moderation during pregnancy. Eating sweets or junk foods full of empty calories won't do you or your baby any good. Instead, replace these treats with nourishing choices, such as a piece of fruit or a slice of fresh whole-wheat bread. You'll satisfy your hunger and your nutritional needs at the same time.

Other Food Facts

✣ Junk Food

You may have to forgo most junk food while you're pregnant. "Junk food" is high-calorie, high-fat food that contains little nutrition for you or your baby. It's probably fine to eat some now and then, but don't make it a regular part of your diet.

Avoid chips, sodas, cookies, pie, chocolate, candy, cake and ice cream. Instead, select foods that are high in fiber and low in sugar and fat; choose fruits and vegetables, legumes, dairy products and whole-grain crackers and breads.

✤ Food Cravings

Cravings for particular foods during pregnancy are normal for many women. (Sometimes the chosen foods appear a little strange to other people!) Cravings can be both good and bad. If you crave foods that are nutritious and healthful, go ahead and eat them in moderate amounts. If you crave foods that are high in sugar and fat, loaded with empty calories, be very careful about eating them. Sometimes you can get rid of a craving by eating fresh fruits and vegetables.

We don't know why women sometimes crave unusual foods or food combinations during pregnancy. Hormonal and emotional changes that occur during pregnancy may have something to do with it.

❧❧❧❧

Megan began having food cravings early in her pregnancy. Her craving for ice cream could have been a problem. She knew if she ate it as often as she wanted to, her weight would be out of control. She found that by using self-control and by substituting lowfat yogurt for higher-calorie ice cream, she was able to have a treat once in a while and still manage her weight.

Some foods you love normally may make you sick to your stomach during pregnancy. This is common. The hormones of pregnancy have a significant impact on the gastrointestinal tract, which can affect your reaction to certain foods.

What do pregnant women crave?
A recent study of pregnant women found they craved:

- Chocolate (33% of the time they craved foods)
- Other desserts and ice cream (20% of the time)
- Citrus (19% of the time)

✤ Caffeine

Caffeine is a component of many beverages and foods, including coffee, tea, cola drinks and chocolate. Some medications, such as cough medicines and headache preparations, contain a lot of caffeine. Caffeine is of no known benefit to you or the fetus.

Caffeine is a central-nervous-system stimulant that can affect calcium metabolism in both you and your baby. Four cups of coffee a day (800mg of caffeine) by a pregnant woman have been associated with decreased birth weight and a smaller head size in newborns. An exact "toxic" amount for caffeine has not been determined, but it makes sense to limit your caffeine intake.

Read labels on foods, beverages and over-the-counter medications to determine caffeine content. Eliminate as much caffeine from your diet as possible.

❧ Making and Drinking Tea

Recently news reports have questioned the safety of drinking brewed tea. (The reports do not apply to herbal tea, which is grown and harvested differently.) Much of the tea we drink in North America is grown in Asia and India, where human feces are used to fertilize tea plants. Residue from the fertilizer gets on the tea leaves and may not be washed off during processing. The residue can cause a bacterial infection, called *fecal coliform*, if the tea has not been prepared properly. Fecal coliform causes diarrhea, cramps and bloating.

Many restaurants brew tea in a way that promotes bacterial growth. The problem arises when regular tea is steeped for long periods in hot (not boiling) water. Restaurants typically use a large amount of water, and the tea sits all day long in a warm state that provides the perfect medium for bacterial growth. Choose another drink at a restaurant, unless you know the tea was prepared safely.

Brewing "sun tea" at home may duplicate these conditions. With sun tea, the water and tea bags sit in the sun for long periods. The water becomes very warm, but does not boil. This supplies the perfect medium in which the fecal coliform bacteria can grow.

The problem does not seem to occur when you make yourself a cup of tea by boiling the water on the range or in the microwave, or when you use a hot-water tap. Boiling kills the bacteria in the former instance; in the latter case, the tea doesn't sit long enough to give the bacteria time to grow.

✈ Herbal Teas

Herbal tea is not affected by fecal coliform bacteria. Some types of herbal tea are good for you and help relieve certain pregnancy discomforts, which makes herbal tea a good alternative to coffee or regular tea. The herbal teas listed in the box below are delicious. Each is safe to use during pregnancy.

Herbal Teas and Their Benefits	
Tea	*Benefit*
Chamomile	helps digestion
Dandelion	helps reduce water retention and soothe an upset stomach
Ginger root	helps ease nausea and nasal congestion
Nettle leaf	rich in iron, calcium and other vitamins and minerals that are good for a pregnant woman
Peppermint	relieves gas pains and calms stomach acids; can be used alone or mixed with chamomile
Red raspberry	helps relieve nausea and stabilize hormones

Some herbs and herbal teas are *not* safe to use during pregnancy because they could harm your developing baby. Herbs and teas to *avoid* during pregnancy include blue or black cohosh, pennyroyal leaf, yarrow, goldenseal, feverfew, psillium seed, mugwort, comfrey, coltsfoot, juniper, rue, tansy, cottonroot bark, large amounts of sage, senna, cascara sagrada, buckthorn, male fern, slippery elm and squaw vine.

❧ Artificial Sweeteners

Studies to date have not shown any harm to pregnancy from aspartame (Nutrasweet®). The phenylalanine in aspartame contributes to phenylalanine in your diet, so if this is a problem for you, avoid foods and beverages sweetened with aspartame. Phenylalanine is discussed on page 172.

Saccharin® is an artificial sweetener found in some foods and beverages; its effect on pregnancy is still being tested. My advice is to avoid artificial sweeteners or use them in moderation during pregnancy.

❧ Late-night Snacks

Late-night nutritious snacks are beneficial for some women, especially if they must eat many small meals a day. However, many women should not snack at night because they don't need the extra calories. For others, food in the stomach late at night can cause distress, especially if heartburn or nausea and vomiting are problems.

❧ Your Cholesterol Level

During pregnancy and lactation, the level of cholesterol in your blood rises naturally because of hormone changes. It probably won't make sense to have your cholesterol tested while you're pregnant or nursing.

❧ Nausea during Pregnancy

Eating can be a problem if you suffer from nausea, also called *morning sickness,* during early pregnancy. Eating smaller meals frequently helps. You should be able to eat nutritious foods, even if you have morning sickness. For a few women, nausea becomes serious because it prevents them from eating an adequate amount of food or drinking enough fluid. See page 155 for further information about nausea and morning sickness.

ᕗ Eating Out

It's fine to eat out at restaurants; just be careful about what you eat. Avoid raw meats or raw seafood, such as sushi. Avoid foods that may not agree with you right now.

ᕤᕤᕤᕤ

May had a habit of going out for fast food every day for lunch before she got pregnant. But during her pregnancy, she found she was very tired by midday and needed to rest. She discovered that if she brought a sack lunch to work she could eat a healthful meal, then lie down on a couch in the staff lounge for 45 minutes. She got some rest and enjoyed her afternoon work a lot more.

At a restaurant, your best choices may be fish, fresh vegetables and salads, but be careful with calorie-loaded salad dressings if you are concerned about excessive weight gain. Avoid highly spiced foods or foods that contain a lot of sodium. Chinese food often contains large amounts of monosodium glutamate (MSG, a sodium-containing product). You may retain water after eating these foods.

ᕗ Other Special Precautions

Phenylketonuria (PKU). PKU is a condition in which the body is unable to use phenylalanine properly, and it accumulates in body fluids. The accumulation can lead to mental retardation and other nervous-system disorders in you or your developing baby.

If you suffer from phenylketonuria, you will need to follow a diet low in phenylalanine. Avoid the artificial sweetener aspartame.

Salmonella poisoning. Salmonella are bacteria that can cause problems ranging from mild gastric distress to a severe, sometimes fatal, food poisoning. This situation can be serious for a pregnant woman and her developing baby if it prevents her from getting enough fluid or eating nutritiously. Almost 1400 strains have been identified. Any form of salmonella could be dangerous to a pregnant woman.

We have long known that cracked raw eggs can be contaminated with salmonella organisms. These organisms are found in uncracked eggs as well, if a hen's ovaries are contaminated. Salmonella bacteria can be found in raw chicken and other raw poultry.

Salmonella are destroyed in cooking, but it's prudent to take additional precautions against salmonella poisoning.

- Clean counters, utensils, dishes and pans with a disinfecting agent and wash your hands after preparing any poultry or products made with raw eggs. You could pick up salmonella from these surfaces on your hands and transfer it to your mouth or another surface.
- Thoroughly cook all poultry.
- Avoid foods made with raw eggs, including salad dressings (Caesar salad), hollandaise sauce, eggnog, homemade ice cream made with eggs or any other food made with raw or undercooked eggs.
- Boil eggs 7 minutes for hard-cooked eggs.
- Poach eggs for 5 minutes.
- Fry eggs for 3 minutes on *each* side.
- Avoid "sunny-side up" eggs (those not turned during frying). It's important to cook the entire egg thoroughly, not just part of it.

❧ If You Need Information

The National Center for Nutrition and Dietetics' Consumer-Nutrition Hotline is an excellent source of information on all aspects of nutrition, whether or not you are pregnant. Call 800-366-1655 to speak with a dietitian.

Facts About Fish

We know that eating fish is healthful, but it's particularly good for you during pregnancy. Fish contains omega-3 fatty acids, which help prevent some heart problems; during pregnancy, this substance also seems to help prevent pregnancy-induced hypertension and pre-eclampsia, which are both greater risks for older pregnant women.

Women who eat a variety of fish during pregnancy have longer pregnancies and give birth to babies with higher birth weights, according to some studies. This is important because the longer a baby stays in the uterus, the better its chances are of being strong and healthy at delivery.

Many fish are safe to eat, and you should include them in your diet. Most fish is low in fat and high in vitamin B, iron, zinc, selenium and copper. Many fish choices are an excellent, healthful addition to your diet, and you can eat them as often as you like. See the chart below for a list of good choices.

Good Fish and Shellfish Choices

Below is a list of fish that we know are good choices for you during pregnancy. You can eat these fish as often as you like.

bass	marlin
catfish	ocean perch
cod	orange roughy
croaker	Pacific halibut
flounder	pollack
freshwater perch	red snapper
haddock	salmon
herring	scrod
mackerel	sole

You may eat the following shellfish as often as you like, if they are thoroughly cooked. You can steam, bake or broil any of them.

clams	oysters
crab	scallops
lobster	shrimp

✎ Omega-3 Fatty Acids

Some researchers now believe that eating fatty fish or ingesting omega-3 fatty acids in another form (such as fish-oil capsules) may enhance your baby's intellectual development. Studies have shown that fish oil is important to fetal neurological development. One recent study of pregnant women demonstrated that when a pregnant woman eats fish oil, it actually reaches the brain of the developing fetus.

Include omega-3 fatty acids in your eating plan, but don't exceed 2.4g of omega-3 fatty acids a day. Fish high in these oils are salmon, mackerel, herring and tuna. Discuss the matter with your healthcare provider.

✎ Methyl-mercury Poisoning

Some fish are contaminated with a dangerous substance as the result of man-made pollution. People who eat these fish are at risk of methyl-mercury poisoning. Mercury is a naturally occurring substance as well as a pollution by-product. Mercury becomes a problem when it is released into the air as a pollutant. It settles into the oceans and from there winds up in some types of fish.

The FDA has determined that a certain level of methyl mercury in fish is dangerous for humans. However, we do not know if this level is harmful to a fetus. Researchers do know that methyl mercury can pass from mother to fetus across the placenta.

Physicians caution pregnant women and those trying to conceive not to eat some kinds of fish more than once a month. These fish include shark, swordfish and tuna (fresh or frozen). If you're nursing, limit your consumption to once a week. Canned tuna is safer but don't eat more than two 6-ounce cans a week.

Some freshwater fish may also be risky to eat, such as walleye and pike. To be on the safe side, consult local or state authorities for any advisories on eating freshwater fish.

✎ Other Problems to Know About

Other environmental pollutants can appear in fish. Dioxin and PCBs (polychlorinated biphenyls) are found in some fish, such as bluefish or lake trout; avoid them.

Parasites, bacteria, viruses and toxins can also contaminate fish. Eating infected fish will make you sick, sometimes severely so. Sushi and ceviche are fish dishes that could contain viruses or parasites. Raw shellfish, if contaminated, could cause hepatitis-A, cholera or gastroenteritis. Avoid *all* raw fish.

Other fish to avoid during pregnancy include some found in warm tropical waters, especially Florida, the Caribbean and Hawaii. Avoid the following "local" fish from those areas: amberjack, barracuda, bluefish, grouper, mahimahi, snapper and fresh tuna.

If you are unsure about whether you should eat a particular fish or if you would like further information, call the Food and Drug Administration on its toll-free telephone hotline: 800-332-4010.

Drink Enough Fluids

Water enables your body to process nutrients, develop new cells, sustain blood volume and regulate body temperature—all very important during pregnancy! Your blood volume increases during pregnancy; drinking extra fluids helps you keep up with this change. You may feel better during pregnancy if you drink more liquid than you normally do.

Research has shown that for every 15 calories you burn, your body needs about 1 tablespoon of water. If you burn 2000 calories a day, you need 133 tablespoons—2 quarts—of water! Because you need more calories during pregnancy, you also need more water.

Drink 6 to 8 glasses of liquid or more every day. Water is the best source of fluid; however, other fluids will satisfy your needs. Foods and drinks that can help you get enough fluid include vegetables, milk and milk products, meats, grain products, fruits and juices. Avoid coffee, tea and diet cola as fluid sources—they can contain sodium and caffeine, which act as diuretics.

Two quarts a day may seem like a lot of liquid to consume, but you can do it. Some women drink water, one glass at a time, throughout the day. (Decrease your intake later in the day so you don't have to go to the bathroom all night long.)

Many pregnant women who suffer from headaches, uterine cramping and other problems find that by increasing their water or fluid intake, they relieve some symptoms. Drinking plenty of water also helps avoid bladder infections.

Water is important in regulating body temperature. In fact, for each degree above 98.6F (37C), drink an extra pint of water (or other fluid) each day to help bring down a fever.

To determine if you're drinking enough fluid, check your urine. When it is light yellow to clear, you're getting enough water. Dark-yellow urine is a sign you need to increase your fluid intake.

Thirst is not a good indication of how much water you need. By the time you get thirsty, you've already lost 1% of your body's water. Don't let yourself become thirsty!

When you exercise, drink a cup of water before you begin your routine. Then drink 1/2 cup to 1 cup of water every 20 minutes while you are exercising to help prevent dehydration.

Salt, Sodium and Pregnancy

Sodium is a chemical that maintains the proper amount of fluid in your body. (Table salt, a compound comprised of sodium and chloride, is about half sodium.) During pregnancy, sodium can also affect your baby's system. Using too much or too little of it can cause problems. You need some sodium; you just don't need a lot.

Sodium is found in salty foods (such as potato chips, nuts and dill pickles) and in many processed foods, from soups to meats. It can be found in carbonated beverages and sports drinks.

During pregnancy, keep your consumption of sodium under 3g (3000mg) a day. Consuming too much sodium can cause fluid retention, swelling and high-blood-pressure problems.

You can't avoid something unless you know where to find it. With sodium, that can be tricky. It's in the salt shaker and in salty-tasting foods, such as pretzels, chips and salted nuts. It's frequently used as a preservative in foods that don't taste salty, such as canned and processed products, fast foods, cereals, desserts—even some medications. Read nutrition labels. You can also buy inexpensive pamphlets at larger grocery stores and bookstores that list the sodium content of common foods and fast foods.

The Challenge of Being Vegetarian during Pregnancy

Some women choose to eat a meatless diet; other women find that during pregnancy, the sight of meat makes them sick. Many of my patients want to know if a vegetarian plan—a food plan without meat—is safe during pregnancy. Following a vegetarian diet while you're pregnant can be safe and healthful, if you pay close attention to the foods and combinations of foods you eat.

Most women who eliminate meat from their diets eat a more nutrient-rich variety of foods than those who eat meat. This may be true because these women make an extra effort to include more fruits and vegetables in their food plans when they eliminate meat products.

If you choose a vegetarian eating plan, be sure you eat enough calories to fuel your pregnancy. During pregnancy, you need to consume between 2200 and 2700 calories a day, depending on your prepregnancy weight. See page 190 for a chart about weight gain during pregnancy.

Besides eating enough calories, be sure you are eating the right kind of calories. Choose fresh foods that provide a variety of vitamins and minerals. Avoid too many fat calories because you may gain extra weight. If you are a vegetarian, discuss your daily diet with a healthcare provider at your first prenatal visit. He or she may want you to see a nutritionist if you have any pregnancy risk factors.

ஜ Different Vegetarian Diets

There are different vegetarian nutrition plans, with unique characteristics. If you are a lacto vegetarian, your diet includes milk and milk products. If you are an ovo-lacto vegetarian, your eating plan includes milk products and eggs. A vegan diet includes only foods of plant origin, such as nuts, seeds, vegetables, fruits, grains and legumes. A macrobiotic diet limits foods to whole grains, beans, vegetables and moderate amounts of fish and fruits. A fruitarian diet is the most restrictive; it allows only fruits, nuts, olive oil and honey.

Macrobiotic and fruitarian diets are too restrictive for pregnant women. They do not guarantee the optimal intake of the vitamins, minerals, protein and calories you need for proper fetal development. Other vegetarian diets can provide complete nutrition for you and your growing baby; vegan diets, lacto diets or ovo-lacto diets can work if you eat a wide variety of foods in the right quantities.

✤ Concerns When You Eat "Vegetarian"

If you are vegetarian, your goal is to consume enough calories to maintain and to gain weight during pregnancy. You don't want your body to use protein for energy because you need it for your growth and your baby's growth.

Minerals are also a concern. By eating a wide variety of whole grains, legumes, dried fruit, lima beans and wheat germ, you should be able to get enough iron, zinc and other trace minerals. If you don't drink milk or include milk products in your diet, you must find other sources of vitamins D, B_2, B_{12} and calcium. See the discussion of vitamins and minerals in the section that follows.

Vitamins and Minerals during Pregnancy

Vitamins and minerals—in the right quantities—are a major part of good nutrition. Eating a nutritious, varied diet helps ensure you get all the vitamins and minerals you need. Your healthcare professional may ask you to take a prenatal vitamin every day. Vegetarians may need to pay special attention to getting enough of some vitamins and minerals.

✤ Iron Supplementation

Iron is one of the most important elements for your body; women need more iron than men because of menstruation. However, most women do not get enough iron in their diet. Research has shown that between the ages of 20 and 50, American women consume only about two-thirds (10mg/day) of the Recommended Daily Allowance (RDA) of iron (15mg/day). The average woman's diet seldom contains enough iron to meet the increased demands of pregnancy (30mg/day).

It's very important that you meet your increased iron needs during pregnancy. Needs are higher because your blood volume increases by half to support the oxygen needs of your baby and the placenta. In the third trimester, your need for iron increases even more. Your baby draws on your stores of the mineral to create its own stores for the first few months of its life.

You will also need adequate iron reserves to draw on during your baby's birth. The uterus' oxygen requirements increase with labor contractions, and you will lose some blood during a normal delivery.

How can you recognize an iron deficiency? There are distinct symptoms. You feel tired, have trouble concentrating, get sick easily or suffer from headaches, dizziness or indigestion. An easy way to check for iron deficiency is to examine the inside of your bottom eyelid—it should be dark pink. Or look at your nail beds; if you're getting enough iron, they will be pink.

In a healthy woman, only 10 to 15% of the iron she consumes is absorbed by the body. To ensure you have enough iron in your diet, eat a variety of foods that are rich in iron. These foods include:

- chicken
- lean red meat
- dried fruits
- organ meats, such as liver, heart and kidneys
- egg yolks
- spinach
- kale
- tofu

Your body stores iron efficiently, so you don't need to eat these foods every day. However, you do need to eat them on a regular basis. Eat vitamin-C foods and iron-rich foods together because iron is more easily absorbed by the body when consumed with vitamin C. (A spinach salad with orange sections is a nutritious example.)

Prenatal vitamins contain about 60mg of iron. You may not need extra iron if you eat a healthful diet and take your prenatal vitamins every day. Discuss it with your healthcare provider.

The iron you ingest can cause constipation. Work with your doctor to minimize this side effect while making sure you are getting enough iron.

Vegetarians and others who eat very little meat are at greater risk of iron deficiency during pregnancy. If you are a vegetarian, pay close attention to this aspect of your diet. Fish, poultry and tofu are all excellent sources of iron. Most legumes and peas also contain significant amounts of the mineral. Many breakfast foods and breads are now iron fortified.

Dried fruit and dark leafy vegetables are good sources of iron. Cook in cast-iron pans because traces of iron will attach to whatever you're cooking. If you are a lacto or ovo-lacto vegetarian, do not drink milk with foods that are iron rich; calcium reduces iron absorption. Don't drink tea or coffee with meals because tannins present in those beverages inhibit iron absorption by 75%.

❧ Getting Enough Calcium

Calcium is important in the diet of every woman, especially women in their 30s and 40s. If you are pregnant, your needs increase because your developing baby requires calcium to build strong bones and teeth, and you need calcium to keep your bones healthy. The daily requirement for a nonpregnant woman is between 800 and 1000mg of calcium. During pregnancy, your needs increase to 1200mg a day.

Dairy products are excellent sources of calcium and vitamin D, which is necessary for calcium absorption. It may be difficult for you to get enough calcium without eating dairy foods. Most prenatal vitamins contain only a small amount of the calcium you need. If your calcium intake is inadequate, your baby may draw needed calcium from your bones, which increases your risk of developing osteoporosis later in life.

If you are lactose intolerant and unable to drink milk, a condition that is more frequent among older women, you may be able to eat hard cheeses and yogurt. Lactose-reduced dairy products are also available. You may be able to use Lactaid®, a preparation that helps your body deal more efficiently with lactic acid. Discuss the situation with your healthcare provider.

You may also choose nondairy sources of calcium; it is found in legumes, spinach, some fish, nuts and other foods. Read nutrition labels. The chart below lists some common calcium-containing foods.

Calcium Sources in Some Foods		
Food	Serving Size	Amount of Calcium
Almonds	1/4 cup	95mg
Beans, dried, cooked	1 cup	90mg
Bok choy	1/2 cup	79mg
Collards	1/2 cup	179mg
Milk, 2%	8 oz.	300mg
Orange juice, calcium-fortified	6 oz.	300mg
Sardines, with bones	3 oz.	324mg
Spinach, cooked	1/2 cup	140mg
Tofu processed with calcium sulfate	4 oz.	434mg
Trout	4 oz.	250mg
Waffle	1 medium	180mg
Yogurt, fruit	8 oz.	345mg
Yogurt, plain	1 cup	400mg

If you need to watch your calories and avoid unnecessary fats, choose your calcium sources wisely. Select lowfat products and those with reduced-fat content. Skim milk and lowfat, fat-free and part-skim cheeses are better choices than whole milk and regular cheese.

Some foods interfere with your body's absorption of calcium. Be very careful about consuming salt, protein, tea, coffee and unleavened bread with a calcium-containing food.

Many women grow tired of drinking milk or eating cheese or yogurt to meet their calcium needs during pregnancy. Below are some suggestions that can add calcium to your diet.

• Make fruit shakes with milk and fresh fruit.
• Drink calcium-fortified orange juice, available commercially.
• Add nonfat-dried-milk powder to recipes.
• Cook brown rice or oatmeal in lowfat or nonfat milk instead of water.
• Drink calcium-fortified skim milk.
• Make soups and sauces with undiluted evaporated nonfat milk instead of cream.
• Eat calcium-fortified breads.

If you and your healthcare provider decide calcium supplements are necessary, you will probably take calcium carbonate combined with magnesium, which aids calcium absorption. Avoid any supplement derived from animal bones, dolomite or oyster shells because they may contain lead.

⁓ Folic Acid

Some women may need folic acid (a term used interchangeably with *folate*) in addition to prenatal vitamins. Deficiency in folic acid can result in a type of anemia called *megaloblastic anemia*. Additional folate may be necessary for situations in which pregnancy requirements are unusually high, such as a pregnancy with twins or triplets, alcoholism or Crohn's disease.

Prenatal vitamins have 0.8mg to 1mg of folic acid in each dose, sufficient for a woman with a normal pregnancy. Most women do not need extra folic acid during pregnancy.

A neural-tube defect called *spina bifida* afflicts nearly 4000 babies born in the U.S. every year. It develops in the first few weeks of pregnancy, when the fetus is highly susceptible to some substances or to the lack of them. Research has proved that nearly 75% of all cases of spina bifida can be prevented if the mother takes 0.4mg of folic acid a day, beginning 3 or 4 months *before* pregnancy. Folic acid is required only through the first 13 weeks of pregnancy.

If a woman gives birth to a baby with spina bifida, she may need extra folic acid in subsequent pregnancies to reduce her chances of having another baby with the same problem. Some researchers now recommend that all women of childbearing age take 0.4mg of folic acid a day, in hopes of significantly decreasing the chances of this serious problem.

Folic acid is obtained through many foods. Although it is difficult to get enough folic acid through food intake alone, a varied diet can help you reach this goal. Common foods that contain folic acid are listed below.

Getting enough folic acid (vitamin B9) is usually not a problem for vegetarians. Folic acid is found in many fruits, legumes and vegetables (especially dark leafy ones).

Eating a breakfast of 1 cup of fortified cereal, with milk, and a glass of orange juice supplies about half of your daily requirement of folic acid.

Foods with Folic Acid

Get the folic acid you need by enjoying any of these foods:

asparagus	green beans	plantains
avocados	lentils	spinach
bananas	liver	strawberries
black beans	oranges and	wheat germ
broccoli	other citrus	whole-wheat
egg yolks	peas	bread
fortified cereals		yogurt

❧ Vitamin A

Vitamin A is essential to human reproduction. Vitamin-A deficiency in North America is rare; most women have adequate stores of the vitamin in the liver.

What concerns doctors now is the *excessive use* of vitamin A before conception and during early pregnancy. (This concern extends only to the retinol forms of vitamin A, often derived from fish oils. The beta-carotene form, usually derived from plants, is believed to be safe.) Studies indicate that elevated levels of the retinol form of vitamin A during pregnancy may cause birth defects, including cleft palate and hydrocephalus ("water on the brain").

The RDA of vitamin A is 2700 international units (IU) a day for a woman of childbearing age (5000IU is a maximum dosage). The requirement is the same whether a woman is pregnant or not. Most women get the vitamin A they need during pregnancy from the foods they eat. Supplementation during pregnancy is not recommended. Be cautious about taking *any* substances that you have not discussed with your healthcare provider. This includes vitamin A. See pages 215 to 216 for particular cautions.

❧ Vitamin B

The B vitamins—B_6, B_{12} and folic acid (B_9)—influence fetal development of nerves and red-blood-cell formation. If your vitamin-B_{12} level is low, you could develop anemia during pregnancy. Milk, eggs, tempeh and miso provide vitamins B_6 and B_{12}. Other good sources of B_6 include bananas, potatoes, collard greens, avocados and brown rice.

❧ Vitamin E

Vitamin E is important during pregnancy because it helps metabolize polyunsaturated fats and contributes to building muscles and red-blood cells. Vitamin E appears in adequate quantities in meats, but if you don't eat meat, it can be harder to come by in the rest of the diet. If you are a vegetarian, you may need to pay particular attention to getting enough of it to meet the minimum requirements.

Unbleached, cold-pressed vegetable oils (such as olive oil), wheat germ, spinach and dried fruits are all good sources of vitamin E. Ask your healthcare provider if your prenatal vitamin contains 100% of the RDA for vitamin E.

✧ Zinc

Zinc stabilizes the genetic code in cells and ensures normal tissue growth in the fetus. It helps prevent miscarriage and premature delivery and can help regulate blood sugar in you and your baby.

Some women, especially thin ones, can increase their chances of giving birth to bigger, healthier babies by taking zinc supplements during pregnancy. In one study, babies born to thin women who took zinc during pregnancy were an average 4.5 ounces heavier, and head circumference was 0.16 inch larger. Zinc also plays a critical role in immune functions.

Zinc is found in many foods, including seafood, meat, nuts and milk. Prenatal vitamins include 15 to 25mg of zinc, an adequate amount for most women.

If you are a vegetarian, you are more likely to have a zinc deficiency, so pay close attention to getting enough zinc every day. Lima beans, whole-grain products, nuts, dried beans, dried peas, wheat germ and dark leafy vegetables are all good sources of this mineral.

✧ Fluoride

The benefit of fluoride supplementation during pregnancy is controversial. Some researchers believe fluoride supplementation during pregnancy results in improved teeth in your child, but not everyone agrees. Fluoride supplementation during pregnancy has not been found to harm the baby. Some prenatal vitamins contain fluoride.

Weight Management

Every woman needs to gain a certain amount of weight during her pregnancy. Proper weight gain helps ensure that you and your baby are healthy at the time of delivery.

Today, recommendations for weight gain during pregnancy are higher than they were in the past; normal weight gain is 25 to 35 pounds. If you are underweight at the start of your pregnancy, expect to gain between 28 and 40 pounds. If you're overweight before pregnancy, you probably should not gain as much as other women during pregnancy. Acceptable weight gain for you is between 15 and 25 pounds. Recommendations vary, so discuss the matter with your doctor. Eat nutritious, well-balanced meals during your pregnancy. Do *not* diet now!

As an average for a normal-weight woman, many healthcare providers suggest a weight gain of 2/3 of a pound (10 ounces) a week until 20 weeks, then 1 pound a week through the 40th week. This recommendation is only an average; actual suggestions vary according to the individual.

It isn't unusual not to gain weight or even to lose a little weight early in pregnancy. Your healthcare provider will keep track of changes in your weight.

Watch your weight, but don't be obsessive about it. If you're in good shape when you get pregnant, with an appropriate amount of body fat, and you exercise regularly and eat healthfully, you shouldn't have a problem with excessive weight gain.

ஃ Increasing Your Caloric Intake

During pregnancy, you will be told to increase your calorie consumption; the average recommended increase is about 300 calories a day. Some women need more calories; some women need fewer. If you are underweight when you begin pregnancy, you will probably have to eat more than 300 extra calories each day. If you're overweight, you may have less need for extra calories.

The key to good nutrition and weight management is to eat a balanced diet throughout your pregnancy. Eat the foods you need to help your baby grow and develop. Choose wisely. For example, if you're overweight, avoid high-calorie peanut butter and other nuts as a protein source; choose water-packed tuna or lowfat cheeses instead. If you're underweight, high-calorie ice cream and milkshakes are acceptable dairy sources.

ஃ Be Prepared to Gain Weight

Getting on the scale and seeing your weight increase is hard for some women, especially those who watch their weight closely. You must acknowledge at the beginning of your pregnancy that it is all right to gain weight; it's for the health of your baby. You can control your weight gain by eating carefully and nutritiously, but you must gain enough weight to meet the needs of your pregnancy. Your doctor knows this; that's why your weight is checked at every prenatal visit.

In the past, women were allowed to gain a very small amount of weight during pregnancy, sometimes as little as 12 to 15 pounds for an entire pregnancy. With the benefit of research and advances in technology, we have learned these restrictive weight gains were not in the best interests of mother or baby.

ஃ Where Does the Weight Go?

A weight gain of 25 to 35 pounds may sound like a lot when the baby only weighs about 7 pounds; however, weight is distributed between you and your baby. Weight gained normally during pregnancy is distributed as shown in the chart on the next page.

Distribution of Pregnancy Weight	
7 to 10 pounds	Maternal stores (fat, protein and other nutrients)
4 pounds	Increased fluid volume
2 pounds	Breast enlargement
2 pounds	Uterus
7-1/2 pounds	Baby
2 pounds	Amniotic fluid
1-1/2 pounds	Placenta

✎ Obesity Brings Special Cautions

If you are overweight as you begin pregnancy, you face special challenges. Being overweight can contribute to a variety of problems, including a greater chance of developing gestational diabetes or hypertension. You may have more problems with backaches, varicose veins and fatigue. Gaining too much weight (above the normal, expected amount) may increase your chances of a Cesarean delivery, especially for older women.

Women who are overweight may need to see their healthcare provider more often during pregnancy. Ultrasound may be needed to pinpoint a due date because it is harder to determine the size and position of your baby. Abdominal fat layers make manual examination difficult.

You may be screened for gestational diabetes. Diagnostic tests may also be done on your baby as your delivery date approaches.

General Weight-gain Guidelines for Pregnancy	
If You Are Currently . . .	*You Should Gain Approximately . . .*
Underweight	28 to 40 pounds
Normal weight	25 to 35 pounds
Overweight	15 to 25 pounds

Gain weight very slowly. Weigh yourself weekly, and watch your food intake closely. Eat nutritious, healthful foods, and eliminate those with mostly empty calories. The quality of the food you eat is more important than ever when you are pregnant.

Exercise can be beneficial, but be sure to discuss your plans with your healthcare provider before you begin an exercise program. If you have never exercised before, walking and swimming may be the safest for you and your baby.

When You're Eating for More Than Two

When you are eating for yourself and more than one baby, you face an even greater nutritional challenge. Taking your prenatal vitamin every day provides some assurance that you are getting the nutrients you need, but the best source of nutrients and calories for you and your developing babies is the food you eat. Proper food choices can provide you with adequate protein, calories and calcium.

When you are expecting more than one baby, nutrition and weight gain are important. If you don't gain weight early in pregnancy, you are more likely to develop pre-eclampsia. Your babies are more likely to be significantly smaller at birth than others.

✀ Target Weight Gain with Multiples

The target weight gain for women carrying more than one baby is quite a bit higher than that for women carrying one baby. The desireable weight gain for women expecting twins is about 44 pounds.

Usually women who gain the targeted amount of weight during their pregnancies lose it after delivery. One study showed that women who gained the suggested amount of weight during a twin pregnancy were close to their prepregnant weight 2 years after delivery. You do not have to carry the extra weight forever, so don't worry about it now.

When you consider the average size of the babies (about 7-1/2 pounds each) and the weight of the placenta(s) (1-1/2 pounds for each), plus the weight of the additional amniotic fluid, you can see where the extra weight gain goes. Don't be alarmed when your healthcare provider discusses this target weight gain with you, even if it seems like a lot.

Research shows that higher weight gains (within targeted ranges) are associated with better fetal growth. Better fetal growth means healthier babies.

✀ Eat the Right Foods

The food pyramid is a good place to begin when making food choices (see page 163). Adjust the number of portions you consume to get the extra calories you need. Eat an extra serving of a dairy product and an extra serving of a protein because you need more calcium, protein and iron when you carry multiples.

Chapter 13

Exercise During and After Pregnancy

Pregnant women often ask me if they can exercise safely. Experts agree that exercise during pregnancy is safe and beneficial for most pregnant women, if it is done properly. Exercise can be even more beneficial for women who are pregnant in their late 30s and early 40s. It can help you feel more energetic and help you deal more effectively with the demands of pregnancy, career and family.

Discuss exercise with your healthcare provider at your first prenatal visit. If you decide later to start exercising or to change your current exercise program, be sure to talk with your physician before you begin.

Some women should not exercise during pregnancy. If you experience any of the following, do not exercise:

• a history of incompetent cervix, preterm labor or repeated miscarriages
• high blood pressure early in pregnancy
• multiple fetuses (twins, triplets, more)
• diagnosed heart disease
• pre-eclampsia
• vaginal bleeding

In the past, exercise was not always approved for a pregnant woman. Doctors were concerned about the redirection of blood flow from the fetus to the mother's muscles during exercise. We now know this occurs to a small degree, but it is not harmful to the fetus.

Any exercise that involves joint movement forces water in the tissues back into the blood and helps pump blood back to the heart. If you experience the normal swelling of pregnancy, such as swollen ankles or legs, exercise can help with the problem. Stationary bicycling is excellent for relieving these symptoms.

If You Exercise Regularly

Many women love to exercise and are willing to juggle hectic schedules to fit it into their daily routine. They believe exercise is necessary to help them feel fit, control their weight and look their best. They don't want to give up exercising and its benefits because of pregnancy.

If you exercised on a regular basis before you became pregnant, you may need to modify your exercise goals and take things a little easier during pregnancy. The goal of exercising at this time is overall good health. Exercise makes you feel better physically, and it can give you an emotional boost, but don't overdo it.

There are benefits to continuing a moderate exercise program during your pregnancy. The box on page 195 identifies some of them.

The Exercise Payoff

Exercise during pregnancy can help you feel more in control of your body and relieve some of the common aches and pains of pregnancy. Exercise improves circulation. Exercise definitely helps you adjust to carrying the extra weight you gain during pregnancy. Regular, moderate exercise can also help:
- relieve backache
- prevent constipation and varicose veins
- strengthen muscles needed for delivery
- make you feel better about yourself
- ease labor and delivery
- leave you in better shape after delivery
- may help control weight gain

Some doctors believe that women who exercise during pregnancy enjoy a shorter recovery time after birth. Because exercise keeps you fit, you may "bounce back" more quickly.

You may have to change or to modify your exercise program during pregnancy because of changes in your body. Your center of gravity shifts, so you need to adjust your exercise for that. As your abdomen grows larger, you may not be able to do some activities very comfortably and you may have to eliminate others.

During pregnancy, your heart rate is higher; you don't have to exercise as vigorously to reach your target-heart-rate range. Be careful not to put too much stress on your cardiovascular system. If your heart rate is too high, slow down but don't stop completely. Continue exercising at a moderate rate. If your heart rate is too low and you don't feel winded, you may pick up the pace a bit, but don't overdo it. Check your pulse rate frequently to make sure you aren't overexerting.

I am often asked by women who jog or run regularly whether they can continue this activity during pregnancy. If you are used to jogging and have been involved in regular jogging before pregnancy, you can continue to jog in moderation during pregnancy. Listen to your body when it tells you to slow down—don't get overheated, stop if you feel tired, and drink lots of water.

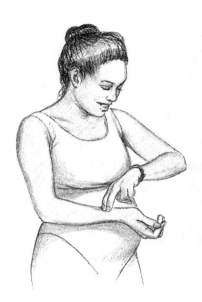

If You've Never Exercised Before

I have patients who do not like to exercise or who do not exercise on a regular basis. When many of these women discover they are pregnant, they begin to think about the benefits of exercise; they want to know whether it is safe to begin an exercise program during pregnancy. If you've never exercised before, you must discuss it with your healthcare provider before you begin.

❧❧❧❧

Suzy never liked regular exercise, but she found that being pregnant gave her the incentive and motivation to engage in a program specifically designed for pregnant women at a health club. It helped her feel more in control of her health while she was pregnant—she felt she was doing something positive for her body. After she delivered her baby, she continued exercising. She found she really missed it if she didn't.

Yes, it is possible to start exercising now; however, begin gradually. Your age may affect your ability to exercise slightly. If you've never exercised before, you may find it a little more difficult to begin because of less flexibility and tighter muscles.

If your pregnancy is uncomplicated, you should be able to exercise as long as you are comfortable doing so. The key is not to do too much, too fast. Don't be afraid that exercising might do something to hurt your developing baby; most moderate exercise is safe.

If exercise is approved for you, start with *moderate* exercise if you do not have a regular exercise routine. Walking is an excellent form of exercise. Riding a stationary bike can be enjoyable. Swimming and other water exercises are also good for a beginner; the water provides your body with a lot of support.

Swimming and Water Exercises

I've had women tell me that while they are pregnant, the only time they really feel comfortable is in the water. Being in the water has a calming effect on some women, and it can help reduce swelling related to pregnancy.

Because it supports you, you will feel much lighter in the water, and you won't have to worry about keeping your balance. Because the water also supports the weight of the fetus, your lower back is relieved of some stress. That enables you to adopt a more-relaxed posture and enjoy a greater range of motion while in the water.

Being in the water reduces the effect of gravity, which in turn reduces pressure on your joints—a great temporary relief for some women. In addition, exercising in the water makes it significantly easier for the heart to pump blood. That's a real benefit, especially if you have hypertension.

You can also get a good workout in the water. Water exerts 12 times the resistance of air on limbs—you'll expend more energy moving through water than you would walking down the street.

Your baby is well protected inside your body while you are in the water. There are actually three barriers that provide protection—the amniotic membrane that surrounds the baby, the cervix and the vagina. Don't be concerned about water getting to the baby. However, if your bag of waters has broken, do not exercise in the water.

Consider these suggestions if you want to work out in water or swim as part of your exercise regimen.

- Be sure pool water is warm enough but not hot. The ideal temperature of the water should be between 80 and 84F (26.5 and 29C). Avoid hot tubs and spas because water is too hot for the fetus.
- Drink plenty of fluids before you begin exercising and during exercise. Dehydration can occur even in a pool.
- Eat easily digested foods 1/2 to 1 hour before you work out; choose fruit or a whole-wheat product.
- To help you keep your footing when you exercise in the pool, wear aquatic shoes, tennis shoes or jogging shoes. Be sure the shoe has a good tread so you don't slip.

Are There Risks to Exercising during Pregnancy?

Exercise during pregnancy isn't without some risks, including increased body temperature, decreased blood flow to the uterus and possible injury to you. Your age is probably not an important factor, however. Most experts recommend you reduce your exercise to 70 to 80% of your prepregnancy level. If you have problems with bleeding or cramping or have had problems in previous pregnancies, you must modify or eliminate your exercise with your doctor's advice.

We know the increased hormone levels of pregnancy soften connective tissues, which can make your joints more susceptible to injury. Avoid full situps, double leg raises and straight-leg toe touches.

It was once believed that exercise could cause preterm labor because of a temporary increase in uterine activity following exercise. However, studies prove that this isn't a problem in a normal pregnancy. The fetal heart rate increases somewhat during and immediately after exercise, but it stays within the normal fetal range of 120 to 160 beats a minute. A moderate exercise program should not cause any problems for you or your baby.

Your Exercise Experience during Pregnancy

You may notice some changes in how your body responds to exercise during pregnancy. Your growing abdomen can put a strain on your respiratory system; you may feel out of breath sooner than usual. When you exercise, don't work to the point that you cannot talk or have trouble breathing. At that point, you are working too strenuously; cut back on your workout.

Avoid becoming overheated during your workout. Work out in a well-ventilated room, and drink lots of water while you exercise. See the fluid-intake discussion on page 176.

Which Exercises during Pregnancy?

Keep in mind a few general precautions about exercising during pregnancy that apply to most pregnant women. Your healthcare provider may want to discuss additional precautions that apply specifically to you.

If you are used to participating in a competitive sport, such as tennis, you may be able to continue, but expect to change the level at which you play. The point to remember is not to get carried away or to overwork yourself. The goal is not to win the game but to maintain fitness and have a good time! You may want to pick a less-strenuous sport to participate in during pregnancy. Some are listed below; most are considered acceptable for women of any age in a normal, low-risk pregnancy.

- walking
- swimming
- low-impact aerobics designed specifically for pregnancy
- water aerobics
- stationary bicycling
- regular cycling (if you're experienced)
- jogging (if you jogged regularly before pregnancy)
- tennis (played moderately)
- yoga (don't lie on your back after the 16th week of pregnancy)

Avoid the following sports during pregnancy:

• scuba diving
• water skiing
• surfing
• horseback riding
• downhill skiing
• cross-country skiing
• any contact sport

❧ Pregnancy Aerobics Classes

Aerobics classes designed for pregnant women are a good exercise choice. They concentrate on your unique needs, such as strengthening abdominal muscles and improving posture. When choosing a class, be sure the instructor has proper training and the class meets the exercise guidelines developed by the American College of Obstetricians and Gynecologists (ACOG).

❧ Nutritional Needs during Exercise

Because nutritional needs increase during pregnancy and because you burn extra calories during exercise, consume enough calories to ensure a balanced diet. You may need to eat more than a pregnant woman who is not exercising at your level. Discuss how much more you should eat with your healthcare professional. Make sure that any additional calories are nutritious and supply your body with protein, calcium and carbohydrates, not sugar and fat.

Guidelines for Exercising during Pregnancy

As I've stated, consult your healthcare provider before you begin any exercise program. Follow the tips below to keep you healthy and in good shape.

• Try to exercise at least 3 times a week for 20 to 30 minutes each time.

- Start your exercise routine with a 5-minute warm-up, and end with a 5-minute cool-down period.
- Wear comfortable clothes that offer support, such as a support bra and good athletic shoes.
- Drink plenty of water during exercise.
- Don't exercise strenuously for more than 15 to 20 minutes.
- Check your pulse rate frequently; keep it below 140 beats a minute.
- Don't exercise in hot, humid weather.
- After the fourth month of pregnancy, avoid exercises that require you to lie on your back.
- Never allow your body temperature to rise above 100.4F (38C).
- Exercise during the coolest part of the day.
- Stop immediately and consult your physician if you experience any problems.

Be aware of problems that might develop while you exercise. If you notice any unusual occurrences, report them to your doctor immediately. Be careful about the following:

- pain
- bleeding
- dizziness
- extreme shortness of breath
- palpitations
- faintness
- abnormally rapid heart rate
- back pain
- pubic pain
- difficulty walking
- breathlessness that doesn't go away
- chest pain
- loss of fetal movement

Prenatal Exercises to Do at Home or at Work

Sometimes you may find it difficult to exercise outside your home or at a health club. You can do the exercises in this section at home or at work. Try all of them, and incorporate those you like into your regular schedule.

✄ Weightlift with Cans

Next time you're putting away groceries, build up arm muscles by doing a little weightlifting with each can (water bottles also work well). As you put a can away, flex your arm a couple of times to work arm muscles. Alternate arms to give yourself a good workout.

✄ Workout in Line

When you're standing in line at the grocery store, post office or anywhere else, use the time to do some "creative" exercises. Rise up and down on your toes to work your calves. Spread your feet apart slightly, and do subtle knee lunges to give quadriceps a workout. Clench and relax buttocks muscles. Do some Kegel exercises (see page 203) to strengthen vaginal muscles. Contract stomach muscles. These exercises help you develop and strengthen some of the muscles you'll use during labor and delivery.

✄ Standing Stretches

If you're forced to stand in one place for a long time, step forward slightly with one foot. Place all your weight on that foot for a few minutes. If you're still waiting, do the same exercise for the other foot. Alternate the leg you begin with each time.

✄ Reaching-Stretching

You probably have to reach for things at home or at the office. When you do, make it an exercise in controlled breathing. Before you stretch, inhale, rise up on your toes and bring both arms up at the same time. When you are finished, drop back on your heels, and exhale while slowly returning your arms to your sides.

❧ Sitting Quietly

Anytime you are sitting quietly—at home, at the office, in your car, on a bus or a train—do this breathing exercise to strengthen abdominal muscles. Breathe deeply and contract stomach muscles; hold for a couple of seconds, then exhale slowly. Do this whenever you get the chance.

❧❧❧❧

Cindy was concerned because it was hard to find time to exercise regularly. She discovered she could exercise at her desk at work, doing ankle and leg exercises. This helped her keep her legs toned and also helped her with leg cramps and swelling.

❧ Bending to Relieve Backache

While standing at the kitchen counter or a counter at work, bend your knees and lean forward from your hips. Hold the position for a few minutes. This exercise is an excellent way to relieve back stress.

❧ Rising from a Chair

Some women find it difficult to get out of a chair gracefully during pregnancy. This exercise helps you maintain your grace and is also beneficial for you. Use leg muscles to lower yourself into and raise yourself out of a chair. Slide to the front edge of the seat, then push up with your legs to get out of the chair. Use your arms for balance.

❧ Kegel Exercise

The Kegel exercise strengthens pelvic muscles. Practicing it helps you relax your muscles for delivery. While sitting, contract the lowest muscles of your pelvis as tightly as you can. Tighten muscles higher in the pelvis in stages until you reach the muscles at the top. Count to 10 slowly as you move up the pelvis. Hold briefly, then release slowly in stages, counting to 10 again. Repeat 2 or 3 times a day.

You can also do the Kegel exercise by tightening the pelvic muscles first, then tightening the anal muscle. Hold for a few seconds, then release slowly, in reverse order. To see if you're doing the exercise correctly, stop the flow of urine while you are urinating.

Your Pregnancy Workout

Practice the exercises in the previous section, and add the following ones to your routine. You may have to set time aside to do these exercises. If you combine them with some form of aerobic exercise, such as walking, swimming or bicycling, you'll get a thorough workout.

❧ Arm Reaches

Relieves upper backache and tension in shoulders, neck and back

Sit on the floor in a comfortable position. Inhale as you raise your right arm over your head. Reach as high as you can, while stretching from the waist. Bend your elbow, and pull your arm back down to your side as you exhale. Repeat for your left side. Do 4 or 5 times.

❧ Pelvic Curl

Strengthens abdominal muscles and relieves back stress

Kneel on your hands and knees, with your back relaxed. Do not arch your back. Inhale and relax. As you exhale, pull your buttocks under and forward until you feel your back straighten at the waist and your abdomen tighten. Hold for a count of 5, then exhale and relax. Do this exercise 4 or 5 times whenever you can.

☙ Tailor's Seat

Develops pelvic-floor strength

Sit on the floor, bring feet close to your body and cross your ankles. Apply gentle pressure to your knees or the inside of your thighs. Hold for a count of 10, relax and repeat. Do this exercise 4 or 5 times.

☙ Tailor Press

Develops pelvic-floor strength and quadricep strength

Sit on the floor and bring the soles of your feet together as close to your body as you can comfortably. Place hands under your knees, and gently press down with your knees while resisting the pressure with your hands. Count to 5, then relax. Increase number of presses until you can do 10 presses twice a day.

☙ Shoulder Circles

Relieves upper backache and tension in shoulders, neck and back

Inhale while slowly moving your left shoulder forward and upward, to form the top half of a circle. Slowly move the shoulder to the back then down to complete the circle as you exhale. Repeat with right shoulder. Do 4 or 5 times.

☙ Wall Push-Away

Develops upper-back, chest and arm strength, and relieves lower-leg tension

Stand a couple of feet away from a wall, with your hands in front of your shoulders. Place hands on the wall, and lean forward. Bend your elbows as your body leans into the wall. Keep heels flat on the floor. Slowly push away from wall, and straighten. Do 10 to 20 times.

ᘐ Hip-and-Back Stretch

Reduces back tension and increases blood flow to the feet

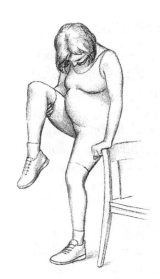

Place one hand on the back of a chair or on a wall. Lift your right knee to the side of your tummy, and put your left hand under your thigh. Round your back, and bring head and pelvis forward. Hold position for count of four, straighten up, then lower leg. Repeat with left leg. Do 2 or 3 times.

ᘐ Side Leg Lifts

Tones and strengthens hip, buttock and thigh muscles

Lie on your left side, with your body in alignment. Support your head with your left hand, and place your right hand on the floor in front of you for balance. Inhale and relax. While exhaling, slowly raise your right leg as high as you can without bending your knee or your body. Keep foot flexed. Inhale and slowly lower your leg. Repeat on right side. Do 10 times on each side.

Your After-pregnancy Workout

After your baby is born, continue the exercises you did during pregnancy. Add some of the following exercises to help you focus on specific areas, especially abdominal muscles. Do these exercises when your healthcare provider gives you permission. Start slowly and gradually work harder.

ᘐ Back Bridge

Strengthens back, legs and buttocks

Lie flat on your back on the floor. Inhale, then slowly lift buttocks and back in straight line. Hold for 4 seconds. Exhale and lower back to floor so your upper back touches floor, then your waist touches, then your pelvis touches last. Do 4 or 5 times.

❧ The Crunch

Strengthens abdominal muscles

Lie on your back on the floor, with knees bent and feet flat. Put your hands on your abdomen. Suck in your abdomen, pulling your navel toward your spine. Hold 4 seconds and release. When you are able to do 8 repetitions, lift your head toward your chest. Hold for 4 seconds, then lower head and hold for 4 seconds. Work up to 10 repetitions.

❧ Leg and Pelvic-floor Strengthener

Strengthens legs and pelvic floor

Lie on your back with arms out at your sides. Cross your right ankle over your left ankle; squeeze legs together. Hold 5 seconds and release. Repeat for other ankle. Do 5 times on each side.

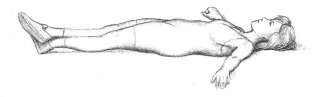

❧ Back Stretch

Strengthens buttocks, back muscles and leg muscles

Kneel on hands and knees, with wrists directly beneath shoulders and knees directly beneath hips. Keep your back straight. Contract abdominals, then extend left leg behind you at hip height. At same time, extend right arm at shoulder height. Hold 5 seconds, and return to kneeling position. Repeat on other side. Start with 4 exercises on each side, and gradually work up to 8.

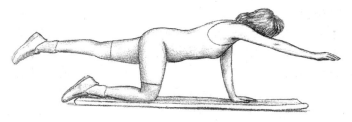

❧ Chair Squat

Strengthens hips, thighs and buttocks muscles

Lightly grasp the back of a chair or a counter for balance. Stand with feet shoulder-width apart. Keep body weight over heels and torso erect. Bend knees, and lower torso in squatting position. Don't round your back. Hold squatting position for 5 seconds, then straighten to starting position. Start with 5 repetitions and work up to 10.

❧ Leg Raises

Good for abdominal muscles

Lie flat on your back. Slowly lift both legs from the hip at the same time, using abdominal muscles. Hold for 5 seconds. Slowly lower both legs together to the floor. Start with 2 repetitions and work up to 6.

Chapter 14

Current Medical Therapy and Medications

It's a fact that the older you get, the more likely you are to develop medical conditions—some serious, most not-so-serious. Medications you use to treat those conditions may affect your baby during your pregnancy. I discuss some of those conditions and treatments in this chapter.

First let me comment on the subject of medication during pregnancy. Many pregnant women seem unconcerned about their use of various medicinal substances during pregnancy. They believe if they can buy it without a prescription, it must be safe to use. Or they believe they can use any amount of vitamins, minerals or herbal substances without hesitation.

Beware this type of thinking! Many substances you use *can* affect your growing baby. Some effects can be serious. Other effects may be subtle and cause minor birth defects. The effects of yet others may not be evident for years.

Researchers once believed the placenta acted as a barrier to any agent the mother was exposed to. Today we know that isn't the case. We have discovered that *most* drugs can cross the placenta and affect the fetus.

Teratogens

Drugs are called *environmental factors* (other things can be termed environmental factors, such as pesticides); environmental factors linked to birth defects are called *teratogens*. The first 13 weeks of development (the first trimester) are the most dangerous time in which to expose a fetus to teratogens. An embryo exposed to teratogens during the first 2 weeks of development may be unaffected; if the embryo is affected, the pregnancy can end in a miscarriage. The most critical period of fetal development during of the first trimester is between the second and eighth weeks.

Although the first trimester is very important, your baby's systems continue to grow and to develop throughout your pregnancy. Exposure to some substances can harm a baby even after the first trimester.

Talk to Your Healthcare Provider

The best time to discuss current healthcare concerns is before you become pregnant, but this isn't always possible. If you discover you are pregnant and are concerned about the medications you use or anything else related to your health, talk to your doctor about it as soon as possible.

At your first visit with your healthcare provider, discuss all medications (prescription and over-the-counter) you take on a regular basis. You may have to stop taking a particular substance or adjust the dosage.

Never stop taking any medication you use for a chronic health problem without first consulting your healthcare provider! Some medication cannot and should not be stopped during pregnancy.

Some Safety Guidelines

You are an important part of your healthcare team, especially during pregnancy. You have to make many decisions about how you will take care of your body during this important time. The suggestions that follow can help you decide what substances you use before and during your pregnancy.

- Don't use any unnecessary drugs while trying to conceive.
- Avoid all medications during the first trimester, if possible. If you must take a medication, consult with your healthcare provider before using it.
- Talk to your healthcare provider openly and honestly about the medications you use. If you have a problem that you normally treat with over-the-counter drugs, ask how to treat it during pregnancy.
- If you must use a prescription medication, ask your healthcare provider to prescribe it in its least-potent strength.

Prescription Medication Use during Pregnancy

Use of some prescription medications is more common than others; the discussion below includes common substances many women must take during pregnancy. Please note—this information does *not* take the place of talking with your doctor.

❧ Hormone-replacement Therapy

Today, the average age of menopause is 50. At menopause, you stop ovulating (necessary for conception) and stop having periods. The change is usually gradual, occurring over years, but it may be sudden. If you still have menstrual periods, you can probably still get pregnant.

In the past, women didn't start taking hormones (hormone-replacement therapy or HRT) until their periods stopped, and they were certain of menopause. Today, more women start HRT at younger ages.

If you become pregnant while taking HRT, advise your healthcare professional immediately. Minor risks are associated with pregnancy when you have been taking female hormones. They are usually not severe enough to warrant terminating the pregnancy.

❧ Thyroid Medication

You will need to continue taking thyroid medication throughout pregnancy. Thyroid hormone is made in the thyroid gland, which is found in the neck. It affects your entire body and is important to your metabolism. Thyroid hormone is also important in your ability to get pregnant.

Thyroxin® (medication for a low-thyroid or hypothyroid condition) can be taken safely during pregnancy. Propylthiouracil (medication for a high-thyroid or hyperthyroid condition) passes to the baby; you will probably be given the lowest amount possible during pregnancy.

❧ Prozac

Today, many women take Prozac® for depression and want to know if they can continue taking the medication during pregnancy. We have little information about its safety for a pregnant woman. Discuss taking Prozac with your physician before you get pregnant or as soon as you discover you are pregnant.

❧ Skin-care Medications

Accutane® (isotretinoin) is a common acne treatment. Do *not* take it if you are pregnant! A woman taking Accutane during the first trimester of pregnancy is at greater risk of miscarriage and fetal malformation.

Retin-A® (tretinoin) is a medication used to help relieve minor wrinkling in the facial area. We don't know its effects on the fetus, so it's probably best to avoid Retin-A during pregnancy until we know more about its effects.

Occasionally steroid cream is prescribed for a skin condition. Before using it during pregnancy, discuss it with your healthcare provider. You may be able to use another preparation that is considered safer during pregnancy.

Tetracycline, an antibiotic, is often prescribed for skin problems. During pregnancy, avoid all tetracyclines! Use of the drug during pregnancy can cause discoloration of your baby's permanent teeth later in life. (Tetracyclines should not be prescribed for children under age 8.)

✥ Other Prescription Medications

Some medications are safe to use during pregnancy but should be prescribed only if absolutely necessary. These substances include Valium, Librium and Tranxene®. Other substances are discussed below.

If you have a headache bad enough to be considered a migraine, call your healthcare provider before you take anything for it. You may have heard of a relatively new medication for migraines called Imitrex®, given by injection or in pill form. Avoid it during pregnancy; we do not know yet whether it is safe.

Common medications used for blood clots or phlebitis, called *anticoagulants,* are heparin and Coumadin®. Heparin doesn't cross the placenta, so it is safe to use during pregnancy. It is administered by injection or I.V. Don't use Coumadin during pregnancy because it causes significant problems in the fetus or newborn.

Many asthma medications are permissible to use during pregnancy. Inhalers, such as Proventil®, can be used safely. For an asthma attack, your doctor may prescribe prednisone; it is approved for use during pregnancy.

Medicines to treat anemia can be important during pregnancy and are safe to use. These medications contain iron, which may cause side effects such as constipation, nausea or upset stomach.

Some older women are taking hormones, including estrogen or progesterone, when they discover they are pregnant. Most doctors recommend that you not take hormones during pregnancy. If you are taking them when you learn you are pregnant, contact your healthcare provider.

In some situations, you may need pain relief during pregnancy. If you do, check with your healthcare provider before taking anything stronger than extra-strength acetaminophen. Acetaminophen with codeine (Tylenol #3®) may be prescribed during pregnancy, but get your doctor's approval before you take it.

Got a cough? You can almost always take cough drops or throat lozenges safely. Robitussin® syrup is usually permissible, but check with your healthcare provider first. Prescription cough medicine may contain codeine. Usually codeine is safe to use for a short period of time, but check with your physician before you use it. Avoid any "nighttime" medicines that contain alcohol. Some are 25% alcohol; you want to avoid alcohol use during pregnancy. Read labels before taking any preparation.

You may become constipated at some point during pregnancy and need a laxative. If you find a laxative is necessary for more than 2 or 3 days, contact your healthcare provider. He or she will probably advise you to make dietary changes to help with the problem.

Some medications can be taken for diarrhea during pregnancy. Imodium® diarrhea preparation is OK to use, but most healthcare providers recommend avoiding the pink bismuth-type preparations during pregnancy. If you have bloody diarrhea or diarrhea that lasts longer than a few days, contact your healthcare provider.

Pregnancy is not the time to use *any* type of diet pill. Over-the-counter diet pills contain large amounts of caffeine. Don't take prescription diet pills during pregnancy because they have not been proved safe. If you are taking diet pills when you find out you're pregnant, stop taking them immediately!

Nonprescription/Over-the-counter Medications

Many people, not just pregnant women, hold the false belief that medications they can buy without a prescription (over-the-counter medications) are harmless. Nothing could be further from the truth. Carelessness with over-the-counter preparations could cause great harm to you and your developing baby.

Take any over-the-counter (OTC) medication with care during pregnancy. Ask your doctor about any medication before you take it, whether it is prescription or nonprescription. Many OTCs contain aspirin, caffeine, alcohol or phenacetin, all of which should be avoided during pregnancy. Cough syrups may contain as much as 25% alcohol (that's "50 proof"!).

Use medications that contain ibuprofen with care; brand-name ibuprofen medications include Advil®, Motrin® and Rufen®. Avoid newer medicines, such as Aleve® (naprosyn) and Orudis® (ketoprofen), until we know more about their safety during pregnancy. Read package labels, and get approval from your healthcare provider or pharmacist before taking anything.

Some OTC medications that are safe to use while you're pregnant include:

• acetaminophen (Tylenol)
• antacids (Amphojel, Gelusil, Maalox, milk of magnesia)
• throat lozenges (Sucrets®)
• decongestants (chlorpheniramine, Sudafed®)
• antidiarrheal preparations (Kaopectate®)
• anti-itch preparations (Benadryl®)
• cough medicine (Robitussin)
• hemorrhoid preparations (Anusol®, Preparation H®)

Don't overuse any product during pregnancy. You can get "too much of a good thing."

Your healthcare provider will not be angry or upset if you call the office with a question about a medication. I can tell you from experience that it's much easier to answer a question and solve a potential problem about a medication *before* a woman takes it than afterwards.

About Vitamin and Mineral Supplements

Be very cautious during pregnancy about taking vitamin and mineral supplements. Often people do not think of vitamins and minerals as harmful, but they can be, especially to your developing baby. Also see the discussion about specific vitamins and minerals beginning on page 179.

Many vitamin supplements and "megavitamins" sold in health-food stores contain extremely high amounts of minerals, vitamins and other substances. Even some foods contain extra vitamins and minerals. Some of these "extra" supplements could affect your developing baby.

One example is vitamin A. Studies indicate that ingesting too much of the retinol form of vitamin A during pregnancy may cause birth defects. Most people get all the vitamin A they need in the foods they eat. Supplementation isn't recommended. Many vitamin supplements and megavitamins sold in health-food stores contain as much as 25,000IU of vitamin A. That's nearly 10 times the amount you need. Even some cereals contain as much as

5000IU per serving. Just eating two bowls a day of fortified cereal could potentially affect your developing baby!

The more vitamin A you consume, the higher the potential danger. A woman taking 20,000IU a day has four times the risk of having a baby with a birth defect than a woman who takes 10,000IU.

To protect yourself and your baby, don't take any vitamins or minerals other than your prenatal vitamin and iron or folic-acid supplements, unless prescribed by your healthcare provider especially for you. Read labels on the foods you eat. Do not "self-medicate" with other vitamins or minerals—you don't need them, and they can be dangerous if taken in excessive amounts.

Prenatal vitamins contain the recommended daily amounts of vitamins and minerals you need during pregnancy. They are prescribed to ensure your health and your baby's health.

✸ Prenatal Vitamins

At your first prenatal visit, your healthcare provider will probably give you a prescription for prenatal vitamins. It's very important that you take these vitamins for your *entire* pregnancy.

❧❧❧❧

Kathy was a busy executive who never had time for breakfast. She might grab a diet cola and a bag of chips for lunch and often ate dinner out with clients. Her plan was to continue this regimen and take a prenatal vitamin during her pregnancy. We had a frank discussion about why her plan wouldn't work. I explained how her baby relied on her for its nourishment. I advised her she couldn't eat that way for the entire pregnancy; she'd feel terrible and not be able to work. With some help, she made a commitment to a healthful eating plan and to take her prenatal vitamins every night after dinner.

Sometimes, late in pregnancy, a woman will stop taking her prenatal vitamins; she gets tired of taking them, or she decides they aren't necessary. Studies show that nearly half of all pregnant women who are prescribed prenatal vitamins do not take them regularly. The vitamins and iron in prenatal vitamins are essential to the well-being of your baby, so be sure you take your prenatal vitamins until your baby is born.

Immunizations and Vaccinations in Pregnancy

Some immunizations are not recommended for a pregnant woman because they may contain substances harmful to a fetus. In other cases, an immunization might be necessary for a woman's health.

Vaccines work by introducing disease components into the body in a very controlled way, which triggers the body to produce antibodies to protect it against the disease in the future. The risk of fetal exposure to various diseases is an important consideration with vaccines during pregnancy, but not all vaccines are harmful.

Don't be immunized without discussing the situation with your doctor first. If you have been exposed to a disease, or exposure is possible, your doctor will weigh the risk of the disease against the risks of the immunization, if any.

ஃ Safe Vaccines

Tetanus, diphtheria and rabies vaccines are all considered safe to take at any time during pregnancy. The flu vaccine is also considered safe to use during pregnancy. If you are in a high-risk group for flu, especially if you suffer from chronic lung problems, kidney disease or cardiovascular disease, your doctor will probably tell you to go ahead and receive the vaccine.

ஃ Vaccines You Should Not Receive

Pregnant women should definitely avoid some vaccines. Live-measles vaccine should never be given to a pregnant woman; this vaccine protects against measles, mumps and rubella (MMR). Don't get a primary vaccine against polio unless your risk of exposure is high—if you are traveling to a high-risk area, for example. Avoid the yellow-fever vaccine, which is also a live-virus vaccine. For added protection, it's wise to have a pregnancy test and be on reliable contraception before receiving MMR, polio or yellow-fever vaccines.

Chapter 15

Pregnancy Affects Your Partner, Too

Getting pregnant and having a baby involves *both* you and your partner. Although it's an exciting time for you, it may be a different experience for your baby's father—it may not be an all-encompassing experience for him.

A first-time pregnancy for you may or may not be a first pregnancy for your partner. However, it will be the first pregnancy he shares with you.

Being pregnant together can teach you a lot about each other. You both will go through many changes during the pregnancy and face new challenges. Your partner may feel anxious about his ability to be a good father or to provide for you and the baby. Other challenges you both may face include making child-care decisions, choosing how each of you will allot your time and delegation of responsibilities, such as who will do what chores.

While your body undergoes changes, and you experience the deep wonder of a new life growing inside you, your partner will watch you change but cannot really know what you are going through. Some men become jealous of the attention their pregnant partners receive. If you notice signs of jealousy, be understanding of your partner's feelings. Offer him support and love, and include him in your pregnancy as much as you can. Help him understand what you and the baby are going through.

Because your partner is less intimately involved with the pregnancy than you are, you may have to adjust your expectations of his enthusiasm and participation. You may need to encourage your partner to become more actively involved, such as by asking him to accompany you to prenatal visits.

Your partner can be a wonderful source of support. He can help prepare you for labor and delivery, and support you as you labor. He can share in the joy of the delivery of your baby. He can support you emotionally during pregnancy, which can be important to you both. Involve him as much as he is willing to be involved, and make him feel he's included in what's going on.

Discuss with him his feelings about the pregnancy. He may have fears and uncertainties he hasn't voiced. Be open and direct with each other about your feelings—it can help both of you.

Some expectant fathers manifest physical problems during their wife's pregnancy. The condition is called *couvade,* a term taken from a Caribe Indian tribe in which every expectant father engages in rituals that enable him to understand some of what his wife is experiencing. In our culture, an expectant father may experience headaches, irritability, back and muscle aches, insomnia, fatigue and depression. Many of these symptoms are the body's way of signaling that the tension level is high and something must be done to relieve the stress.

To help relieve stress, a father can discuss his feelings and fears with other men, such as those who are taking the same childbirth-education classes. Exercise, reading and listening to music may also relieve stress. When a man experiences headaches and shows other stress-related symptoms during his partner's pregnancy, it's time for the couple to start taking better care of each other so they can take care of their baby when it is born.

Some Fears Men Express About Pregnancy

Your husband may feel increased anxiety as your pregnancy progresses. He may be concerned about your health, the health of the baby, sex with you, labor and delivery and his ability to be a good father. Share your own concerns with him; it may be enough to calm his anxieties.

A recent survey of about 200 men revealed common things that men are fearful of as they approach fatherhood, including:

• being able to participate in the birth
• doubts about their personal maturity
• dropping the baby
• having enough time for the baby
• in-laws and parents coming over too often
• losing the relationship they have with their partner after the baby's birth
• losing their freedom
• providing adequately for the family
• the baby's crying
• whether they'll be a good father

Understanding what your partner is feeling can help you adjust to his reactions to your pregnancy.

❧❧❧❧

In my work, nearly all the phone calls I get are from women. When the answering service said they had Fred on the line, I thought they had the wrong doctor. Fred explained his wife Silvia was a patient of mine, due in about 2 months. He was very upset. They had always been open and close during their 10 years of marriage, but now he felt left out. They had also lost some of the intimacy they had always shared. He confessed he wasn't sure what to do or how to get involved in the pregnancy. He feared Silvia didn't need him, and they were drifting apart.

I suggested Fred come with Silvia on her next visit, and I'd help him "break the ice." At the visit, I brought up the topic of sex and intimacy during pregnancy. It turned out they both had some misconceptions. I told them this was a normal reaction. They might need to make some changes in their lovemaking, but they could still be intimate. Silvia had felt Fred was a little aloof but she didn't know what to do about it. It took some effort from both of them, but Fred confided in me at the delivery that things were much better. Silvia really did need him after all.

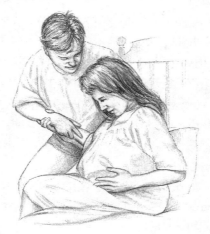

Your Partner Can Help You

Let your partner know there are things he can do for you during pregnancy. Tell him how important he is to you. Be specific about what you want, so he can help you effectively. Some helpful things your partner can do are listed below.

- Keep stress to a minimum.
- Communicate with each other about everything.
- Be patient and supportive.
- Promote good nutrition.
- Encourage exercise, and exercise with you.
- Help around the house when possible, and do the strenuous chores.
- Attend prenatal checkups when possible.
- Plan for the baby's arrival.
- Learn about the birth process.
- Read, study and prepare together.

Ways to Reassure Your Partner

You can reassure your partner and help him grow more comfortable with your pregnancy and the idea of fatherhood. Suggestions my patients have shared with me include the following.

• Reassure your partner about the impending birth. Let him know you are comfortable with whatever level of participation he is willing to give.

• Appreciate his help. He'll probably be more willing to offer his help if he knows it means something to you.

• Listen when he talks. Encourage him to express his hopes, fears and expectations about the baby's birth and being a father.

• Be as supportive of him as you can be. Let him know you have faith in his abilities.

• Talk about how you will divide responsibilities. List what you can do and what your partner can do. If possible, practice before the baby's birth!

• Help inform your partner about the birth and living with a new baby. Together, take childbirth-education classes and other classes that are offered. Share this and other books with him. Tour the hospital, and discuss any questions and concerns you have.

• Encourage your partner to be as involved with the baby as he wants to be. If he wants to take paternity leave from work, encourage it. Help him learn about diapering, feeding and bathing, and living with a new baby.

☙❧☙❧

Jeannie thought her pregnancy couldn't have come at a worse time. She had just been promoted, with more pay and greater responsibilities. She came to her first visit feeling unhappy and discouraged. She wanted a baby but not right now. I told her that her reaction was not unusual; many of my patients have "accidents" or unplanned pregnancies. I encouraged her to look at the positive things about her pregnancy. She admitted her husband was thrilled; he had assured her things would be fine. Later in the pregnancy, Jeannie expressed amazement about how she felt early on and about how well things were working out. I think she felt guilty about her feelings earlier and the time she lost feeling down about her pregnancy.

How a Father's Health Can Affect Pregnancy

It was once believed that a man had little to do with a pregnancy, other can contributing sperm to fertilize an egg. Today, we know a father-to-be can affect his baby even before it is born. Research has proved that reproduction and fetal development may be affected if a man is exposed to various chemical hazards before conception. Exposure to alcohol, cigarettes, certain drugs and some environmental hazards by the father can harm an unborn baby. Usually male exposure is most harmful if it occurs just before or at the time of conception (rather than months or years before).

The age and health of your baby's father is also important. If he is over 50, doctors suspect there is an increased risk of Down syndrome, although we do not have a great deal of evidence to support this theory.

Some researchers believe heavy alcohol consumption by the baby's father may produce fetal alcohol syndrome (FAS) in the baby. Chapter 6 has more information on FAS. Alcohol intake by the father has also been linked to intrauterine-growth retardation.

A nonsmoking pregnant woman and her unborn baby who are exposed to secondary smoke are exposed to chemicals that can harm both. If your partner smokes, ask him to stop during your pregnancy or at least to smoke outside your home.

Even substances on your partner's work clothes could be harmful to you or your developing baby. If you think you may be exposed to hazardous substances in this manner, be sure to discuss it with your healthcare provider.

A Father Can Bond with Baby

Bonding between parent and child is very important. It's easy for a mother to bond with her baby; they are linked in a number of physical ways. It's more difficult for a man to bond with the baby, but you can help your partner do this. He can begin bonding with the baby before birth and continue after the baby is born. Encourage your partner to:

- Talk to the baby while it is in the uterus.
- Talk to the baby soon after birth. Babies bond to sound very quickly.
- Hold the baby close and make eye contact; a baby makes associations based on sight and smell.
- Feed the baby. It's easy if you bottlefeed. If you breastfeed, let him give the baby a bottle of expressed breast milk or water.
- Help with daily chores, such as changing diapers, holding the baby when it is restless, bathing and dressing the baby.

❧❧❧❧

Steve came with Liz for an ultrasound exam, and he couldn't wait to tell me he thought he had a new "medical breakthrough." He said he had been a little nervous about the pregnancy, afraid to touch Liz or her tummy. But one night, while they were lying in bed, he saw Liz's bellybutton move. He decided to feel it gently. He felt a foot or an arm, and when he pushed it, it pushed back! For the next 20 minutes, he continued the gentle pushing and feeling. This had become a regular activity that he looked forward to. He felt he was getting to know his baby's personality. Some nights it would want to "play" for 10 minutes, sometimes longer. Steve wanted to know if this was OK or harmful. I reassured him that it was fine, and that many couples bond with their baby in this way before it is born.

Sex during Pregnancy

Most couples are concerned about sexual activity during pregnancy; however, men are more often concerned with this aspect of a relationship. It's an important topic, so discuss it with your healthcare provider. You will need to rule out any complications and ask for individual advice. Most doctors agree sex can be a part of a normal, low-risk pregnancy.

Sex doesn't just mean sexual intercourse. There are many ways for couples to be sensual together, including giving each other a massage, bathing together and talking about sex. Whatever you do, be honest with your partner about how you're feeling—and keep a sense of humor!

❧ Can Sex during Pregnancy Hurt the Baby?

Sexual activity doesn't harm a growing baby. Neither intercourse nor orgasm should be a problem if you have a low-risk pregnancy.

The baby is well protected by the amniotic sac and amniotic fluid. Uterine muscles are strong, and they also help protect the baby. A thick mucus plug seals the cervix, which helps protect against infection. Discuss sexual activity with your healthcare provider, if your partner goes with you to your appointments. If he doesn't, assure him there should be no problems, if your healthcare provider gives you the go-ahead.

Frequent sexual activity should not be harmful to a healthy pregnancy. Usually a couple can continue the level of sexual activity they are used to. If you are concerned, discuss it with your healthcare provider.

❧ How Pregnancy Affects You Sexually

Generally, women experience one of two sex-drive patterns during pregnancy. One is a lessening of desire in the first and third trimesters, with an increase in the second trimester. The second is a gradual decrease in desire for sex as pregnancy progresses.

During the first trimester, you may experience fatigue and nausea. During the third trimester, your weight gain, enlarging abdomen, tender breasts and other problems may make you desire sex less. This is normal. Tell your partner how you feel, and try to work out a solution that is satisfactory to you both.

Pregnancy actually enhances the sex drive for some women. In some cases, a woman may experience orgasms or multiple orgasms for the first time during pregnancy. This is due to heightened hormonal activity and increased blood flow to the pelvic area.

Some women feel less attractive during pregnancy because of

their size and the changes in their bodies. Discuss your feelings with your partner. Tenderness and understanding can help you both.

You may find new positions for lovemaking are necessary as pregnancy progresses. Your abdomen may make some positions more uncomfortable than others. In addition, physicians advise you not to lie flat on your back after 16 weeks until the baby's birth because the weight of the uterus restricts circulation. You might try lying on your side or in a position that puts you on top.

☞ When to Avoid Sexual Activity

Some situations should alert you to abstain from sex during pregnancy. If you have a history of early labor, your healthcare provider may warn against intercourse and orgasm; orgasm causes mild uterine contractions. Chemicals in semen may also stimulate contractions, so it may not be advisable for a woman's partner to ejaculate inside her. See the list below for other times to avoid sexual activity.

If you have a history of miscarriage, your doctor may caution you against sex and orgasm. However, no data actually links the two. Avoid sexual activity if you have any of the following problems or conditions:

- placenta previa or a low-lying placenta
- incompetent cervix
- premature labor
- multiple fetuses
- ruptured bag of waters
- pain with intercourse
- unexplained vaginal bleeding or discharge
- you can't find a comfortable position
- either partner has an unhealed herpes lesion
- you believe labor has begun

☞ Sexual Practices to Avoid

Some practices should be avoided during sex when you're pregnant. Don't insert any object into the vagina that could cause injury or infection. Blowing air into the vagina is dangerous because it can force a potentially fatal air bubble into a woman's bloodstream. (This can occur whether or not you are pregnant.) Nipple stimulation releases oxytocin, which causes uterine contractions; you might want to discuss this practice with your doctor.

Bed Rest and Your Partner

In some situations, a woman may be ordered to bed for part of her pregnancy. (See the discussion of bed rest starting on page 233.) She may also have to abstain from sex. Bed rest can be unpleasant for the woman; however, it may be just as difficult for her partner.

Partners of women with pregnancy complications carry a heavy load. In addition to worrying about their partner and the growing baby, they may also have to handle housework, cooking, childcare and care of their partner. It can be difficult for a man to handle his work and the added responsibility at home. Resentment is common.

If you are ordered to bed, make sure you consider your partner's feelings about it. Let him know how valuable he is to you. Be supportive (this can be tough when you're the one in bed!), and try not to ask for too much. Arrange for others to help out when possible.

For all the inconveniences and disruptions in your life that bed confinement causes, the experience may strengthen your relationship. When he gives his time and attention to this demanding task, your partner is really offering you support and love. Let him know how much you appreciate it.

Part 4

If You Have a Problem

Chapter 16

Pregnancy Problems and Warning Signs

Pregnancy is usually a happy time, but you may experience situations that cause you some concern. Some diagnoses, such as for diabetes and hypertension, are not unusual and cause no noticeable discomfort but are always serious and must be treated for your health and that of your baby.

If you feel uncomfortable or have questions, don't be afraid to ask for help. Call your healthcare provider to discuss your concerns. This part of the book can help you formulate the questions you may want to ask.

Although you may believe it's easier to get advice or information from family members or friends, *don't* rely on them for medical advice. Your healthcare provider has probably dealt with the same situation many times. The answers he or she gives you will be right for your particular pregnancy.

If you experience any of the following signs or symptoms, call your healthcare provider immediately. General warning signs include:

- vaginal bleeding
- severe swelling of the face or fingers
- severe abdominal pain
- loss of fluid from the vagina (usually a gushing of fluid but sometimes a trickle or a continual wetness)

- a big change in the movement of the baby or a lack of fetal movement
- high fever—more than 101.6F (38.7C)
- chills
- severe vomiting or an inability to keep food or liquids down
- blurred of vision
- painful urination
- a headache that won't go away or a severe headache
- an injury or accident that hurts you or gives you concern about the well-being of your pregnancy, such as a fall or an automobile accident

❧ If You Fall

A fall is the most frequent cause of minor injury during pregnancy. Fortunately, a fall usually doesn't cause serious injury to the fetus or to the mother. Movement of the baby after a fall is reassuring. A possible problem after a fall may be indicated by any of the following:

- bleeding from the vagina
- a gush of fluid from the vagina, indicating rupture of membranes
- severe abdominal pain

If you fall, contact your doctor; you may require attention. If you had a very bad fall, your doctor may advise monitoring the baby's heartbeat or order an ultrasound for further evaluation.

❧❧❧❧

It was a late-night call, and Jan apologized for bothering me. She was 34 weeks pregnant and had fallen in her driveway bringing in groceries. She had landed squarely on her bottom. She was OK but was concerned about the baby. The baby hadn't moved since the fall and that scared her. She said she wasn't bleeding or leaking any fluid, but her uterus was tightening. She didn't know if it was contractions, but it was uncomfortable. I reassured her that her baby was cushioned very well, better than she was, but it was something to be concerned about.

Even though it was late and cold outside, I asked her to go to the hospital to check things out. We all felt better after Jan had a nonstress test, and the baby was fine. The contractions stopped, and Jane was able to take some Tylenol for her bumps and bruises. At her next visit, I told Jan not to apologize for calls like that—it was the right thing to do.

Bed Rest

Bed rest is ordered for a woman to improve her chances of giving birth to a healthy baby. Today, one in five women spends at least one week in bed during pregnancy. If the condition is severe, hospitalization may be advised.

When a woman has to rest in bed, it can disrupt the normal routines of her family, especially when it lasts more than a short time. Adjusting to around-the-clock bed rest can be difficult.

A woman may be advised to rest in bed when certain conditions threaten the baby's or mother's health. These conditions include:

- a history of premature labor
- early rupture of the membranes
- pre-eclampsia
- high blood pressure
- multiple fetuses, especially triplets or more
- incompetent cervix
- premature labor
- risk of miscarriage
- intrauterine-growth retardation
- chronic heart condition
- diabetes, with complications

❧ How Bed Rest Works

Resting in bed works two ways. First, resting on your side maximizes the blood flow to your uterus, which brings more oxygen and nutrients to the baby. Second, lying down takes the pressure of the baby's weight off the cervix, which can help when a woman experiences premature labor.

❧ If You Are Ordered to Bed

Bed rest can seriously disrupt your routine. You may not be able to work, and you may have to curtail other activities. Bed rest can be difficult when you have young children. Changing your routine can be stressful for people around you, including family members and co-workers. Staying in bed may be hard, but it is better to do it at home than in the hospital!

Ask your healthcare provider what you can and cannot do while you are on bed rest. Sometimes you aren't allowed to get out of bed except to eat, go to the bathroom and go to prenatal appointments. At other times, bed rest may be less strict. You may be able to sit up or be a little more active for part of the day. You may have to take medication and limit your activities.

You may be advised to lie only on your left side to increase blood flow to the uterus. This position relieves pressure on the vena cava and increases blood flow to the legs and uterus. You may be allowed to alternate between sides. However, you may *not* lie on your back. Lying on your back puts too much pressure from your uterus on the vena cava.

❧ Surviving Bed Rest

Staying in bed isn't fun, especially if you haven't yet prepared for your baby's arrival. You may feel resentful. You may have to abstain from sex, which can add stress to an already-difficult situation. You can make the experience more bearable if you plan for your time of confinement. If you work, ask your healthcare provider if you can read or work on projects at home. The following suggestions may help you get through your time in bed.

• Spend the day in a room other than your bedroom. Use the living room or den sofa for daytime activities.

- Use foam mattress pads and extra pillows for comfort.
- Keep a telephone close at hand.
- Keep reading material, the television remote control, a radio and other essentials nearby.
- Establish a daily routine. When you get up, change into daytime clothes. Shower or bathe every day. Comb your hair, and put on lipstick. Nap if you need it. Go to bed when you normally do.
- Keep food and drinks close at hand. Use a cooler to keep food and drinks cold. Use an insulated container for hot soup or coffee.

For support, contact other women who have been on bed rest. A national support group helps women with high-risk pregnancies. They can provide you with information and put you in touch with other women who have had the same experience. Contact Sidelines at 714-497-2265.

✎ If You Have Children

Bed rest can be especially hard for a pregnant woman with young children at home. Try some of the following suggestions to help you make the experience more tolerable.

- Have someone come to your home to help during the day.
- If you can't find someone to come to your home, see if a friend or neighbor can take your children for all or part of the day.
- Keep books and toys nearby to help entertain kids when they are with you.
- Ask your children to help you. A child can put toys away or get something for you. Children love to feel important, and asking a child to help you can make him or her feel very grown up.
- Do some quiet activities with your child; look at photo albums or read books together.

If you must rest in bed, stay positive! No matter how long you have to rest in bed—a few days or weeks—the goal is a healthy baby and a healthy mom. You may be upset or feel anxious. Keep in mind that you are doing this for you and your baby, and give yourself a pat on the back.

Bleeding during Pregnancy

Bleeding during pregnancy is not unusual and doesn't always mean a problem; about one woman in five bleeds sometime in early pregnancy. Most of the time we cannot say what causes bleeding, but we do know it is not usually a problem. Always tell your doctor about any bleeding; he or she may want you to have an ultrasound.

Bleeding later in pregnancy raises concerns regarding premature labor, premature rupture of the membranes, placenta previa or placental abruption. If you bleed late in pregnancy, call your healthcare provider *immediately*. Your problem may not be serious, but it must be evaluated by your doctor.

Most women who experience bleeding during pregnancy want to know if they can take medicine or do something to stop the bleeding. Bed rest may help. Unfortunately, no surgery or medicine will help. You may be scheduled for an ultrasound. An ultrasound won't stop the bleeding, but it may provide reassurance. Your doctor will make treatment decisions based on your individual history. Follow his or her instructions.

Blood Clots

Some women develop blood clots, usually in their legs, during pregnancy. These clots may break loose, travel through the blood system and lodge elsewhere in the body, such as the lungs. Blood clots are an uncommon problem and occur only once in every 3000 to 7000 pregnancies. However, it is a serious complication and can affect you and your baby.

Clots occur in pregnancy because of changes in blood circulation. The most likely cause of a blood clot in the legs is decreased blood flow, called *stasis*. Blood flow slows because of pressure from the uterus on blood vessels and changes in the blood and its clotting mechanisms.

A blood clot in the legs is not always a serious problem. Unlike deep-vein clots, clots created in the superficial veins of the leg are treated with mild pain relievers, heat, elevation of the leg and support of the leg with an ace bandage or support stockings.

Conditions that refer to blood-clotting problems are also called *venous thrombosis, thromboembolic disease, thrombophlebitis* and *lower deep-vein thrombosis.*

✄ Deep-vein Thrombosis

Clotting in the deep veins of the legs, called *deep-vein thrombosis* or *phlebitis,* is serious. A blood clot that forms deep in the leg is more likely to break loose and travel to another part of the body, such as the lungs, heart or brain, where it can indirectly damage those tissues. Signs and symptoms of deep-vein thrombosis vary widely and include:

• abrupt onset
• paleness of the leg
• leg is cool to the touch
• a portion of the leg may be tender, hot and swollen
• there may be red streaks over the veins of the leg
• squeezing the calf or walking may be very painful

In a pregnant woman, an ultrasound of the legs is the only test, other than a physical exam, with which a doctor diagnoses phlebitis. At other times, X-ray or ultrasound is used.

✄ Treating Deep-vein Thrombosis

Deep-vein thrombosis is usually treated by hospitalization and the administration of heparin, a blood thinner. While heparin is given, the woman is required to stay in bed. Heat is applied to the elevated leg.

Heparin is safe to use during pregnancy. It is administered by injections that you give yourself 2 or 3 times a day, by an intravenous drip attached to your arm or by device called a *heparin pump.*

Warfarin (Coumadin) cannot be given during pregnancy because it crosses the placenta and is not safe for the baby. After you deliver, you may be given warfarin for a few weeks, depending on the severity of the blood clot.

If you have had a blood clot with a previous pregnancy or at any other time, such as after surgery, be sure to share that information with your healthcare provider as soon as you know you are pregnant. You will probably need heparin during this pregnancy.

Breast Lumps

Sometimes a woman develops lumps in her breasts during pregnancy. Because your breasts go through so many changes in pregnancy, it may be harder for you to discover a lump. It's a good idea to examine your breasts every 4 or 5 weeks throughout your pregnancy.

If you discover a lump, tell your doctor immediately. It's normal for breasts to change and to grow larger during pregnancy, but don't ignore a breast lump and hope it will go away. Lumps need to be checked out.

After examination by your doctor, you may undergo a mammogram or an ultrasound. If you are supposed to have a mammogram, tell the technician you are pregnant, so your abdomen is shielded properly with a lead apron.

A lump in the breast usually can be drained or aspirated. If not, a doctor may have to perform a biopsy (take a sample of the tissue involved). Depending on those findings, surgery or other treatment may be needed.

There is controversy about whether pregnancy causes breast cancer to grow faster. Most researchers do not believe pregnancy accelerates the course or growth of a breast cancer.

Diabetes

Diabetes was once a very serious medical problem during pregnancy for a woman of any age. It continues to be an important complication of pregnancy, but today many diabetic women can go through pregnancy safely if they have proper medical care, watch their diet and follow their doctor's instructions. If you know you are diabetic, inform your healthcare provider of the fact as soon as you become pregnant—or before, if possible.

We believe diabetes can appear during pregnancy for two

reasons—the mother's body decreases its production of insulin for some reason, or the mother is unable to use insulin appropriately. (Insulin is used to break down blood sugar.) In either case, the mother's blood-sugar levels rise to unacceptable levels.

Pregnancy problems are more likely for diabetic women. There is a 3 to 6% increase in the risk of major fetal abnormalities, including heart, genitourinary and gastrointestinal problems. Miscarriages occur more often. Symptoms of diabetes include:

- an increase in urination
- blurred vision
- weight loss
- dizziness
- increased hunger

Diabetes is diagnosed with a blood test, sometimes called a *fasting blood-sugar* or *glucose-tolerance test*. If your doctor finds sugar in your urine during routine tests at his or her office, it does not always mean you have diabetes. Pregnant, nondiabetic women commonly have a small amount of sugar in their urine, called *glucosuria*, because of the way sugar is handled in the kidneys during pregnancy.

✤ Pregnancy-induced Diabetes

Some women develop diabetes only during pregnancy, called *gestational diabetes*. Diabetes that occurs during pregnancy can be a greater problem for older women.

Gestational diabetes affects about 10% of all pregnancies. After pregnancy, nearly all women with gestational diabetes return to normal, and the problem disappears. However, more than half of all women who experience diabetes during pregnancy become diabetic later in life. A woman who develops gestational diabetes in one pregnancy has a good chance of developing it in a subsequent pregnancy.

Women at greatest risk of developing gestational diabetes are overweight, with family members who have insulin-dependent or diet-controlled diabetes. Occasionally a woman with no known personal or family risk factors develops the problem. Gestational diabetes is triggered when the usual hormone changes of pregnancy, combined with dietary factors, result in higher blood-sugar levels.

Children of diabetic women are more likely to develop diabetes themselves. Daughters of women who developed gestational diabetes are likely to become diabetic during their own pregnancies. If your mother developed gestational diabetes, be sure to share this information with your physician.

✿ How Gestational Diabetes Affects You

During pregnancy, diabetes can cause several medical complications, including kidney, eye, blood and vascular problems. Any of these can be serious for you and for your baby. If diabetes goes untreated, you and your baby will be exposed to a high concentration of sugar in the blood, a condition called *hyperglycemia*. This is not healthy for the baby.

Gestational diabetes sometimes causes *polyhydramnios* (production of excessive amounts of amniotic fluid), which can develop at any time during pregnancy. The condition may cause premature labor because the uterus becomes overdistended.

A woman may experience a very long labor because the baby is large. Sometimes a baby cannot fit through the birth canal, and a Cesarean delivery is required.

If your blood-sugar level is elevated, you may experience more infections during pregnancy. The most common infections involve the kidneys, the bladder, the cervix and the uterus.

✿ How Gestational Diabetes Affects Your Baby

All of a baby's nutrition comes from its mother. If an expectant mother's blood-sugar levels are high, the baby's insulin output increases to try to process the excess and re-establish a balance. However, the baby's insulin can't cross the placenta, back to the mother, so the effort doesn't help balance their shared blood chemistry. The extra insulin remains in the amniotic sac, and the baby's growth may be exaggerated because of it. In some cases, the baby grows so large it cannot be delivered safely by vaginal birth.

After birth, a baby may also have very low blood sugar, called *hypoglycemia,* because the baby's body now controls its own blood sugar. Every baby is checked for the condition immediately after delivery. If the blood-sugar level is low, the baby may be given some sugar.

The baby may be born with hyperbilirubenemia (severe jaundice). Some babies have weak or high-pitched cries, appear shaky and tire quickly. A baby may be unable to nurse well or for long enough to get adequate nutrition, which can affect its growth.

⋙ Treating Gestational Diabetes

The best way to treat diabetes during pregnancy is to eat properly. If you are diabetic, your healthcare provider will probably recommend a six-meal, 2000- to 2500-calorie/day eating plan and may have you see a dietitian.

Under a typical plan, you eat six small meals a day of lowfat, sugar-free, high-fiber foods. Eating this way enables your body to keep sugar production at a more-constant level.

Getting regular exercise and drinking lots of water every day are also very important in this plan. If you have gestational diabetes, your blood-sugar level may be tested at prenatal office visits and by you at home.

Ectopic Pregnancy

Ectopic pregnancy, sometimes called a *tubal pregnancy*, is not common; it occurs only about once in every 100 pregnancies. An ectopic pregnancy occurs when the fertilized egg implants outside the uterine cavity, usually in the Fallopian tube. One of the most common signs of ectopic pregnancy is pain. It isn't unusual to have mild pain early in pregnancy from a cyst on the ovary or stretching of the uterus or ligaments. However, if pain is severe and causes you concern, call your doctor.

⋙ Factors that Increase the Risks of Ectopic Pregnancy

You cannot prevent an ectopic pregnancy. However, some factors increase its likelihood, including:

• pelvic infections (PID; pelvic inflammatory disease)
• previous ruptured appendix

- previous ectopic pregnancy
- surgery on your Fallopian tubes (such as reversal of a tubal
  ligation or infertility surgery)
- use of an IUD for contraception

❧ Diagnosing an Ectopic Pregnancy

Diagnosis of an ectopic pregnancy can be very difficult. It may require a couple of tests and some waiting; tests used include ultrasound, quantitative HCG and laparoscopy (a type of minor surgery). It may take a few days or weeks to make a definitive diagnosis.

Sometimes a doctor orders a couple of quantitative HCG tests a few days apart. A quantitative HCG (human chorionic gonadotropin) test is a special pregnancy blood test. HCG is produced when you're pregnant; it increases rapidly early in pregnancy. A quantitative HCG tells how far along in pregnancy you are by assigning a number to your developmental stage. The numbers aren't exact, but they increase in a way that can help your doctor decide if it is a normal or abnormal pregnancy. The HCG test is not used in normal pregnancies but can be very helpful when there is concern about an ectopic pregnancy.

❧ Treatment of Ectopic Pregnancy

An ectopic pregnancy cannot be carried to full term. Surgery is almost always required to correct the problem, which results in loss of the pregnancy.

Hypertension

Hypertension is the most common chronic illness in older pregnant women. About one pregnant woman in 10 experiences the condition during pregnancy; however, women in their 30s and 40s have a higher incidence of pregnancy-induced hypertension than younger women. (Hypertension is also called *high blood pressure*.) Most women who are hypertensive during pregnancy do not have high blood pressure when they are not pregnant. Other women enter pregnancy with the problem.

✂ How Hypertension Affects You and Your Baby

Blood vessels in the uterus supply the developing baby with nutrients and oxygen. High blood pressure constricts uterine blood vessels, which can slow the passage of nutrients and oxygen from the mother to the baby, which in turn slows fetal development. Hypertension increases the risk of placental abruption (separation of the placenta from the wall of the uterus before delivery). This situation can cause heavy bleeding and shock, which are dangerous conditions for you and your baby.

Hypertension has other effects. About 20% of all women who experience chronic hypertension (high blood pressure before pregnancy) develop pre-eclampsia. About 25% of those women who develop pregnancy-induced hypertension also develop pre-eclampsia. (By comparison, 6% of women who begin pregnancy without hypertension develop pre-eclampsia.) A discussion of pre-eclampsia begins on page 248.

Pregnancy-induced hypertension occurs only during pregnancy and disappears after the baby is born. The condition is treated with bed rest, increased fluid intake and by avoiding salt and sodium-heavy foods. Medications to lower blood pressure may be prescribed if diet changes don't work. Women who do not respond to these measures may be hospitalized.

Miscarriage

A *miscarriage* is a loss of a pregnancy before 20 weeks of gestation. An embryo or a fetus is delivered before it can survive outside the womb. At some time during pregnancy, nearly every woman thinks about the possibility of miscarriage.

Having a miscarriage is an emotional experience for any woman. It may also be an emotional loss for your partner. Many women mistakenly blame themselves when a miscarriage occurs. It isn't your fault, so don't blame yourself.

❧ Causes of Miscarriage

When a miscarriage occurs with one of my patients, one of the first questions I am asked is, "Did I cause it?" Patients also want to know, "What could I have done to prevent it?"

Most of the time we don't know why a miscarriage occurs; it can happen for many different reasons. The most common finding studies done of early miscarriages is abnormal development of the embryo. Research indicates that more than half of these miscarriages have chromosomal abnormalities.

Outside factors, such as radiation and some chemicals (drugs or medications), may cause a miscarriage. Maternal factors may also result in a miscarriage. Several maternal factors that have been identified include:

- unusual infections
- a progesterone deficiency (treatable if detected early)
- genital infections
- antibodies produced in the body that attack the fetus or disrupt the function of the placenta
- smoking
- alcohol or drug use (especially cocaine)

In some cases, the uniting of the couple's sperm and egg results in a miscarriage. Let me explain. When the couple's genes unite at fertilization, the union can produce genetic abnormalities that cause a miscarriage. Genetic screening can reveal this problem; a discussion of genetic counseling begins on page 255.

❧ Types of Miscarriage

Different medical descriptions of miscarriages actually describe different types of miscarriage. Medically speaking, there are five basic types.

A *threatened miscarriage* occurs when there is a bloody discharge from the vagina during the first half of pregnancy. Bleeding may last days or weeks. A woman may or may not experience cramping and pain. The pain may feel like a menstrual cramp or mild backache. Resting in bed is about all a woman can do, although being active does not cause miscarriage. (In most instances early in pregnancy, the bleeding or spotting stops and everything is fine.)

An *inevitable miscarriage* occurs with rupture of membranes, dilatation of the cervix and passage of blood clots and tissue. Loss of the pregnancy is almost certain under these circumstances. The uterus usually contracts, expelling the embryo or products of conception.

With an *incomplete miscarriage,* the entire pregnancy may not be expelled. Part of the pregnancy may be passed while the rest remains inside the uterus. Bleeding may be heavy and continues until the uterus is empty.

A *missed miscarriage* can occur when an embryo that has died earlier is retained in the uterus. A woman may not bleed or have any other symptoms. The period between the failure of the pregnancy until the time the miscarriage is discovered is usually weeks.

Habitual miscarriage usually refers to three or more consecutive miscarriages.

❧ Warning Signs

The first warning sign of a miscarriage is bleeding from the vagina, followed by cramping. Call your healthcare provider if you experience this! Unfortunately, in nearly all instances, there is little you or your doctor can do to stop a miscarriage from happening. No surgical technique or medicine can stop a miscarriage.

Most physicians recommend bed rest and decreased activity. (See the discussion of bed rest that begins on page 233.) Some recommend use of the hormone progesterone, but not all doctors agree with its use. Ultrasound and blood tests may help your healthcare provider determine whether you are going to miscarry, but you may have to wait and see.

If you pass all of the pregnancy, bleeding stops and cramping goes away, you may be done with it. If everything is not expelled, it is necessary to perform a D&C (dilatation and curettage), which is minor surgery to empty the uterus. A D&C is recommended so you won't bleed for a long period of time, risking anemia and infection.

If you're Rh-negative and have a miscarriage, you will need to receive the medication RhoGAM. This applies *only* if you are Rh-negative.

The Placenta

The placenta is very important during pregnancy. It carries nourishment and oxygen from you to your developing baby and carries away the baby's waste products. More information on the placenta and its function begins on page 000. Problems occasionally develop with the placenta, especially for older women, including *placenta previa*, *placental abruption* and *retained placenta*.

❧ Placenta Previa

When a woman has placenta previa, the placenta covers part or all of the cervix. The placenta may separate from the uterus as the cervix begins to dilate (open) during labor. This causes heavy bleeding, which can be dangerous for the mother and the baby. Placenta previa affects about 2 to 3% of all women in the last trimester of pregnancy.

Signs and symptoms of placenta previa vary, but the most characteristic symptom is painless bleeding. If you experience painless bleeding, your doctor may order an ultrasound exam to determine the location of the placenta, if he or she is concerned about placenta previa. Your physician will not perform a pelvic exam because it may cause heavier bleeding. If you see another doctor or when you go to the hospital, tell whomever you see that you have placenta previa and you should not have a pelvic exam.

If your doctor determines you have placenta previa, you will have to curtail certain activities. Most physicians recommend avoiding intercourse and not traveling in addition to avoiding pelvic exams.

With placenta previa, the baby is more likely to be in a breech position. For this reason, and to avoid bleeding, a physician will almost always perform a Cesarean delivery.

❧ Placental Abruption

Placental abruption occurs when the placenta separates from the wall of the uterus before birth. Normally the placenta does not separate until after delivery of the baby. Separation of the placenta before birth can be dangerous for mother and baby.

Placental abruption occurs about once in every 80 deliveries. Its cause is unknown; however, certain conditions may make it more likely to occur. These include:

- trauma to the mother, such as from a fall or a car accident
- an umbilical cord that is too short
- very sudden change in the size of the uterus, as with the rupture of membranes
- hypertension
- dietary deficiency in the mother
- an abnormality of the uterus, such as a band of tissue in the uterus called a *uterine septum*

The symptoms of placental abruption include the following signs, not all of which may be present:

- heavy bleeding from the vagina
- uterine tenderness
- uterine contractions
- premature labor
- lower-back pain

Ultrasound may help establish the diagnosis of placental abruption in some cases. If bleeding is severe, a woman experiencing placental abruption may go into shock because her blood doesn't clot properly.

The most common treatment of placental abruption is delivery of the baby. However, the decision of when to deliver the baby varies, based on the problem's severity. Sometimes a Cesarean section is necessary, but each case is handled individually.

You may be able to help prevent placental abruption. A folic-acid deficiency may play a role in causing placental abruption, so you may be required to take extra folic acid during pregnancy. Many foods contain folic acid, including oranges, beans, whole-wheat bread and strawberries. Include them in your diet.

Maternal smoking and alcohol use may increase the risk of placental abruption. If you smoke cigarettes or drink alcohol, you will be advised to stop both activities (it's also advisable for many other reasons). Cocaine use also causes placental abruption.

❧ Retained Placenta

Some women have problems with the placenta after their baby is born. Usually the placenta separates with contraction of the uterus from the implantation site on the uterus a few minutes after delivery. When the placenta does not deliver following the birth of the baby, we call it a *retained placenta.*

In some cases, the placenta doesn't separate because it is attached to the wall of the uterus. This can be very serious and cause heavy blood loss. In other cases, part of the placenta may deliver while part is retained. Your doctor will check the placenta after delivery to be sure it has all been delivered.

The most significant problem with a retained placenta is heavy bleeding after delivery, which can be severe. If the placenta cannot be delivered, your doctor may attempt to remove the placenta by D&C. If the placenta is attached through the wall of the uterus, it may be necessary to remove the uterus by performing a hysterectomy; this is rare.

Reasons for a retained placenta include a placenta attaching over a previous C-section scar or other incision scar on the uterus, attaching in a place that has been previously curetted, such as for a D&C or abortion, or attaching over an area of the uterus that was infected.

Pre-eclampsia

Pre-eclampsia, also called *toxemia of pregnancy,* can be a serious complication of pregnancy. Pre-eclampsia occurs *only* during pregnancy; left untreated, it poses a serious threat to you and your baby. Older women are more likely to develop pre-eclampsia.

Most cases are mild and treatable. With mild pre-eclampsia, your blood pressure is slightly elevated. (Hypertension is discussed on page 242.) The only other obvious symptom of mild pre-eclampsia might be swelling of the legs, hands and face.

If pre-eclampsia worsens, it can quickly progress to a serious condition called *eclampsia*, which is accompanied by seizures or convulsions. A woman can also go into a coma. A *seizure* is a loss of body control, such as passing out, and often includes twitching or shaking. (A *convulsion* is a severe seizure.) If you think you've had a seizure, contact your doctor immediately.

❧ Causes

We don't really know what causes pre-eclampsia. When a woman suffers from pre-eclampsia, her body may be producing too much thromboxane A and too little prostacyclin, both blood chemicals. Thromboxane A constricts blood vessels; prostacyclin dilates them. A diet that is too low in protein may increase your risk of developing pre-eclampsia.

❧ Women at Risk

Some women are at greater risk of developing pre-eclampsia than others. Your chance of getting the problem increases if any of the following applies to you:

- 35 or older
- family history of pre-eclampsia
- first pregnancy
- kidney disease
- lupus
- diabetes
- a multiple pregnancy
- overweight
- personal history of pre-eclampsia, combined with high blood pressure before pregnancy

The best way to reduce the risk of developing pre-eclampsia or eclampsia is to keep all your prenatal appointments. Your physician will follow changes in your blood pressure throughout your pregnancy. With your help and cooperation, your healthcare provider can usually treat pre-eclampsia before it becomes a serious problem.

❧ Warning Signs of Pre-eclampsia

Pre-eclampsia may develop after the 20th week of pregnancy, though most cases occur after 30 weeks. Symptoms include:

- hypertension
- protein in the urine
- sudden weight gain
- swelling
- changes in muscle reflexes

Certain signs indicate a worsening condition. Contact your healthcare provider *immediately* if you have pre-eclampsia and develop any of these signs:

- pain under the ribs on the right side
- headache
- see spots or notice other vision changes

If your legs or feet are swollen, it does *not* mean you have pre-eclampsia. Most pregnant women experience some swelling, but a diagnosis of pre-eclampsia includes the other symptoms described.

❧ Treating Pre-eclampsia

For a mild case of pre-eclampsia, your doctor will probably order bed rest until your blood pressure stabilizes. You will be advised to drink lots of water and to avoid salt and foods containing large amounts of sodium.

You will need to visit your healthcare provider more frequently if you are diagnosed with pre-eclampsia. In some cases, you are given medication to lower your blood pressure. You may be given medication to protect against seizures, including magnesium sulfate, or you may be prescribed antiseizure medicines, such as phenobarbital.

If pre-eclampsia worsens, you may be admitted to the hospital for observation. Your blood pressure is measured several times a day, and your weight and the level of protein in your urine are recorded. Your developing baby is also monitored. Fetal movements are recorded every day, and a nonstress test is done.

If your blood pressure continues to rise and other symptoms worsen, the baby may need to be delivered to protect you from serious complications, including convulsions, stroke, liver damage and kidney damage. Before delivery, you may receive magnesium sulfate intravenously to prevent convulsions during labor and baby's birth.

Emergency Surgery during Pregnancy

Emergencies occur, even during pregnancy. When you are pregnant, a medical emergency must be dealt with in a way that is best for you and your developing fetus. Sometimes surgical procedures are necessary. Some common reasons for surgery during pregnancy are gall-bladder removal, appendicitis, ovarian cysts, broken bones and dental emergencies.

✿ Gall-bladder Problems

Inflammation of the gall bladder, also called *cholecystitis*, occurs most often in women in their 30s and 40s. Treatment consists of pain medication and surgery. If you're pregnant, your doctor will try to avoid surgery until after the baby is born, when possible. However, if your pain is severe and does not improve with pain medication, surgery may be necessary.

The ideal time to perform gall-bladder surgery during pregnancy is the second trimester. The risk of miscarriage or premature delivery is lower.

The surgical procedure for gall-bladder removal requires general anesthesia and an incision, with a hospital stay of up to 2 or 3 days. If laparoscopy is used to remove the gall bladder, the surgeon makes three or four small incisions, and the gall bladder is examined and removed. The hospital stay is about 1 day. In most cases, laparoscopy isn't recommended after 20 weeks of pregnancy.

Risks to the fetus from gall-bladder surgery include premature labor, infection and risks associated with anesthesia. If surgery is required, you will be monitored very closely to watch for and prevent premature labor.

✣ Appendicitis

The incidence of appendicitis in pregnancy is about 1 in every 2000 pregnancies. Diagnosis of appendicitis is more difficult during pregnancy because some of the symptoms, including nausea, vomiting and a high white-blood cell count, are the same as those for normal pregnancy or other problems. Pregnancy can also make diagnosis difficult because as the uterus grows larger, the appendix moves upward and outward, so pain and tenderness are in a different location than usual. (See the illustration below.) Diagnosis of appendicitis during pregnancy requires a physical exam, blood tests and ultrasound.

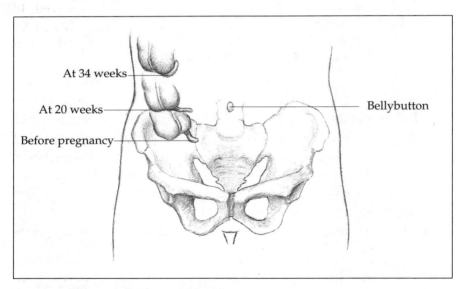

Location of the appendix during pregnancy

Surgery is performed immediately. It is major abdominal surgery and often requires a few days in the hospital. Laparoscopy is used in some situations, but it may be more difficult to perform during pregnancy because of the enlarged uterus.

Risks to the developing fetus with appendicitis include the risks associated with general anesthesia, infection and premature labor.

৵ Ovarian Cysts

Ovarian cysts can be a serious complication during pregnancy. A *cyst* is a sac that develops in the ovary and consists of one or more fluid-containing chambers. It may have to be surgically removed because of pressure, twisting, bleeding or blockage of the birth canal. Ovarian cysts that develop in pregnancy are almost always benign.

Ovarian cysts can cause pain, bloating and abdominal swelling. A physical exam and ultrasound are used to diagnose the problem. Treatment is usually pain medication and observation; surgery is usually avoided unless absolutely necessary.

If surgery is necessary, the cyst may be drained or removed. In some cases, the doctors must remove the entire ovary. If surgery can be postponed, the safest time to do it is after the first trimester has ended.

Risks to the fetus vary, depending on when surgery is performed. In early pregnancy, loss of an ovary could mean loss of hormones necessary to support the pregnancy. Late in pregnancy, a cyst could block the birth canal, requiring a Cesarean delivery. Other risks include those associated with general anesthesia, infection and premature delivery.

৵ Broken Bones

A fall or accident can break a bone, which may require X-rays or surgery. Treatment cannot be delayed until after pregnancy; the problem must be dealt with immediately. If you break a bone, insist that your OB-GYN be contacted before any test or treatment is done.

If X-rays are required, technicians should shield your pelvis and abdomen. If the pelvis and abdomen cannot be shielded, the need for the X-ray must be weighed against the risks it potentially poses to the fetus.

Anesthesia or pain medication may be necessary for a simple break that requires setting or pinning. Keep its use to a minimum. It is best for you and the baby to avoid general anesthesia if possible. If general anesthesia is required, doctors will monitor the baby closely throughout surgery.

✥ Dental Emergencies

Dental emergencies can occur during pregnancy. Some emergencies you might face include root canal, tooth extraction, a large cavity, an abscessed tooth or problems resulting from an accident or injury. Any of these emergencies can occur during pregnancy; it might be unwise to postpone treatment until after your baby is born.

If you have a dental problem, contact your dentist and your healthcare provider before doing anything else. Your dentist and your healthcare provider may find it helpful to talk before any decisions are made.

Dental X-rays may be necessary and can be done during pregnancy. Be sure your abdomen is shielded with a lead apron before X-rays are taken. If possible, wait until after the end of the first trimester to have dental work done.

Avoid gas or general anesthesia for a dental procedure. Local anesthetics are fine, as are many antibiotics and pain medications. Be sure to consult your healthcare provider before taking any medications.

If you have a serious dental problem, such as an abscess, get it treated. Problems, such as infection, that could result from not treating it are more serious than the normal risks associated with treatment.

Chapter 17

Special Concerns of the Older Pregnant Woman

Most women over 30 have problem-free, healthy pregnancies and deliver healthy babies. However, for women who are 30 or older, age can be a factor in pregnancy. If you experience any of the situations covered in this chapter, discuss it with your health-care provider.

Chromosome Abnormalities Discovered by Genetic Counseling

Genetic counseling can identify some chromosome abnormalities. Chromosome abnormalities can occur in any cell, and they can occur as an abnormal chromosome number or as an abnormality in the structure of the chromosome itself. With Down syndrome, an individual has 47 chromosomes instead of the normal 46. With Turner's syndrome, one chromosome is missing; the individual has 45 chromosomes. For more information about Down and Turner's syndromes, see pages 258 and 257.

A loss, a gain or a repositioning of the chromosome material identifies a structural abnormality. Terms used to describe these various conditions include *additions, duplications, deletions, inversions* and *translocations*.

✿ Causes of Chromosome Abnormalities

Chromosomal abnormalities are usually attributed to one of three conditions: advanced parental age; radiation exposure of mother, father or fetus; or gene regulation problems.

"Advanced parental age" usually refers to the mother's age, but research has also implicated the father's age. Age is a factor for the mother because females are born with all the eggs they will ever have. They are exposed to radiation and other teratogens in the environment throughout life. The exposures have an additive effect—the more teratogens a woman is exposed to, the greater her chance of damaging the eggs.

Radiation exposure, such as X-rays, can damage genetic material and affect gene function and regulation. This is serious because genes control development of the fetus, its organs and growth. Three of the most common examples of chromosomal abnormalities are discussed below.

- *Down syndrome* is the most common chromosome abnormality; it occurs in about 1 in 600 births. The syndrome is caused by an extra chromosome. Those born with Down syndrome can live fairly long lives and may be moderately to severely mentally retarded. About half have congenital heart disease; particular physical abnormalities are common to the syndrome. For a more-complete discussion, see page 258.
- *Trisomy 18 (Edwards' syndrome)* is a severe chromosome abnormality occurring in approximately 1 in 6000 births. Babies with trisomy 18 have multiple abnormalities of major organs, including mental retardation, microcephaly (small head), heart problems, kidney problems and gastrointestinal problems. The syndrome is caused by an abnormal chromosome 18. Most babies born with the problem die within the first year of life.
- *Trisomy 13 (Patau's syndrome)* occurs about once in 5000 births. The syndrome is caused by an extra chromosome 13. Babies born with trisomy 13 may have multiple abnormalities,

including mental retardation, microcephaly, cleft palate, cleft lip, heart problems and gastrointestinal problems. The prognosis for these infants is poor; most die by the age of 3.

Sex-chromosome Abnormalities

Abnormalities of the sex chromosomes are relatively common and are seen in 1 of every 500 live births. It is believed this type of abnormality causes about 25% of all miscarriages. The two most common sex-chromosome abnormalities are Turner's syndrome and Klinefelter's syndrome.

Turner's syndrome occurs about once in 10,000 female births. It is the most common chromosome abnormality identified in miscarriages. Instead of having two X chromosomes, a baby girl born with Turner's syndrome has only one X chromosome, called *45X*. The mature girl with Turner's syndrome is short and has a webbed neck, very small ovaries, is underdeveloped sexually, and often has heart and kidney problems. The condition may not be identified until she reaches puberty.

Klinefelter's syndrome is found in approximately 1 in every 1000 newborn males. The most common characteristic is very tall stature when the boy reaches maturity. These boys are born with an extra sex chromosome, thus the *47XXY* label. A boy is very tall, underdeveloped sexually and has small testes.

Fragile-X syndrome (also called *X-linked*) is one of the most common causes of mental retardation in males. Major physical characteristics include large ears, large hands and language-development delays.

Environmental Causes of Malformations

A birth defect (congenital malformation) results from abnormal tissue differentiation during early development stages or abnormal interaction of developing cells during fetal development of organs and organ systems. About 10% of all birth defects are caused by environmental factors, called *teratogens*. These include drugs, chemicals, radiation, congenital infection and the pregnant woman's environment. See teratogens, page 210.

✿ Congenital Infections

Rubella was one of the first maternal infections researchers identified as the cause of fetal malformations. Other infections that have been identified that can cause malformations include cytomegalovirus (CMV), toxoplasmosis, herpes simplex, parvo virus 19 and syphilis.

Congenital infections can cause a wide spectrum of problems in a baby. These range from major malformations, such as heart defects, to newborn infection at birth.

Down Syndrome

Nearly every woman who experiences pregnancy receives information on Down syndrome. When you're older, you are offered various tests to determine whether the fetus you carry is affected by the condition. If tests determine a woman is carrying a child with Down syndrome, she will be offered counseling.

Down syndrome was given its name by British physician J. Langdon Down in the nineteenth century. He found that babies born with the syndrome have an extra chromosome 21. Symptoms of the condition are present to some degree in all babies born with the syndrome. These symptoms include mental retardation, a sloping forehead, short, broad hands with a single palm crease, a flat nose or absent nose bridge, low-set ears and a generally dwarfed physique.

Through medical research, we know some women are at higher risk of giving birth to a child with Down syndrome than others. Women with increased risk include older women, those who have given birth previously to a child with Down syndrome and those who have Down syndrome themselves.

The statistical risk of delivering a baby with Down syndrome increases with age. If you're 45, you have a 97% chance of *not* having a baby with Down syndrome. If you're 49, you have a 92% chance of delivering a child *without* Down syndrome. Your risk of delivering a child with Down syndrome, depending on your age, looks like this:

• at age 25 the risk is 1 in 1300 births
• at 30 it is 1 in 965 births
• at 35 it is 1 in 365 births
• at 40 it is 1 in 109 births
• at 45 it is 1 in 32 births
• at 49 it is 1 in 12 births

✿ Diagnosing Down Syndrome before Birth

Many tests are available that can help diagnose Down syndrome in a developing fetus. They are not offered to every woman; they are usually offered only to women at high risk or those over 35. Some women with higher risk choose not to take the tests because they would not terminate their pregnancy even if the child had Down syndrome.

Tests performed for Down syndrome include:

• maternal alpha-fetoprotein test
• amniocentesis
• chorionic villus sampling (CVS)
• triple-screen test (assessment of HCG, unconjugated estriol and alpha-fetoprotein)
• quad-screen test (assessment of HCG, unconjugated estriol alpha-fetoprotein and inhibin-A)
• ultrasound

If you are concerned about Down syndrome and you believe you would choose to terminate a pregnancy if the fetus were afflicted, I suggest having one or more of these tests. Testing might be indicated even if you would not terminate the pregnancy; you might have the test if you and your partner (and the rest of the family) wanted to be mentally and emotionally prepared for this special child.

Some patients have told me they would welcome any child into their lives, no matter what. If this is your attitude, enjoy your pregnancy and don't worry about it.

⁂ Down Syndrome Children Are Special

People often ask me if there are any positive aspects of giving birth to a child with Down syndrome. I always answer "Yes!" to anyone who asks.

As a society, we have come to realize that those born with Down syndrome bring a special, valuable quality of life into our world. Down children are well known for the love and the joy they bring to their families and friends. They remind us of the pleasure in accomplishing simple tasks when they learn new skills. They embody the concept of unconditional love, and we can often learn how to cope and to grow as we interact with them.

Rearing a child with Down syndrome can be challenging, but many of my patients and others I know who have faced this challenge are positive about the impact these special children have in their lives. If you have a child with Down syndrome, you may work harder for every small advancement in your child's life. You may experience frustration and feelings of helplessness at times, but every parent has these feelings at some time.

Many physicians present only the negative side of Down syndrome. They describe the worst-case scenario and never look at another side of the issue. All women carrying a child with Down syndrome need to know the following facts.

- The average IQ for a child with Down syndrome is between 60 and 70. Most are in the low, mildly retarded range.
- Some children with Down syndrome have normal IQs.
- IQ scores for those with Down syndrome have risen steadily in the last 100 years.
- Less than 5% of those with Down syndrome are severely to profoundly retarded.
- The reading levels of those with Down syndrome who are in special-education programs in public schools range from kindergarten to 12th grade. The average is about 3rd grade.
- Nearly 90% of all those with Down syndrome are employable as adults.
- Most adults with Down syndrome are capable of living independently or in group homes.

- A person with Down syndrome has a life expectancy of 55 years, if he survives infancy.
- Many families are on waiting lists to adopt children with Down syndrome.
- A child with Down syndrome usually makes a positive impact on a family.

❧❧❧❧

A few years ago, I delivered a Down syndrome child for a patient of mine in her early 40s. We did an amniocentesis early in the pregnancy and knew to expect Down syndrome. A year later she reported to me the joy and love this special child had brought the entire family. She told me, "I don't know what our family would have been like without the blessing of this very special child. We cherish her."

❧ It's Your Decision

After testing, if you are advised that you are carrying a child with Down syndrome, you and your partner have many aspects of the situation to consider. Some couples elect to terminate the pregnancy. Many others welcome the birth of this special child into their families.

Whatever decision you make, it must be *your* decision. Do not allow yourself or your partner to be pressured into making any decision without your full understanding of the situation. Seek information. Talk to parents of children with Down syndrome. Make your decision based on the feelings you and your partner share. There are positive and negative aspects to consider, as there are with any child. Whatever decision you make may be difficult for you. Involve your physician and your partner in the process.

Cancer during Pregnancy

Most women don't need to be concerned about contracting cancer during pregnancy; it is rare. However, because many women today wait until they are older to have babies, and cancer strikes more older women, it's good to have this information available so you can discuss the situation with your healthcare provider if you are concerned about it.

Cancer at any time is stressful; during pregnancy, it can be devastating. Many issues must be considered before a course of treatment is decided upon, including the following.

• Must the pregnancy be terminated?
• Can the malignancy affect the developing baby?
• Can therapy be delayed until after the baby is developed or delivered?
• How do medications, chemotherapy or radiation used to treat the cancer affect the fetus?

The most common cancer discovered during pregnancy is breast cancer. Gynecologic cancers, leukemia, lymphoma, melanoma and bone tumors have also been found.

Cancers may appear during pregnancy for a couple of reasons. Some cancers arise from tissues or organs that are influenced by the increase in hormone levels caused by the pregnancy. In others, increased blood flow and changes in the lymphatic system in pregnancy are thought to contribute to the transfer of cancer to other parts of the body.

❧ Breast Cancer

Breast cancer is the type of cancer discovered most often during pregnancy. Unfortunately, it is harder to find breast cancer at this time because of changes in the breasts, including tenderness, increased size and even lumpiness. About 2% of all women who have breast cancer are pregnant when it is diagnosed.

Breast cancer can be treated during pregnancy. Treatment varies, depending on the woman; surgery, chemotherapy or radiation, or all three, may be required.

๛ Gynecologic Cancers

Various cancers of the female organs, including the cervix, the uterus, the vagina, the ovaries, the bladder and the Fallopian tubes, have been reported during pregnancy. Let me reassure you—these cancers are very rare during pregnancy, no matter what your age.

Cervical cancer occurs only about once in 10,000 pregnancies. However, about 1% of the women who have cancer of the cervix are pregnant when the cancer is diagnosed. Cancer of the cervix is extremely curable, especially when discovered early. That's one reason your Pap smear is important before and during pregnancy.

๛ Cancer Treatments

Treating cancer during pregnancy can be difficult because of the effects various substances and procedures have on mother and fetus. Treatment can cause a variety of problems, including miscarriage, fetal death, fetal malformations and fetal-growth retardation. The pregnant woman may also experience side effects.

Discuss any questions about cancer treatment during pregnancy with your doctor. He or she can give you the best answers and help reassure you.

๛ Other Cancers in Pregnancy

Other types of cancer, such as Hodgkin's disease, leukemia or melanoma, may or may not complicate pregnancy. If you are diagnosed with *any* form of cancer, you and your doctor will discuss ways to treat it.

Part 5

Laboring and Delivering Your Baby

Chapter 18

Labor and Delivery

Many of my patients in their 30s and 40s want to know if labor and delivery will be different for them than for younger women. Labor may be longer for a woman in her 30s and 40s than for a woman under 30 because the cervix does not dilate as easily as it does in a woman under 30. We also know that more older women need a Cesarean delivery.

Just as your uterus may not contract as readily during labor, it may not contract as quickly as it would for a younger woman after delivery. Postpartum bleeding may last longer and be heavier.

However, your labor and delivery will be unique to you, no matter what your age. Every woman labors differently, and there is often a difference in the way a woman labors from one birth to another.

You don't have a lot of control over the kind of labor you will have. But you *do* have control over other areas related to your delivery. You can prepare for delivery in advance and be ready to go. Have your bag packed and ready. Have your insurance papers filled out and available. At best, your prenatal classes will be over, and you will have visited the labor and delivery area of the hospital you have chosen. You will have made arrangements for your older children to be cared for by someone you trust. You will have everything at work organized so you can leave with a clear conscience. Doing these tasks will help reassure you and put you in the best possible frame of mind. This chapter can also help you prepare for your baby's birth.

Before Labor Begins

By now, you may be impatient for your baby's birth. When the day finally comes, you will experience new sensations as your body prepares to labor and to deliver your baby. Signs you may notice include:

• increase of Braxton-Hicks contractions (described below)
• feeling the baby "drop" lower into your pelvis
• weight loss or a break in weight gain
• increased pressure in the pelvis and rectum
• changes in vaginal discharge
• diarrhea

Braxton-Hicks contractions are painless, nonrhythmical contractions you may feel when you place your hand on your abdomen. They can begin early in pregnancy and continue until your baby is born. They occur at irregular intervals and may increase in number and strength when your uterus is massaged.

The feeling of having your baby drop, also called *lightening*, means the baby's head has moved deep into your pelvis. It is a natural part of the birthing process and can happen a few weeks or a few hours before labor begins or during labor. Often a woman feels she has more room to breathe when the baby descends into the pelvis, but this relief may be accompanied by more pelvic pressure and discomfort.

When Your Water Breaks

Your baby is surrounded by amniotic fluid in the uterus. As labor begins, the membranes that surround the baby and hold the fluid ("waters") may break, and fluid leaks from your vagina. You may feel a gush of fluid, followed by slow leaking, or you may just feel a slow leaking, without the gush of fluid. A sanitary pad helps absorb the fluid.

Not every woman's water breaks before she goes into labor. Usually, the physician must rupture the membranes. Occasionally the bag of waters breaks before a baby is ready to be born. There are several ways a doctor can confirm if your membranes have ruptured.

- *By your description of what happened.* For example, if you describe a large gush of fluid from your vagina.
- *With nitrazine paper.* Fluid is placed on the paper; if membranes have ruptured, the paper changes color.
- *With a ferning test.* Fluid is placed on a glass slide, allowed to dry, then examined under a microscope. A fern-like appearance indicates it is amniotic fluid.

If you believe your water has broken, contact your healthcare provider immediately. You may be advised to go to the hospital.

If you are not near term, your doctor may ask you to come to the office for an examination. You may not be ready to deliver your baby yet, and your doctor will want to confirm that your water has broken and to prevent any infection. The risk of infection increases when your water breaks.

Preterm Birth

Preterm birth refers to a baby born prematurely (more than 4 weeks early); it is also called *premature birth*. About 10% of all babies are born prematurely. Some preterm births are linked to the mother's health, such as when a mother suffers from high blood pressure or has an infection. Usually we do not know the reason a baby is born early.

Preterm delivery of a baby can be dangerous because a baby's lungs and other systems may not be ready to function on their own. Your doctor may take steps to halt contractions if you go into labor too early. Most doctors start with bed rest and increased fluids to stop labor. Some medications, given orally, by injection or intravenously, also help stop labor.

❧ Causes of Premature Labor

While the cause of premature labor is unknown in most cases, we do know that premature labor can start for these reasons:

- a uterus with an abnormal shape
- a large uterus
- hydramnios
- an abnormal placenta
- premature rupture of the membranes
- incompetent cervix
- multiple fetuses
- abnormalities of the fetus
- fetal death
- retained IUD
- serious maternal illness
- incorrect estimate of gestational age

❧ Treating Premature Labor

Your baby needs to remain inside your uterus until it is ready to be born. The goal in treating premature labor is to reduce the risks of problems related to premature delivery.

The treatment most often prescribed for premature labor is bed rest, which means lying on your side in bed. Either side is OK, but the left side is best. See the bed-rest discussion beginning on page 233.

Doctors advise bed rest because it works in many cases. However, bed rest means you may have to stop or to modify activities. Bed rest was once the only treatment for premature labor; now we have medications available, too. However, even if you take medication, you will probably be advised to rest in bed. Three types of medications relax the uterus and decrease contractions: magnesium sulfate, beta-adrenergics and sedatives or narcotics. These drugs are taken orally or intravenously.

Packing for the Hospital

Packing for the hospital can be unnerving. You don't want to pack too early and have your suitcase staring at you. But you don't want to wait till the last minute, throw your things together and take the chance of forgetting something important.

. It's probably a good idea to pack about 3 weeks before your due date. Pack things you'll need during labor for you and your labor coach and items you and the baby will need after delivery, as well as for the hospital stay.

One advantage to packing early for your trip to the hospital is that you will have time to really think about what you want to take with you. You will avoid "panic packing" and perhaps including items you don't need while forgetting more important ones.

There are a lot of things to consider, but the list below should cover nearly all of what you might need:

- completed insurance or preregistration forms and insurance card
- heavy socks to wear in the delivery room
- an item to use as a focal point
- 1 cotton nightgown or T-shirt for labor
- lip balm, lollipops or fruit drops, to use during labor
- light diversion, such as books or magazines, to use during labor
- breath spray
- 1 or 2 nightgowns for after labor (bring a nursing gown if you are going to breastfeed)
- slippers with rubber soles
- 1 long robe for walking in the halls
- 2 bras (nursing bras and pads if you breastfeed)
- 3 pairs of panties
- toiletries you use, including brush, comb, toothbrush, toothpaste, soap, shampoo, conditioner
- hairband or ponytail holder, if you have long hair
- loose-fitting clothes for going home
- sanitary pads, if the hospital doesn't supply them

You may also want to bring one or two pieces of fruit to eat after the delivery. Don't pack them too early!

It's also a good idea to include some things in your hospital kit for your partner or labor coach to help you both during the birth. You might bring the following:

- a watch with a second hand
- talc or cornstarch for massaging you during labor
- a paint roller or tennis ball for giving you a low-back massage during labor
- tapes or CDs and a player, or a radio to play during labor
- camera and film
- list of telephone numbers and a long-distance calling card
- change for telephones and vending machines
- snacks for your partner or labor coach

The hospital will probably supply most of what you need for your baby, but you should have a few things:

- clothes for the trip home, including an undershirt, sleeper, outer clothes (a hat if it's cold outside)
- a couple of baby blankets
- diapers, if your hospital doesn't supply them

Be sure you have an approved infant car seat in which to take your baby home. It's important to start your baby in a car seat the very first time he or she rides in a car! Many hospitals will not let you take your baby home without one.

Going to the Hospital

You may want to preregister at the hospital a few weeks before your due date. It will save you time checking in when you are actually in labor and may reduce your feelings of stress at the same time. Preregister with forms you receive from your doctor's office or from the hospital. Even if you don't actually take them to the hospital before labor, it's a good idea to fill out the forms early. If you wait until you are in labor, you may be in a hurry or concerned with other things.

Be sure you have your insurance card or insurance information with you—put it on top of the things you pack in your bag. It's also helpful to know your blood type and Rh-factor, your doctor's name, your pediatrician's name and your due date.

Ask your healthcare provider how you should prepare to go to the hospital; he or she may have specific instructions for you. You might want to ask the following questions.

• When should I go to the hospital once I am in labor?
• Should I call you before I leave for the hospital?
• How can I reach you after regular office hours?
• Are there any particular instructions to follow during early labor?

Going to the hospital to have a baby can make anyone a little nervous, even an experienced mom. Make some plans before you go so you'll have less to worry about.

• Tour the labor and delivery area of your hospital.
• Preregister at the hospital.
• Talk to your healthcare provider about what will happen during your labor.
• Find out who might cover for your doctor if he or she cannot be there for the birth.
• Plan the trip, and have your partner drive it a couple of times.
• Make alternative plans in case your partner cannot be with you.
• Know how to get in touch with your partner 24 hours a day.
• Pack your bag with items for you, your labor coach or partner, and the baby.

❧ After You Are Admitted to the Hospital

After you're admitted to the hospital, you will probably be settled into a labor room. You are checked to see how much your cervix has dilated. A brief history of your pregnancy is taken. Vital signs, including blood pressure, pulse, temperature and your baby's heart rate are noted. You may receive an enema, or an intravenous drip may be started; blood will probably be drawn. You may have an epidural put in place, if you request one.

You may have your pubic hair shaved, although this is not always necessary. I have had patients, who chose not to have their pubic hair shaved, tell me later they experienced discomfort when their pubic hair became entangled in their underwear because of the normal vaginal discharge after the birth of their baby. It may be something to consider.

Intravenous drip (I.V.). Some women are concerned about having an intravenous drip started in their arm. An I.V. is necessary with an epidural painkiller; however, if you have chosen not to have an epidural, an I.V. is not always required. Most physicians agree an I.V. is helpful if a woman needs medications or fluids during labor. It is also a good safety precaution for problems, such as bleeding; if a woman bleeds heavily before or during labor, medications or blood can be administered quickly. If you are concerned about having an I.V., discuss it with your healthcare provider before the birth of your baby.

Enemas. Many of my patients also want to know if they will have to have an enema to empty their bowels. Not every woman is required to have an one; usually it's a choice.

There are benefits to having an enema in labor. It decreases the amount of fecal contamination during labor and at the time of delivery. It may also help you after delivery if you have an episiotomy because having a bowel movement very soon after delivery can be painful. Discuss any concerns you have about enemas with your healthcare provider at one of your prenatal appointments.

If your doctor isn't available. In some cases, when you get to the hospital you will learn your doctor is not available and someone else will deliver your baby. If your doctor believes he or she might be out of town when your baby is born, ask to meet doctors that "cover" when your doctor is unavailable. Although your physician would like to be there for the birth of your baby, sometimes it is not possible.

Labor

Nearly every woman wants to know if labor will be painful. The only fact I can give you, which is true for every labor, is that no two labors are alike, not even for the same woman. Because

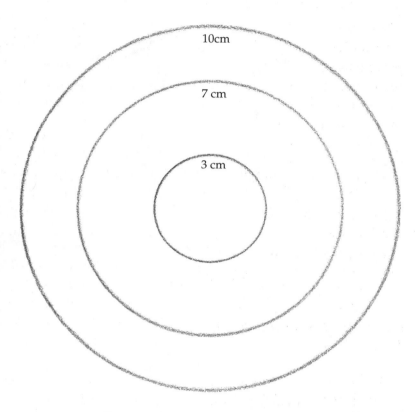

Dilatation of the cervix from 3 to 10cm (shown actual size)

labor is different for every woman, no one can predict what your labor will be like before it begins.

Labor is defined as the dilatation (stretching and expanding) of your cervix. The cervix opens while your uterus, a muscle, contracts to push out your baby.

Some women experience long, intense labors; others have short, relatively pain-free labors. I have found that if a woman understands the labor process and what causes childbirth pain, she has a better chance of reducing it.

Your uterus is a muscular sac shaped like an upside-down pear. This muscle tightens and relaxes during labor (contractions) to expel the baby. During labor, your bladder, rectum, spine and pubic bone receive strong pressure from the uterus as it tightens and hardens with each contraction. The weight of the baby's head as it moves down the birth canal also causes pressure.

❧ The Stages of Labor

Labor is divided into three stages—each stage feels distinctly different and has a specific purpose. See the chart on pages 278 to 280 to see what you might expect during labor and delivery.

❧ Signs Labor Is About to Begin

You may bleed a small amount following a vaginal exam late in pregnancy or at the beginning of labor. This *bloody show* occurs as the cervix stretches and dilates. If it causes you concern or appears to be a large amount of blood, contact your healthcare provider immediately.

Along with light bleeding, you may pass some mucus, sometimes called a *mucus plug*. Passing mucus doesn't always mean you'll have your baby soon or that labor is beginning.

True Labor or False Labor?		
Considerations	*True Labor*	*False Labor*
Contractions	Regular	Irregular
Time between contractions	Come closer together	Do not get closer together
Contraction intensity	Increases	Doesn't change
Location of contractions	Entire abdomen or back	Various locations
Effect of anesthetic or pain relievers	Will not stop labor	Sedation may alter frequency or stop contractions
Cervical change	Progressive cervical change (effacement and dilatation)	No cervical change

❧ Timing Contractions

It's important for your doctor to know how often contractions occur and how long each one lasts. Knowing this, he or she can help you decide if it's time to go to the hospital. Contractions are timed to see how long a contraction lasts and how often contractions occur.

Ask your doctor how he or she prefers you to time your contractions. There are two ways to do it.

Method 1. Start timing when the contraction starts, and time it until the next contraction starts. This is the most common method.

Method 2. Start timing when the contraction ends, and note how long it is until the next contraction starts.

❧ Your Partner's Involvement

Well before your delivery date, sit down and talk with your partner about how you will stay in touch as your due date approaches. Some of my patients' partners rent personal pagers for the last few weeks. (Some hospitals or health-maintenance organizations supply pagers for expectant couples.) Arrange for a backup support person, in case your partner cannot be with you or you need someone else to take you to the hospital.

Your partner can be a big help now. He can help prepare you for labor and delivery and support you as you labor. He can share the joy of your baby's delivery. He can support you emotionally, which is very important to you both.

Your partner may choose to be your labor coach. A labor coach can do a lot to help you through labor. He or she can:

- time your contractions so you are aware of labor's progress
- encourage and reassure you during labor
- help create a mood in the labor room
- keep a watch on the door, and protect your privacy
- report symptoms or pain to the nurse or doctor
- help you deal with physical discomfort

Stages of Labor

Stage 1—Early Phase

What's happening
- Cervix opens and thins out due to uterine contractions
- Cervix dilates to about 2cm
- This phase can last 1 to 10 hours

Mother is experiencing
- Membranes may rupture, accompanied by gush or trickle of amniotic fluid from vagina
- Pinkish discharge may appear ("bloody show")
- Mild contractions begin at 15- to 20-minute intervals; they last about 1 minute
- Contractions become closer together and more regular

What Mother or Partner can do
- Mother should not eat or drink anything once labor begins
- Mother may be able to stay at home, if she is at term
- Begin using relaxation and breathing techniques learned in childbirth class
- If water has broken, if labor is preterm, if there is intense pain, if pain is constant or there is bright-red blood, contact doctor immediately!

Stage 1—Active Phase

What's happening
- Cervix dilates from about 2cm to 10cm
- Cervix continues to thin out
- This phase can last 20 minutes to 2 hours

Mother is experiencing
- Contractions become more intense
- Contractions come closer together
- Contractions are about 3 minutes apart and last about 45 seconds to 1 minute

What Mother or Partner can do
- Keep practicing relaxation and breathing techniques
- An epidural can be administered during this phase

Stage 1—Transition Phase

What's happening	• Stage 1 begins to change to Stage 2 • Cervix is dilated to 10cm • Cervix continues to thin out • This phase can last a few minutes to 2 hours
Mother is experiencing	• Contractions are 2 to 3 minutes apart and last about 1 minute • Mother may feel strong urge to push; she shouldn't push until cervix is completely dilated • Mother may be moved to delivery room, if she is not in a birthing room
What Mother or Partner can do	• Relaxation and breathing techniques help counteract mother's urge to push

Stage 2

What's happening	• Cervix is completely dilated • Baby continues to descend into the birth canal • As mother pushes, baby is delivered • Doctor or nurse suctions baby's nose and mouth, and clamps umbilical cord • This stage can last a few minutes to a few hours (pushing the baby can last a long time)
Mother is experiencing	• Contractions occur at 2- to 5-minute intervals and last from 60 to 90 seconds • With an epidural, mother may find it harder to push • An episiotomy may be done to prevent tearing vaginal tissues as baby is born
What Mother or Partner can do	• Mother will begin to push with each contraction after cervix dilates completely • Mother may be given analgesic or local anesthetic • Mother must listen to doctor or nurse when baby is being delivered; doctor or nurse will tell mother when to push • As mother pushes, she may be able to watch baby being born, if mirror is available

Stages of Labor, *continued*

Stage 3

What's happening	• Placenta is delivered • Doctor examines placenta to make sure all of it has been delivered • This stage can last a few minutes to an hour
Mother is experiencing	• Contractions may occur closer together, but be less painful • Doctor repairs episiotomy
What Mother or Partner can do	• You'll meet and hold your baby • You may need to push to expel the placenta • You may be able to hold your baby while the doctor repairs your episiotomy • Nurse will rub or massage the uterus through the abdomen to help it contract to control bleeding

Stage 4

What's happening	• Placenta has been delivered • Uterus continues to contract, which is important to control bleeding • This stage usually lasts a couple of days

❧❧❧❧

Maria was upset at her 32-week visit. Her husband's reserve
unit had been activated, and he would be gone for at least
6 months. Maria was sure she would not be able to deliver
without her husband as her labor coach. We talked about
other possible coaches. Maria didn't know that someone else
could act as her coach. When she came in 2 weeks later,
Maria was happy to report that her sister (who had delivered
a year earlier) was thrilled and honored to help. They had
even been to a prenatal class together to get ready.

❧ Eating and Drinking during Labor

During labor, you are not allowed to eat or drink anything.
Women often get nauseated during labor, which could cause
vomiting. For your safety, keep your stomach empty. You may be
able to sip water or to suck on ice chips.

❧ Back Labor

Some women experience "back labor;" it occurs in about 30%
of all deliveries. Back labor means most of the pain is concentrat-
ed in the back. The cause of back labor is a baby facing toward
the mother's front—the baby presses against the mother's lower
spine. Each contraction forces the baby's head against the mother's lower spine, resulting in strong pain that does not completely
disappear between contractions.

Back labor may mean that delivery takes longer. The doctor
may have to rotate the baby's head so it comes out facing the
conventional way—looking down at the ground rather than up at
the sky.

❧ Tests during Labor

Tests done on your baby during labor give your healthcare
provider a great deal of information. These tests include fetal blood
sampling, external fetal monitoring and internal fetal monitoring.
These tests are discussed on pages 135 and 136.

Coping with the Pain of Labor and Childbirth

Today, healthcare providers encourage frank discussions about the pain of labor and delivery. Childbirth is usually accompanied by pain, and pain varies among women, from very little to a great deal. Research shows that the *expectation* of pain can, in itself, evoke fear and anxiety. The best way to deal with pain is to become informed about it.

Many women believe they'll feel guilty after their baby is born if they ask for pain relief during labor. Sometimes they think the baby will be harmed by the medication they take. Some women believe they'll deprive themselves of the "complete" birth experience. Others are concerned about cost and believe they can't afford an epidural if their insurance doesn't cover it.

You learn out about pain and pain relief through several channels. Childbirth-education classes are good sources of information. You can learn about pain-relief methods that don't require medication, such as breathing methods and relaxation techniques.

Talk to your doctor about pain relief. I've found that using medication for pain relief is usually a personal choice, not a medical decision.

Keep an open mind about using medication for pain relief during labor. Your labor may be harder (or easier) than you expect. You may have a greater or lesser need for pain relief than you think. You can always change your mind if you need to or want to.

❧❧❧❧

Martha was certain she wouldn't need an epidural. At one of her visits late in the pregnancy, she tried to make me promise I wouldn't make her have one. I explained an epidural was an option, not a requirement, and no one would make her have one. I knew she thought I was trying to talk her into it, but I wasn't. Experience has taught me that no matter how much a woman prepares, no one knows what labor will be like for her. I try to help them keep an open mind about the experience. Among her other requests, Martha didn't want an I.V., an enema and certainly not an episiotomy. Martha's labor turned out to be an adventure—a long one. At 3cm, she was screaming for relief. She got to 5cm and stayed there for quite a while. In the end, I had to do a C-section for her 9-pound, 4-ounce healthy baby boy.

I wasn't sure what her reaction was going to be after the birth. When I saw her the next day, Martha was in good spirits and very happy. She felt her expectations before delivery had been misdirected. She jokingly said to me, "The only thing on my list that didn't happen was an episiotomy."

Pain Relief without Medication

Some women do not want medication during labor to relieve pain. They prefer to use different laboring positions, massage, breathing patterns, relaxation techniques or hypnotherapy to relieve their pain.

Breathing patterns and relaxation techniques are usually learned in a childbirth-education class. See page 42 for a discussion of various options.

Different laboring positions and massage enable a woman and her partner (or labor coach) to work together during labor to find relief. This interaction can help you feel closer, and it lets you share the experience. I've had patients tell me that using these methods brought them closer to their partner and made the birth experience a more joyful one.

Laboring Positions

Most women in North America and Europe give birth on their backs, in bed. However, some women are trying different positions to find relief from pain and to make the birth of their baby easier.

In the past, women often labored and gave birth in an upright position that kept the pelvis vertical, such as kneeling, squatting, sitting or standing up. Laboring in this position enables the abdominal wall to relax and the baby to descend more rapidly. Because contractions are stronger and more regular, labor is often shorter.

Today some women use different laboring positions, such as the one shown above, to help them find pain relief. Discuss it with your healthcare provider if you're interested in trying a different position for labor.

Today, many women are asking to choose the birth position that is most comfortable for them. Freedom to choose the birth position can make the woman feel more confident about managing birth and labor. Women who choose their own methods may feel more satisfied with the entire experience.

If this is important to you, discuss the matter with your healthcare provider. Ask about the facilities at the hospital you will use; some have special equipment, such as birthing chairs, squatting bars or birthing beds, to help you feel more comfortable. Positions you might consider for your labor are described below.

- *Walking and standing* are good positions to use during early labor. Walking may help you breathe more easily and relax more. Standing in a warm shower may provide relief. When walking, be sure someone is with you to offer support (both physical and emotional).
- *Sitting* can decrease the strength and frequency of contractions and can slow labor. Sitting to rest after walking or standing is acceptable; however, sitting can be uncomfortable during a contraction.
- *Kneeling on hands and knees* is a good way to relieve the pain of back labor.
- *Kneeling against a support,* such as a chair or your partner, stretches your back muscles. The effects of kneeling are similar to those of walking and standing.

- When you can't stand, walk or kneel, *lie on your side.* If you receive pain medication, you will need to lie down. Lie on your left side, then turn to your right.
- Although *lying on your back* is the most common position used for labor, it can decrease the strength and frequency of contractions, which can slow the process. It can also make your blood pressure drop and cause your baby's heart rate to drop. If you lie on your back, elevate the head of the bed and put a pillow under one hip so you are not flat on your back.

❧ Massage for Relief

Massage is a wonderful, gentle way to help you feel better during labor. The touching and caressing of massage helps you relax. One study showed that women who were massaged for 20 minutes every hour during active labor felt less anxiety and less pain.

Many parts of the body of a laboring woman can be massaged. Massaging the head, neck, back and feet can offer a great deal of comfort and relaxation. The person doing the massage should pay close attention to the woman's responses to determine correct pressure.

Different types of massage affect a woman in various ways. You and your partner may want to practice the two types of massage described below before labor and for use during labor.

Effleurage is light, gentle fingertip massage over the abdomen and upper thighs; it is used during early labor. Stroking is light, but doesn't tickle, and fingertips never leave the skin.

Start with hands on either side of the navel. Move the hands upward and outward, and come back down to the pubic area. Then move the hands back up to the navel. Massage may extend down the thighs. It can also be done as a crosswise motion, around fetal-monitor belts. Move fingers across the abdomen from one side to the other, between the belts.

Counterpressure massage is excellent for relieving the pain of back labor. Place the heel of the hand or the flat part of the fist (you can also use a tennis ball) against the tailbone. Apply firm pressure in a small, circular motion.

Massage at any time in pregnancy and during labor and delivey helps a woman relax.

❧ Analgesics and Anesthetics

There are many different types of pain relief. *Analgesia* is pain relief without total loss of sensation. *Anesthesia* is pain relief with partial or total loss of sensation.

Analgesia is injected into a muscle or vein to decrease the pain of labor, but you remain conscious. It provides pain relief but can make you drowsy, restless or nauseous. You may find concentrating difficult. Analgesia may slow the baby's reflexes and breathing, so this medication is usually given during the early and middle parts of labor. Examples of analgesia are Demerol® (meperidine hydrochloride) and morphine.

There are two types of anesthesia—local anesthesia, sometimes called *regional anesthesia,* and general anesthesia. You remain completely unconscious under general anesthesia, so it is used only for some Cesarean deliveries and emergency vaginal deliveries. Using a general anesthesia has certain disadvantages. Sometimes the mother vomits or aspirates vomited food or stomach acid into her lungs. The baby is also anesthetized and needs to be resuscitated after delivery. General anesthesia is not used very often for childbirth today. Its advantage is that it can be administered quickly in an emergency.

Local or regional anesthesia affects a small area and is useful for an episiotomy repair. It rarely affects the baby and usually has few lingering effects. The three most common types of regional anesthesia are pudendal block, spinal block and epidural block.

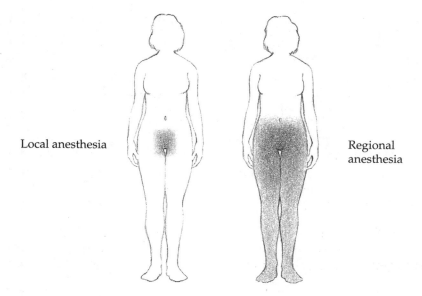

Local anesthesia

Regional anesthesia

A *pudendal block* is medication injected into the pudendal nerve area in the vagina to relieve pain in the vaginal area, the perineum and the rectum. You remain conscious, and side effects are rare. Pudenal block is considered one of the safest forms of pain relief; however, it does not relieve uterine pain.

Medication is injected into spinal fluid in the lower back with a *spinal block,* which numbs the lower part of the body. You remain conscious. This type of block is administered only once during labor, so it is often used just before delivery or for a Cesarean section. It works quickly and is an effective pain inhibitor.

A tube is inserted into a space outside your spinal column in the lower back for an *epidural block.* Medication is administered through the tube for pain relief, and you remain conscious during delivery. The tube remains in place until after the baby is born so medication can be readministered when necessary; sometimes medication is delivered continuously by pump. An epidural causes some loss of sensation in the lower part of the body. It helps relieve painful uterine contractions, pain in the vagina and rectum as the baby passes through the birth canal and the pain of an episiotomy. A woman with an epidural still feels pressure sensations so she is able to push during vaginal delivery. However, an epidural may make it harder to push, so vacuum extraction or forceps may be necessary during delivery.

A spinal block or an epidural block may cause a woman's blood pressure to drop suddenly, which in turn can cause a decrease in the baby's heart rate. These blocks are not used if a woman is bleeding heavily or if the baby has an abnormal heartbeat. One other possible side effect from these blocks is severe headache, if the insertion needle punctures the covering of the spinal cord; this is an unusual complication, however.

A *walking spinal,* also called *intrathecal anesthesia,* can be given to women who suffer extreme pain in the early stages of labor (dilated less than 5cm). A small amount of narcotic, such as Demerol, is injected through a thin needle into the spinal fluid, which eases the pain and causes few side effects. Because the dose is small, neither mother nor baby becomes overly drowsy. Sensory and motor functions remain intact, so the mother can walk around with help, sit in a chair or go to the bathroom.

Cesarean Delivery

When you have a Cesarean delivery (also called a *C-section*), your baby is delivered through an incision made in your abdominal wall and uterus. Research has shown that women in their 30s and 40s have the highest rate of Cesarean deliveries.

While there are many reasons for doing a C-section, the main goal is to deliver a healthy baby and have a healthy mother. Particular reasons for performing a Cesarean include:

• a previous Cesarean delivery
• to avoid rupture of the uterus
• the baby is too big to fit through the birth canal
• fetal distress
• compression of the umbilical cord
• baby is in the breech position
• placental abruption
• placenta previa
• multiple fetuses—twins, triplets or more

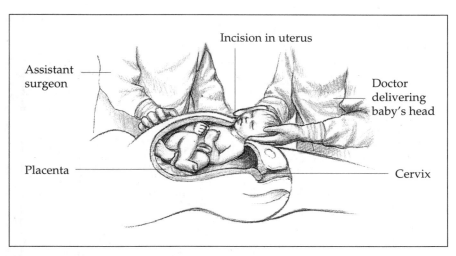

Cesarean delivery

The rate of C-sections done in the U.S. has increased. In 1965, only 4% of all deliveries were Cesarean. Today, nearly 25% of all deliveries are Cesarean deliveries. For women over age 35, the rate is 31%.

We can point to many reasons for the increase. We believe it is related to better monitoring during labor and safer procedures for C-sections. Women are also having bigger babies. Another factor influencing this increase may be rising malpractice rates and doctors' fears of litigation.

A woman often wants to know in advance if she will need a Cesarean delivery. A doctor doesn't usually know the answer to this question before labor begins, unless the woman had a previous C-section. (Also see discussion below of vaginal birth after Cesarean delivery.) We usually have to wait for labor contractions to begin before we can tell if the baby is stressed by them or if the baby fits through the birth canal.

It's a good idea to discuss Cesarean delivery with your healthcare provider several weeks before your due date. Ask why he or she would do a C-section. Let your healthcare provider know your wishes and concerns in regard to having a Cesarean delivery.

❧ How a Cesarean Is Performed

When a Cesarean delivery is performed, an incision is made through the skin of the lower abdomen down to the uterus, and the wall of the uterus is cut. Next, the amniotic sac containing the baby and placenta is cut, and the baby is removed through the incisions. After the baby is delivered, the placenta is removed. The uterus is closed in layers with absorbable sutures (they don't have to be removed). Finally, the abdomen is sewn together.

With many C-sections, an anesthesiologist administers an epidural or spinal anesthetic so you remain awake. You can see and hold your baby immediately after birth, and your partner can be with you.

A Cesarean delivery is major surgery and carries with it certain risks, including infection, bleeding, shock through blood loss, the possibility of blood clots and the possibility of injury to other organs, such as the bladder or rectum.

You will probably have to stay in the hospital for a couple of extra days. Recovery is slower with a Cesarean than with a vaginal delivery. Full recovery normally takes 4 to 6 weeks.

❧ Vaginal Birth after Cesarean (VBAC)

Today, many women who have had a C-section with one pregnancy deliver vaginally with a later pregnancy. This is called *vaginal birth after Cesarean (VBAC)*. A high percentage of these deliveries are successful. About 70% of women who had a Cesarean because of a situation that is not a factor in this pregnancy can expect a successful vaginal delivery.

A number of factors in your situation must be considered. Ask your healthcare provider for information before making this decision. Certain criteria must be met before you can have a VBAC, including the following.

• The type of uterine incision from the previous Cesarean delivery is important. (This incision may or may not be similar to the incision made in your abdomen.) With a classical incision, which goes high up on the uterus, labor is *not* permitted in subsequent pregnancies.

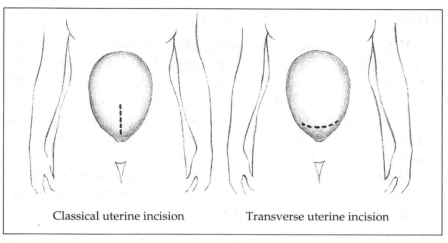

Classical uterine incision   Transverse uterine incision

The incision in the uterus for a Cesarean delivery is not always the same as the one made in the abdomen.

- The size of your pelvis is important. If you are small and your baby is large, it may cause problems.
- You have no medical complications, such as diabetes or high blood pressure.
- You are expecting only one baby.
- Your baby is entering the birth canal head first.

If you are considering a vaginal birth with this pregnancy, the American College of Obstetricians and Gynecologists has made some recommendations about the birthing facility. It should offer the ability to perform an emergency C-section within 30 minutes, the ability to monitor the fetus continuously and a fully equipped, 24-hour blood bank.

If you are interested in a vaginal birth, discuss VBAC with your doctor well in advance of labor so plans can be made. Discuss the benefits and risks, and ask your doctor for his or her opinion as to your chances of a successful vaginal delivery. He or she knows your health and pregnancy history. Include your partner in the decision-making process.

Is an Episiotomy Always Necessary?

An *episiotomy* is a surgical incision in the area behind the vagina, above the rectum; it is made during delivery to avoid tearing or lacerating the vaginal opening or rectum, and to allow room for the baby to fit through the birth canal. Many women do not want an episiotomy for the delivery of their baby; they believe the procedure is unnecessary.

Whether you must have an episiotomy is something to discuss with your doctor at prenatal visits. Ask if an episiotomy is routine or if it is done only when necessary. Some situations do not require an episiotomy, such as a small or premature baby. However, your doctor may not be able to make this decision until delivery.

An episiotomy is not necessary for every woman. The more children a woman has, the less likely it is she will need one; it depends on the size of the baby. Factors leading to an episiotomy include the size of the mother's vaginal opening, the size of the baby's head and shoulders, the number of babies previously delivered and whether it is a forceps or vacuum delivery.

✥ Types of Episiotomies

Episiotomies are described according to the relative depth of the incision.

- *1st degree*—cuts only the skin
- *2nd degree*—cuts the skin and underlying tissue, called *fascia*
- *3rd degree*—cuts the skin, underlying tissue and rectal sphincter, the muscle that goes around the anus
- *4th degree*—goes through the three layers described above and the rectal mucosa

✥ If You Have an Episiotomy

After delivery of your baby, the most painful part of the entire birth process might be your episiotomy. Don't be afraid to ask for pain medication. Ice, sitz baths and laxatives can also help relieve episiotomy pain.

The Baby's Birth Position

Most babies enter the birth canal head first, which is the best position for labor and delivery. However, some babies enter the birth canal in other positions.

A *breech position* means the baby is not in a head-down position; its legs or buttocks come into the birth canal first. If your baby is breech when it is time to deliver, your doctor may try to turn the baby or you may need a Cesarean delivery.

One of the main causes of a breech presentation is prematurity of the baby. Near the end of the second trimester, the baby is commonly in the breech presentation. As you progress through the third trimester, the baby usually turns into the head-down presentation for birth.

For a long time, breech deliveries were performed vaginally. Then it was believed the safest delivery method was a C-section; many doctors still prefer to do a Cesarean for a breech presentation. However, some physicians believe a woman can deliver a breech baby without difficulty if the situation is right.

✿ Abnormal Birth Presentations

There are three different breech presentations and three other atypical presentations.

Frank breech—Occurs when lower legs are flexed at the hips and extended at the knees. Feet are up by the face or head.

Complete breech presentation—One or both knees are flexed (not extended).

Incomplete breech presentation—A foot or knee enters the birth canal ahead of the rest of the baby.

Face presentation—The baby's head is hyperextended so the face enters the birth canal first.

Transverse lie—The baby is lying almost as if in a cradle in the pelvis. The head is on one side of the mother's abdomen, and the bottom is on the other side.

Shoulder presentation—The baby's shoulder enters the birth canal first.

❧ Can My Baby Be Turned?

Some doctors try to turn a baby in the breech position. If your baby is in a breech position, your physician may attempt to change its position by using external cephalic version (ECV).

With ECV, the doctor places his or her hands on your abdomen. Using gentle movements, he or she manually tries to shift the baby into the head-down position. An ultrasound is usually done first so the doctor can see the position of the baby and again during the procedure to guide the doctor in changing the baby's position.

A physician usually uses this method before labor begins or in the early stages of labor. It is successful in about half of the cases in which it is used. Not every doctor is trained in the procedure.

Delivery of Your Baby

After you have labored through the first stage, you are ready to deliver your baby. You will finally meet your child, whom you have carried for so long.

The actual delivery of the baby and placenta (not including the laboring process) in stage 2 takes from a few minutes to an hour or more. However, the part that takes the longest is not the birth of the baby. Stitching closed the various skin and muscle layers after the baby is born may take the greatest amount of time.

In a forceps delivery, the doctor uses an instrument to help remove the baby from the birth canal. Forceps look like two metal hands. They are not used as frequently as they were in the past; today, physicians more often use a vacuum extractor.

A *vacuum extractor* is a plastic cup that fits on the baby's head by suction. When you push during labor, your doctor is able to pull gently and deliver the baby's head and body more easily.

After Your Baby Is Born

Things happen quickly when your baby emerges into the world. First, the baby's mouth and throat are suctioned. Then the doctor clamps and cuts the umbilical cord (or your partner may cut the cord).

The baby is wrapped in clean blankets and may be placed on your abdomen. Apgar scores are recorded at 1 minute and 5 minutes after birth. An identification band is placed on the baby's wrist or ankle. Usually a brief physical exam or an assessment is done right after delivery. The baby receives drops in its eyes to prevent infection and is given a vitamin-K shot to prevent bleeding.

You will be asked if you want your baby to receive the hepatitis vaccine. Discuss this with your healthcare provider before the birth; the vaccine protects your baby against hepatitis in the future. Once the initial evaluation is complete, the baby is returned to you. Later, the baby is placed in a heated bassinet for a period of time.

If your partner wants to cut the umbilical cord after the baby is delivered, discuss it with your healthcare provider before you go into labor. What your partner may be allowed to do varies from place to place.

❧ Bleeding after Delivery

After you deliver your baby, the uterus shrinks from the size of a watermelon to the size of a volleyball so it won't bleed. It is not unusual to lose blood during labor and delivery; however, heavy bleeding after the baby is born can be serious. A loss of more than 17 ounces (500ml) in the first 24 hours after your baby's birth, called *postpartum hemorrhage*, is significant. Bleeding is controlled by massaging the uterus (called *Credé*) and medications. Bleeding lessens gradually over time, then stops.

❧❧❧❧

Kay had delivered two days earlier, and she called me because she was concerned. She thought she should be feeling a lot better, and she was afraid something was wrong because she didn't. She said her breasts were sore and ached, it felt as though her uterus were still contracting (especially when she breastfed) and sitting down was an ordeal because her episiotomy was sore. I told her all these things were normal, and we talked about what she could do to help make things better.

In the hospital, she had taken some pain medicine but didn't want to take any more because she was nursing. I told her the prescription she had been given was safe and would probably help a lot. Breastfeeding had stimulated her uterus to contract to help it get smaller so it wouldn't bleed. We talked about sitz baths for her episiotomy, and I reminded her the pain medicine would also help with that discomfort. When I saw her a few weeks later, she said my suggestions had made her life a lot easier.

Heavy bleeding after the birth may be caused by a number of things, including a uterus that won't contract, lacerations or tearing of the vagina or cervix during birth, a large or bleeding episiotomy, a tear or rupture in the uterus, retained placental tissue or clotting or coagulation problems.

If you experience a significant change in bleeding after you go home, contact your doctor. Some bleeding is normal, but it's best to talk to your healthcare provider about it. He or she may want to see you, prescribe medication or determine if the amount of bleeding is normal.

Inducing Labor

Each year, healthcare providers induce labor for about 450,000 births. Labor is induced for a number of reasons, including postdate (overdue) babies, chronic high blood pressure in the mother, pre-eclampsia, gestational diabetes, intrauterine-growth retardation and Rh-isoimmunization.

❧ Postdate Pregnancies

The most common reason for inducing birth is an overdue baby. Babies born 2 weeks or more past their due date are called *postdate births.* Nearly 10% of all babies are born more than 2 weeks late. The majority of these babies are delivered safely. However, carrying a baby longer than 42 weeks can cause some problems for the fetus and the mother, so healthcare providers conduct tests on these babies and induce labor, if necessary.

A healthcare provider can determine if a baby is moving around in the womb and if the amount of amniotic fluid is healthy and normal. If the baby is healthy and active, the mother is usually monitored until labor begins on its own. Tests may be done as reassurance that an overdue baby is fine and can remain in the womb. These tests include a nonstress test, a contraction stress test and a biophysical profile. If signs of fetal stress are found, labor is often induced.

Emergency Childbirth

Emergency childbirth can happen to anyone, so it's a good idea to be prepared. Read and study the information in the boxes on the following pages. Be sure you have the names and telephone numbers of your healthcare provider and those of friends or family near the phone. And if it happens to you, relax and follow the instructions provided.

Emergency Delivery at Home

1. Call **911** for help.

2. Call a neighbor, family member or friend (have phone numbers available).

3. Encourage the woman *not* to push or to bear down.

4. Use blankets and towels to make the woman as comfortable as possible.

5. If there is time, wash the woman's vaginal and rectal areas with soap and water.

6. When the baby's head delivers, encourage the woman to pant or blow, and to concentrate on *not* pushing.

7. Try to ease the baby's head out with gentle pressure. Do not pull on the head.

8. After the head is delivered, gently push down on the head and push a little to deliver the shoulders.

9. As one shoulder delivers, lift the head up, delivering the other shoulder. The rest of the baby will quickly follow.

10. Wrap the baby in a clean blanket or towel.

11. Use a clean cloth or tissue to remove mucus from the baby's mouth.

12. Do not pull on the umbilical cord to deliver the placenta—it is not necessary.

13. If the placenta delivers on its own, wrap it in a towel or clean newspapers, and save it.

14. You don't need to cut the cord.

15. Keep the placenta at the level of the baby or above the baby.

16. Keep both mother and baby warm with towels or blankets until medical help arrives.

Emergency Delivery Alone

1. Call **911** for help.

2. Call a neighbor, close member or friend (have phone numbers available).

3. Try not to push or to bear down.

4. Find a comfortable place, and spread out towels or blankets.

5. If the baby comes before help arrives, try to use your hands to ease the baby out while you gently push.

6. Wrap the baby in a clean blanket or clean towels; hold it close to your body to keep it warm.

7. Use a clean cloth or tissue to remove mucus from the baby's mouth.

8. Do not pull on the umbilical cord to deliver the placenta—it is not necessary.

9. If the placenta delivers on its own, save it.

10. You don't need to cut the cord.

11. Try to keep yourself and your baby warm until medical help arrives.

Emergency Delivery on the Way to the Hospital

1. Stop the car.

2. Try to get help, if you have a cellular phone or a CB radio.

3. Put on your flashing warning lights.

4. Place the woman in the back seat, with a towel or blanket under her.

5. Encourage the woman not to push or to bear down.

6. When the baby's head delivers, encourage the woman to pant or blow, and to concentrate on *not* pushing.

7. Try to ease the baby's head out with gentle pressure. Do not pull on the head.

8. After the head is delivered, gently push down on the head and push a little to deliver the shoulders.

9. As one shoulder delivers, lift the head up, delivering the other shoulder. The rest of the baby will quickly follow.

10. Wrap the baby in a clean blanket or clean towels. Clean newspapers can be used if nothing else is available.

11. Use a clean cloth or tissue to remove mucus from the baby's mouth.

12. Do not pull on the umbilical cord to deliver the placenta—it is not necessary.

13. If the placenta delivers on its own, wrap it in a towel or clean newspapers and save it.

14. You don't need to cut the cord.

15. Keep the placenta at the level of the baby or above the baby.

16. Keep both mother and baby warm until you can get them to the hospital or medical help arrives.

Part 6

Living with
Your Baby

Chapter 19

After the Birth

Your baby has been delivered, and you have a new person in your life who needs care and attention. But you need care and attention, too—and time to pay attention to your own needs. Soon after the birth, you may start thinking about how to get back in shape and feel your best again. Just keep in mind that your body can't recover overnight from 9 months of pregnancy, so don't expect it to. Relax and take your time!

The recovery period following your baby's birth (the first 6 weeks) is called the *postpartum period.* Your body rapidly downsizes as it begins to return to its prepregnancy size. During this time, you go through great physical and emotional adjustments.

You can help yourself during the postpartum period in many ways. Eat nutritiously, allow others to help you and accept the fact you'll have to take it easy for a while. Another way you can help yourself is to learn as much as you can about what to expect after delivery.

After the Baby Is Born

You will probably be discharged from the hospital a day or two after your baby is born, if labor and delivery were normal and the baby is doing well. Some women choose to go home 24 hours

after the birth of their baby or even sooner. If you have a Cesarean delivery, you need to stay a few days longer.

Your blood pressure and bleeding are checked regularly in the first hours after the birth. You will be offered medication for pain relief and encouraged to nurse your baby.

Changes in the Uterus

Your uterus goes through great changes after your baby is born and takes several weeks to return to its original size. The size of your uterus at birth is quite large to accommodate the baby. Immediately after delivery, you can feel the uterus around your navel; it should feel very hard. You are checked frequently to make sure it remains hard after delivery. If it feels soft, you or a nurse can massage it so it becomes firm.

The uterus shrinks about a finger's width every day; this is called *involution*. In the hospital, someone will check you every day; the exam can be a little uncomfortable.

You will probably feel afterpains for several days after the birth as your uterus contracts to prevent heavy bleeding and to return to its normal size. Cramps are eased by lying on your stomach and taking mild pain relievers. An empty bladder enables the uterus to work more efficiently, with less pain, so drink lots of fluids and urinate often.

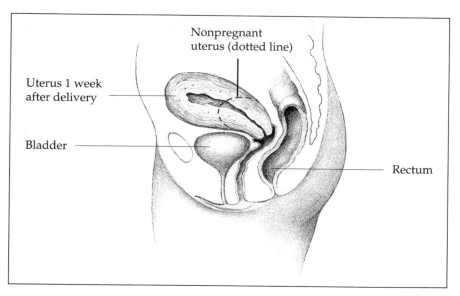

Your uterus shrinks a great deal after delivery. This illustration compares a nonpregnant uterus with a uterus 1 week after birth.

If you breastfeed, you may find that afterpains intensify. When your baby sucks, the pituitary gland is stimulated to release oxytocin, which makes the uterus contract. These extra contractions are good for you, but they may be painful. Mild pain medication can offer relief.

Pain in the Perineum

You may feel pain in the perineum. (The perineum is the area between the vagina and anus.) The area may have been stretched, cut or torn during delivery. Most of the soreness should be gone in 3 to 6 weeks.

If this pain is a problem, ice packs offer some relief in the first 24 hours after delivery. Ice numbs the area and helps reduce swelling. After 24 hours, a warm bath or a soak in a sitz tub can offer relief. Do this several times a day. Other remedies for perineal pain include numbing sprays, walking (to stimulate circulation), witch-hazel compresses and Kegel exercises. See page 203 for Kegel exercises.

Urination may be painful; acidic urine can sting the cut area. You may want to urinate standing up or in the shower with running water washing the area.

Bowel Movements

It's not unusual to have sluggish bowels for a few days after your baby's birth. The digestive system slows down during labor, and pregnancy and delivery stress abdominal muscles. You may have had an enema or emptied your bowel during the pushing phase of labor. Pain medication can cause constipation. These all contribute to bowel habits that are different than normal. I tell my patients not to worry about having a bowel movement for the first 4 or 5 days. Constipation at this time is acceptable.

To help your system work more efficiently, eat a diet high in fiber, and drink lots of fluid. Laxatives are commonly used and available. Drinking prune juice and eating prunes are natural laxatives. Over-the-counter stool softeners also help. If you don't have a bowel movement within a week after delivery or you become uncomfortable, call your healthcare provider.

An episiotomy or hemorrhoids can make a bowel movement more difficult or make you more apprehensive about having one. If you are left with hemorrhoids after delivery, be assured they eventually shrink on their own. If you have problems with them, a compress of witch hazel or commercial compresses can offer relief. Ice packs may also help them shrink.

Your Breasts

After delivery, your breasts may be sore, whether you breastfeed or bottlefeed. If you bottlefeed, your milk still comes in; doctors don't give medication to stop it as they did in the past. Your breasts fill with milk, called *engorgement*. Engorgement lasts a few days and can be very uncomfortable. You can ease discomfort by wearing a support bra or binding your breasts with a towel. Ice packs also help milk dry up.

Don't empty your breasts unless you really have to because of pain—your body will replace the milk with more milk! Avoid nipple stimulation and running warm water over the breasts. These practices stimulate breasts to produce milk.

You may find you have a mild fever with engorgement. Acetaminophen can help reduce the fever and discomfort.

Vaginal Discharge

After delivering your baby, you will experience a vaginal discharge similar to a heavy menstrual flow. This discharge, called *lochia*, lasts from 2 to 4 weeks. The discharge is red for the first 3 or 4 days, then turns pink, then brown and finally white or colorless at around 10 days. You will also have lochia if you have a C-section, although it may be less than appears with a vaginal birth.

If the discharge is foul-smelling, remains heavy or is extremely light the first few days, tell your healthcare provider. He or she may want to examine you.

Research indicates that the incidence of toxic shock syndrome (TSS) occurs more often in the postpartum period. Because tampons are associated with TSS, don't use them to deal with lochia. Use sanitary napkins.

If you do not breastfeed, your first menstrual period occurs within 6 to 8 weeks after giving birth. If you breastfeed, you may not have a regular menstrual period until you wean your baby.

Postpartum Warning Signs

If you take care of yourself after delivery, you should not feel ill after the birth. Occasionally problems do occur. Refer to the list of symptoms and warnings signs below. Call your doctor immediately if you experience:

- unusually heavy or sudden increase in vaginal bleeding (more than your normal menstrual flow or soaking more than two sanitary pads in 30 minutes)
- vaginal discharge with strong, unpleasant odor
- a temperature of 101F (38.3C) or more, except in the first 24 hours after birth
- chills

- breasts that are painful or red
- loss of appetite for an extended period
- pain, tenderness, redness or swelling in the legs
- pain in the lower abdomen or in the back
- painful urination or feeling an intense need to urinate
- severe pain in the vagina or perineum

Your Emotions

Temporary emotional changes are not uncommon during the postpartum period. You may have mood swings, mild distress or bouts of crying. (See the discussion of postpartum distress that begins on page 314.) Mood changes are often a result of birth-associated hormonal changes in your body.

Lack of sleep may play a part in how you feel. Many women are surprised by how tired they are emotionally and physically in the first few months after the birth of the baby. Be sure to take time for yourself, and allow yourself a period of adjustment.

Sleep and rest are essential after your baby is born. To get the rest you need, go to bed early when possible. Take a nap or rest when your baby sleeps.

Exercise after Pregnancy

Many women are eager to begin exercising soon after their baby is born. Exercise helps you feel better, and it can lift your spirits. Start by doing simple isometric exercises the day after delivery. Practice holding in stomach muscles, or start with mild Kegel exercises. See page 203.

When you are up and about again, you can do other forms of exercise. Do something you enjoy, and do it on a regular basis. Walking and swimming are excellent exercises to help you get back in shape. However, before you start any postpartum exercise program, check with your doctor. He or she may have particular advice for you.

Be careful about beginning an exercise program too soon. Don't overtire yourself by choosing a program that is too ambitious. Always get adequate rest.

After a Cesarean delivery, light activity is very important. In the hospital, you'll probably have to practice coughing or deep breathing to keep lungs clear. Wiggle toes to aid circulation. Walking may not be easy, but it helps minimize the chances of developing a blood clot in your lower extremities. Check with your healthcare provider before starting an exercise routine or program of any kind.

Recovering from a Cesarean Section

Recovery from a Cesarean delivery is different than recovery from a vaginal birth. You have undergone major abdominal surgery, so be prepared to take it easy for a while. While you have experienced many of the same situations as someone who has had a vaginal birth, you face some additional restrictions.

You are encouraged to get out of bed as soon as possible after your baby is born. Moving helps prevent blood clots in the legs, lung collapse and pneumonia. Walking helps restore body functions, such as relieving constipation and abdominal gas.

Be careful not to strain stomach muscles. Avoid lifting anything heavy. Once home, keep your incision clean and dry, and watch for infection.

Infection of a Cesarean incision usually occurs 4 to 6 days after surgery. If any of the following signs appear, contact your healthcare provider immediately. Signs of infection include:

• redness that spreads from the edges of the incision
• fever
• hardness around the incision
• discharge from the incision site

Although you did not deliver vaginally, you will probably experience painful uterine contractions for several days after the C-section. This is a sign your uterus is returning to its pre-pregnancy size. If you breastfeed, you may notice the pains when your baby nurses.

You will have lochia with a Cesarean delivery (see page 307). However, your discharge may be lighter than lochia that follows a vaginal birth.

If you are interested in exercising after a Cesarean, you can usually begin light exercise about 3 weeks after birth. You can probably resume full activity between 4 and 6 weeks postpartum.

Resuming Sexual Relations

One concern you and your partner may share after delivery is postpartum sex. Getting back into the swing after the baby is born can be difficult. Your sex drives can be affected by stress, hormonal changes, emotions and fatigue.

We used to advise women to wait at least 6 weeks before having intercourse. If you feel no pain or discomfort and your episiotomy has healed, you can resume sexual relations. Be sure bleeding has ceased. For most women, this will be at least a few weeks after delivery.

If you decide to have intercourse, you need to take precautions if you don't want to become pregnant again. *You can become pregnant before you have a menstrual period.* Discuss birth-control options with your healthcare provider.

Birth Control after Pregnancy

Some women choose to have a tubal ligation done while they are in the hospital after the birth of their baby. Immediately after the birth is probably *not* the time to make a decision about a tubal ligation if you haven't thought seriously about it before. Consider tubal ligation permanent and irreversible. If you have your tubes tied within a few hours or a day after having your baby, then change your mind, you may regret it.

Most women do not choose permanent birth control after delivery; however, contraception is something you should think about. You will probably begin ovulating 6 to 8 weeks after birth, and you could get pregnant again. If you do not want to have another baby very soon, it's important to discuss birth-control options with your healthcare provider in the hospital or at your postpartum checkup.

Breastfeeding protects you against pregnancy to some degree, but breastfeeding is *not* an effective method of birth control. If you breastfeed, it's important to consider birth-control methods if you want to postpone pregnancy.

If you used a diaphragm or cervical cap for birth control in the past, you need to be refitted after delivery. The size of your cervix or vagina may have changed.

You may consider condoms or spermicides if you breastfeed. Neither interferes with breastfeeding.

If you bottlefeed, you may decide on a method that can be started immediately after delivery. These methods include Norplant implants, Depo-Provera® injections, a progestin-only pill or an IUD. If you want to use a combination-birth-control pill, which contains estrogen and progestin, wait at least 2 weeks after delivery to begin.

Common Breastfeeding Problems

Your breasts may become temporarily engorged when your regular milk comes in, which can be painful. To relieve engorgement, continue breastfeeding, wear a supportive bra and apply cold compresses to your breasts for short periods. Take acetaminophen if pain is severe, but consult your doctor if you need something stronger.

When you breastfeed your baby, you may get sore nipples, which occur for various reasons. If your baby doesn't take your nipple fully into his mouth during breastfeeding, his jaws can

compress the nipple and make it sore. Your clothing can also irritate tender nipples. Nipple shields, worn inside your bra between the nipple and fabric, provide some relief. A mild cream can also provide soothing relief. Ask your pharmacist or healthcare provider for the names of products that are approved for use during nursing. Take heart—sore nipples rarely last longer than a couple of days. Continue breastfeeding while your breasts are sore.

Plugged Milk Ducts

Sometimes milk ducts in the breast become plugged. A plugged duct prevents milk from flowing freely and makes some parts of the breast feel tender or firm. These become more painful after breastfeeding.

A plugged duct usually takes care of itself, if you continue to nurse frequently. If it doesn't resolve on its own, apply a warm compress to the affected area or soak the breast in warm water. Then express milk or breastfeed while massaging the tender area. You may take acetaminophen. If problems continue, contact your healthcare provider.

Breast Infections

Large red streaks that extend up the breast toward the armpit or a breast that becomes firm or hard usually indicates a breast infection. Call your healthcare provider immediately. A fever may develop within 4 to 8 hours of appearance of the red streaks. Your doctor will want to start antibiotic treatment quickly because antibiotics work best in the first 12 to 16 hours of infection.

To help prevent an infection, eat right and get enough rest to reduce stress and keep your immune system in top fighting form. Don't wear tight-fitting bras, especially underwire bras, because they block milk flow. This may cause an infection. Empty your breasts on a regular schedule to avoid engorgement. After each feeding or pumping, let nipples air dry for a few minutes. Don't stop nursing if you have a breast infection or think you have one; continue breastfeeding. If you stop, the infection may get worse. Don't be concerned about passing the infection to the baby.

If you have a cold or other virus, it's all right to breastfeed. It's OK to breastfeed if you're taking most antibiotics, as long as you know the drug is compatible with nursing. Ask your healthcare provider or pharmacist if any medication prescribed for you should not be taken while breastfeeding. Ask *before* you begin taking it; some antibiotics should be avoided.

After-pregnancy Changes

After the birth of your baby, you may notice changes in your abdominal shape and skin. Breasts are often affected, too.

ॐ Abdominal-skin Changes

After they give birth, some women find that their abdomen returns to normal naturally. For others, it never quite returns to its prepregnancy state. Abdominal skin is not like muscle, so it can't be strengthened by exercise. Perhaps the most important element affecting your skin's ability to return to its prepregnancy tightness is connective tissue, which provides suppleness and elasticity. As you get older, your skin loses connective tissue and elasticity. Other factors include your fitness level before pregnancy, heredity and how much your skin stretched during pregnancy.

ॐ Breast Changes

After birth, most women's breasts return to their prepregnancy size or decrease a little in size. If you breastfeed, it takes longer for your breasts to return to normal. This is a result of the change in the connective tissue that forms the support system of your breasts. Exercise cannot make breasts firmer, but it can improve the chest area underneath so breasts have better support.

ॐ Weight Changes

It's normal to lose 10 to 15 pounds immediately after your baby is born. You may find you retain 5 pounds of fluid, but it washes out of your system within a few days.

Extra weight may be harder to lose. Your body stored about 7 to 10 pounds of fat as energy for the first few months after birth.

If you eat properly and get enough exercise, these pounds will slowly come off.

If you breastfeed, all the nutrients your baby receives depend on the quality of the food you eat. Breastfeeding places more demands on your body than pregnancy. Your body burns up to 1000 calories a day just to produce milk. When breastfeeding, you need to eat an extra 500 calories a day. Be sure they are nutritious, not empty, calories (eat fruits, vegetables and breads—stay away from junk food). Keep up fluid levels, too.

Postpartum Distress

After your baby is born, you may feel sad or moody. You may wonder if having your baby was a good idea. Many women experience some degree of postpartum distress; in fact, up to 80% of all women get the "baby blues." It usually appears between 2 days and 2 weeks after the baby is born. The good news is that the situation is temporary and tends to leave as quickly as it comes.

Today, many experts consider some degree of postpartum distress a normal occurrence. Symptoms include:

- anxiety
- crying for no reason
- exhaustion
- impatience
- irritability
- lack of confidence
- lack of feeling for the baby
- low self-esteem
- oversensitivity
- restlessness

If you believe you may be suffering from some form of postpartum distress, contact your healthcare provider. Every postpartum reaction, mild or severe, is usually temporary.

ॐ Forms of Postpartum Distress

The mildest form of postpartum distress is called the *baby blues*. The baby blues last only a couple of weeks, and symptoms do not worsen.

A more serious version of postpartum distress is called *postpartum depression* (PPD); it affects about 10% of all new mothers.

The difference between baby blues and postpartum depression lies in the frequency, intensity and duration of the symptoms. Sleep problems are one way to distinguish between the two. If the mother can sleep while someone else tends the baby, it is probably baby blues. If she cannot sleep because of anxiety, it's probably PPD.

PPD can occur from 2 weeks to 1 year after birth. A mother may have feelings of anger, confusion, panic and hopelessness. She may experience changes in her eating and sleeping patterns. She may fear she will hurt her baby or feel as if she is going crazy. Anxiety is one of the major symptoms of PPD.

The most serious form of postpartum distress is *postpartum psychosis*. The woman may have hallucinations, think about suicide or try to harm the baby.

Causes of Postpartum Distress

At this time, no one is sure what causes postpartum distress; not all women experience it. We believe a woman's individual sensitivity to hormonal changes may be the cause, but hormones are only part of it.

A new mother must make many adjustments, and many demands are placed on her. Either or both of these situations may cause distress. Other possible factors include a family history of depression, lack of familial support after the birth, isolation and chronic fatigue.

Dealing with the Problem

One of the most important ways to help yourself is to set up a support system before the birth. Ask family members and friends to help. Have your mother or mother-in-law stay for a while. Ask your husband to take some leave, or hire someone to come in and help each day.

There is no particular treatment for baby blues, but there are ways you can help relieve symptoms. Ask for help. Rest when baby sleeps. Find other mothers who are in the same situation; it helps to share your feelings and experiences. Don't try to be perfect; let some things slide. Pamper yourself. Do some form of moderate exercise every day. Eat nutritiously, and drink plenty of fluids. Go out every day.

With postpartum depression, medication may be necessary in addition to the suggestions made above. About 85% of all women who suffer from postpartum depression require medication. Medications of choice include antidepressants, tranquilizers and hormones; often they are used together.

If you breastfeed, medication selection may be more limited. Certain medications, such as Pamelor® and Norpramin®, can be used by a woman while breastfeeding, if the baby's doctor is aware of it and the baby is monitored for side effects.

✽ Postpartum Distress Can also Affect Dad

Your partner can be affected if you suffer from the baby blues or PPD. It's important to prepare your partner for this situation. Explain to him that if it happens to you, it is only temporary. You might also suggest some things he can do to help himself.

• Advise him not to take it personally.
• Suggest he get support for himself. He can talk to friends, family members, other fathers or a professional.
• He needs to take care of himself by eating well, getting enough rest and exercising.
• Ask him to be patient with you.
• Ask for his love and support during this difficult time.

Your Postpartum Checkup

Your postpartum checkup is the last part of your complete prenatal-care program. This appointment is as important as any during your pregnancy. A postpartum checkup is scheduled between 2 and 6 weeks after delivery, depending on the circumstances of the birth.

At your visit, your healthcare provider will want to hear how you feel. If you have had headaches or experienced increased irritability or fatigue, he or she may prescribe an iron supplement. You will have a physical exam, similar to the one at your first prenatal exam.

Your healthcare provider will do an internal exam. If you had any birth tears or incisions, he or she will examine them to see how they are healing. An internal exam is also done to determine if your uterus is returning to its prepregnant size and position.

This is a good time to discuss birth control, if you haven't already made plans. See the discussion of birth-control options on page 310.

Chapter 20

Back to Work?

Your baby is born, a little person who already brings you great delight. It seems as if the hard work is done, and most of it is. But if you are like many women, you must still address issues related to your work—from the kind of childcare arrangement you choose to whether you will work full time.

Whether to continue working outside the home after the baby's birth is a decision some mothers wish they didn't have to make. Others look forward to returning to jobs and careers they enjoy, even if that day comes sooner than they would prefer. Whatever the reason, returning to work after having a baby is as typical these days as staying at home used to be. More than half of all mothers with preschool-age children work outside the home. For almost all of them, finding adequate child care is a big issue.

Arranging a childcare situation for your new baby can be one of the most important tasks you face before returning to work. The best way to choose the right setting and best care provider is to know your options.

You do have choices. Any of a number of situations could be right for you; examine your needs and those of your child before you decide which to pursue. Let's look closely at some of the most common childcare arrangements.

Childcare Decisions

❧ In-home Care

In-home care is the easiest option for you and your baby. You don't have to get the baby ready before you leave in the morning or take your child out in bad weather. You save commuting time in the morning and evening.

In-home care is an excellent choice for a baby or small child because the environment is familiar. It provides her with a great deal of attention. A relative or nonrelative may provide this care. A potential drawback to in-house care in the toddler years may be that the child won't have the chance to play with others his age.

❧❧❧❧

Lucy had been thrilled to find Irene to care for Harry at home while she worked. Now that Harry was 2, Lucy wanted him to spend some time with other children his age. She decided to ask around about play groups. Maybe Irene and Harry could walk to a nearby group a couple of mornings each week.

When the caregiver is a relative, such as a grandparent or an aunt, you may find the situation somewhat challenging. Can you maintain your relationship with the "relative caregiver" while asking or telling him or her to do things the way you want them done?

If the caregiver is not a relative, the arrangement may be expensive. In addition, you are bringing someone you do not know into your home to tend your child. Ask for references, and check them out thoroughly. Don't rush into an arrangement with a caregiver in whom you aren't completely confident.

✦ Care in a Caregiver's Home

Many parents take their children to someone else's home for care. Often these homes offer small group sizes and scheduling flexibility (for example, you may be allowed to leave your child a little longer if you have an occasional late meeting). They offer a homelike atmosphere, and your child may receive lots of attention.

Home care is not regulated in every state, so check each situation carefully. Contact your state's Department of Social Services, and ask about its requirements. Sometimes local agencies oversee caregivers. Care providers must abide by certain standards or rules, such as the maximum number of children allowed in the home (including their own). They may also have to obtain certification in first aid and CPR (cardiopulmonary resuscitation).

✦ Hiring an In-home Caregiver

Whether you have someone come to your home or take your child to another's home, these steps can help you find the best caregiver.

- *Advertise in local newspapers and church bulletins* to find interview candidates. State how many children are to be cared for and their ages. Give information on days and hours care is needed, experience you are seeking and other particulars.

- *Talk to people over the phone first* to determine whether you want to interview them. Ask about their experience, qualifications, child-care philosophy and what they seek in a position. Then decide if you want to pursue the contact with an in-person interview. Make a list of what to discuss, including days and hours the person is needed, duties to be performed, need for a driver's license and a benefits policy.

- *Check all references.* Have the potential caregiver provide you with the names and phone numbers of people he or she has worked for in the past. Call each of the families, let them know you are considering this person as a caregiver and discuss their experience with the candidate.
- *Keep checking.* After you hire someone, check the situation occasionally by dropping in unannounced. Pay attention to how your child reacts each time you leave or arrive; this can give you a clue as to how he feels about the caregiver.
- *To hire a nanny*, contact a referral agency; they are listed in the yellow pages.

Your responsibilities to your caregiver. Just as your caregiver has certain responsibilities to you, you have responsibilities to him or her. Be on time when you drop off your child or pick him up. Call if you're going to be late, even if the care is in your own home. Pay the caregiver on time. Provide diapers, formula or expressed breast milk, extra clothes and personal items for baby when they are needed.

Taxes are an important consideration. You must pay federal-with-holding, state and local taxes for your care provider, including Social Security and Medicare taxes. If the person works in your home, you may also need to pay workers' compensation and unemployment insurance taxes. These taxes must be paid on a rigid schedule. Failure to pay on time can put you in a serious legal and financial predicament. Contact the Internal Revenue Service and your state Department of Economic Security for further information.

⁂ Childcare Centers

A childcare center is a larger setting in which children receive care. Centers vary widely in the facilities and activities they provide, the amount of attention they give each child, group sizes and childcare philosophy.

Ask about the training required for each childcare provider or teacher. Some facilities expect more from a care provider than others.

You may find that some childcare centers you're interested in do not accept infants. Often centers focus on older children because infants take more time and attention. If the center accepts infants, the ratio of caregivers to children should be about one adult to every three or four children (up to age 2). One adult for every four to six 2-year-olds and one adult for every seven to eight 3-year-olds is considered acceptable.

Don't be fooled by facilities alone in a state-of-the art center. Even the cleanest, brightest place is useless without the right kind of care provider. Visit it by appointment, then stop by unannounced a few times. Meet the person in charge and the people who will care for your child. Ask for references of parents whose children are cared for there currently. Talk to these parents before you make a final decision.

Infant care. Babies have special needs that a preschool cannot meet; be sure the place you choose for your infant meets those needs. A baby must be changed and fed, but he also has other needs. A baby needs to be held and interacted with, and comforted when he is afraid. He needs to rest at regular times each day.

When searching for child care, keep in mind what is required for your child. Evaluate every situation in terms of how it responds to your baby's needs.

Finding day care. Where do you start the search for the right day care for your child? Start with the following ideas.

- *Ask friends, family and co-workers for referrals* to people or places they know about.
- *Talk to people in your neighborhood.*
- *Ask at your church about programs* they may sponsor.

- *Call a local referral agency* or contact Child Care Aware, 800-424-2246, for a local childcare resource.

Whomever you choose to provide care for your child, check references thoroughly before you make a final decision. Ask direct, probing questions as you check references. Share your concerns with the person you are checking with. Beware references who only tell you wonderful things about the caregiver. They could be close friends who have never really used the caregiver you are checking on.

⁓ The Cost of Child Care

Paying for child care can be a big-budget item in your household expenses. The cost of infant and toddler care (through age 3) typically ranges from $100 to $200 a week, depending on the type of care you choose. In-home care can be the most costly, with placement fees and additional charges you negotiate based on extra tasks you want the care provider to perform.

෧෧෧෧

"We were surpised by the costs," Julie said, as her partner, Bill, nodded vigorously. "The monetary benefit we expected from my going back to work became negligible, although personally, that's not the reason I want to go back—I like my career. I'd tell anybody to calculate the actual costs involved with day care and then think about why both parents are working."

Public funding is available for some limited-income families. Title EE is a program paid for with federal funds. Call your local Department of Social Services to see if you are eligible.

Other programs that can help some families with childcare costs include a federal tax-credit program, the dependent-care assistance program and earned-income tax credit. These programs are regulated by the federal government; contact the Internal Revenue Service at 800-829-1040 for further information.

When to Start Looking for Child Care

Finding the best situation for your baby takes time. Start the process several weeks before you need it. For special situations, such as twins, you might want to start the process several months in advance. Often this means finding child care before your baby is born.

You may notice a shortage of quality child care for children under age 2. You may have to get on a waiting list for some arrangements. If you find a care provider you are comfortable with before care is to start, ask to put down a deposit and set a date on which child care begins. Keep in touch with the care provider. Plan to meet again before you place your child in daily care.

Special-care Needs

If your baby has special needs and requires one-on-one care, expect to spend extra time finding qualified child care. A child with special needs may be best cared for by someone who comes to your home. Ask for references from your pediatrician or at the hospital where your child has received care.

Caring for a Sick Child

All children come down with colds, the flu or diarrhea at some time. If you can't take time off from work to stay home with a sick child, you may have other care options.

In many places, "sick-child" day-care centers are available. They are usually attached to a regular day-care facility, although some I have heard of are connected with hospitals. A center provides a comfortable place where an ill child can rest or participate in quiet activities, such as story time.

Often a registered nurse heads the facility; this person can administer medication when necessary. Fees for this type of service run from $25 to $55 a day.

Some cities have "on-call" in-home care providers who come to your home when your child is too sick to be taken anywhere. The program is usually run by an agency that deals with child care, and caregivers charge by the hour. Caregivers are usually assigned on a first-come, first-served basis, so you may have to wait a day for a provider. However, this can be an excellent way to care for some children who are ill.

Going Back to Work

If you're like many women today, you may be concerned about returning to work even after you have dealt with childcare issues satisfactorily. It's important to find ways to ease the transition from home to work. Some co-workers will be supportive; others may not be.

You may find some of your greatest challenges come after work, when you get home. Your baby and partner need your time and attention. Even when you feel tired, you may have household chores to do. Arrange with your partner before you return to work to share these responsibilities. That way, each of you can give your baby undivided attention for some part of the evening. Set aside time just for you and your partner, too!

☙ Managing Your Time

Time is a limited resource; learning to manage your time well is the secret to relishing this busy time in your life. Make a daily plan and stick to it. Do what you can and delegate some responsibilities to others. Change your expectations, if you need to. After that, concentrate on the baby, your partner and other important people in your life. Let less important things go. Enjoy the moment!

❧❧❧❧

"'Yikes, look at the time!' I said that *all* the time the first month after I went back to work. Finally my friend Mary Beth—she has two kids—told me to get a grip before I burned up and disappeared. She was right. I slowed down, let go of the stuff I couldn't control, and did the best I could with everything else. If it didn't get done that day, it got done the next—or thereabouts!"

Can You Modify Your Work Situation?

After having a baby, some women decide to continue working outside the home but not full time or not at their old schedule. You may be happier if you can find a way to work part time or if you can adapt your schedule in some other way. There may be ways to modify your current work situation so everyone is happy—you, your boss, your partner and your baby.

If you want to work part time, you may be able to share a job with someone else in the company who would also like to work part time. Ask your employer.

Find out if flex-time programs are available at your workplace. You may be allowed to modify your work schedule (for example, work four 10-hour days instead of five 8-hour days). Or you may come in early and leave early, or arrive and leave later. You may be able to set your own schedule, as long as you get your work done.

You might be able to work at home part time or full time. Many companies allow employees who work on computers to work at home, connected by modem.

Be aware that if you do work part time or on flex time, childcare may be harder to find. With some centers, you pay by the week, whether your child is there or not. An in-home care provider may need the money that only full-time work offers. But some centers are more flexible than others, and some in-home care providers may be delighted at the prospect of a lighter schedule.

Breastfeeding and Work

You don't have to stop breastfeeding when you return to work, but you may need to make adjustments. If you breastfeed exclusively, you will need to pump your breasts or arrange to see your baby during the day. Or you may nurse your baby at home and provide expressed breast milk or formula for your care provider to give baby when you're away.

One way to smooth the back-to-work transition for you and baby is to begin storing breast milk a couple of weeks before you return to work. Use an electric breast pump to express milk between feedings for about 2 weeks before you return to work. Don't start sooner—you may produce too much milk. A breast pump with a double-pumping feature empties both breasts at once.

Freeze expressed milk in quantities of 1 to 4 ounces. This gives the caregiver options as to how much to thaw for a particular feeding.

You might pump and store breast milk while you are at work. You may be uncomfortable if you don't pump your breasts because your milk continues to come in. Take a breast pump with you, and refrigerate or discard breast milk after it is pumped.

If you remain at home until your baby is between 4 and 6 months old, your baby may be able to skip the bottle and start drinking from a cup. Earlier than 4 months, your baby will need to learn to drink from a bottle. After 4 weeks of nursing exclusively, your baby will be ready to try a bottle without compromising your milk supply or her nursing technique. With the first bottle feedings, let someone else feed the baby when she's not too hungry. Bottlefeed her at the time she will get a bottle once you return to work.

If You Stay Home

You may decide to stay home with your baby. If you do, the change from leaving the house each day to staying at home can be dramatic. You may find that being at home isn't as easy as you thought it would be. It's true you don't have to worry about getting to work or coming home to fix meals and do housework. However, you may find staying home means less companionship, less money and the loss of routine.

Try to anticipate some of these changes and meet them halfway. Don't bury yourself in motherhood and exclude all other activities. Make an effort to get out, meet people and get involved in new experiences with your baby. Consider joining an exercise class designed specifically for new mothers and babies; classes are frequently offered through the YWCA and similar organizations.

If you have worked full time, you may not have met many people in your neighborhood. Once you're home full time, you'll have an opportunity to make friends. If other new mothers are in the neighborhood, you might start an infant play group that meets once a week for an hour or so. Take turns hosting. Babies play and moms talk!

It may be a good idea to stay in touch with your colleagues at work. Drop in to see them, or go out to lunch with a group. See what they are up to, and stay on top of what is happening in your field.

❧

Going back to work takes some planning. Not everything may go smoothly at first, but what adventure does? With the number of childcare options available today and perhaps some creative approaches to your workplace schedule, you will be able to find a truly happy medium—one that works for you, your partner, your employer and your baby.

Chapter 21

Looking Ahead

More couples choose to delay childbearing today, and predictions are that more women over 30 will become pregnant and deliver babies in the years to come. I believe there is reason for optimism for these pregnancies. Pregnancy at any age is an adventure full of risk, physical and emotional challenges, and highs and lows. Any pregnancy can end in miscarriage or birth defects; fortunately most babies are born healthy.

People today have become more aware of the importance of taking care of their health. Fewer people smoke. They use less alcohol and they are more aware of the dangers of drug use. Regular exercise and better eating habits are more often the rule, not the exception. All of these activities help everyone involved prepare for a pregnancy, and the result is healthier pregnancies resulting in healthier babies and moms.

Medical advances are made every year. Two of the greatest areas of growth have been in technology for pregnancy and in care of the premature infant. As a medical resident in training 15 years ago, I remember babies born before 32 weeks seldom survived; if they did, they had major problems. Today, babies born as early as 25 weeks survive, and there are even cases earlier than this surviving and doing well.

In this book I have discussed many technologies—ultrasound, amniocentesis, chorionic villus sampling, fetoscopy—genetic counseling and other advances in obstetrics. All promise more advances in the goal of a healthy baby and a healthy mother.

Each individual (or couple) is different. This is an important fact. A healthy 38-year-old woman who eats right, exercises and takes good care of herself will probably do better during pregnancy than a 23-year-old woman who eats poorly, doesn't exercise and doesn't take care of herself. Every pregnancy is different.

There is much reason for optimism and encouragement in pregnancy for the woman over 30. We have come a long way in our care of the pregnant woman and her developing baby. In the past, many doctors frowned on pregnancy after the age 35, but women decided they were going to have babies anyway. If predictions are correct, this trend will continue.

Despite the risks and possible problems that can occur during a pregnancy, I hope the message has come through that it's much more likely you and your baby will do well. The best things you can do are to plan ahead for pregnancy, exercise regularly, eat right, take care of medical problems before getting pregnant and seek prenatal care early.

Resources

General Information

American College of Obstetricians and Gynecologists
Resource Center
409 12th Street, SW
P.O. Box 96920
Washington, DC 20090-6920
202-638-5577

Child Care Aware
800-424-2246

Internal Revenue Service
(for information on child-care expenses)
800-829-1040

National Organization of Single Mothers
P.O. Box 68
Midland, NC 28107-0068
704-888-KIDS

Sidelines
(for women experiencing complicated pregnancies)
Candace Hurley, executive director: 714-497-2265
Tracy Hoogenboom: 909-563-6199

The Women's Bureau Publications
(for summary of state laws on family leave)
U.S. Department of Labor
Women's Bureau Clearing House
Box EX
200 Constitution Avenue, NW
Washington, DC 20210
800-827-5335

Nutrition Information

Beechnut Nutrition Hotline
800-523-6633

FDA Hotline
(for information on fish)
800-332-4010

Food Guide Pyramid Brochure
USDA
P.O. Box 1144
Rockville, MD 20850

National Center for Nutrition and Dietetics'
Consumer-Nutrition Hotline
(to talk directly with a nutritionist)
800-366-1655

Mother's Health

American Cancer Society
(for dangers of passive smoke)
800-ACS-2345

Group-B Strep Association
P.O. Box 16515
Chapel Hill, NC 27516
919-932-5344

Childbirth Information

American Academy of Husband-Coached Childbirth
(Bradley Method)
P.O. Box 5224
Sherman Oaks, CA 91413
800-423-2397
818-788-6662

American College of Nurse-Midwives (ACNM)
818 Connecticut Avenue NW, Suite 900
Washington, DC 20006
202-728-9860

American Society for Pyschoprophylaxis in Obstetrics
(ASPO/Lamaze)
1200 19th Street NW, Suite 300
Washington, DC 20036-2422
800-368-4404

Association of Labor Assistants and Childbirth Educators
(ALACE)
P.O. Box 382724
Cambridge, MA 02238-2724
617-441-2500

Doulas of North America
1100 23rd Avenue East
Seattle, WA 98112
FAX 206-325-0472

Informed Home Birth
313-662-6852

International Cesarean Awareness Network (ICAN)
1304 Kingsdale Avenue
Redondo Beach, CA 90278
310-542-6400

International Childbirth Education Association
P.O. Box 20048
Minneapolis, MN 55420-0048
612-854-8660

Midwives Alliance of North America (MANA)
P.O. Box 175
Newton, KS 67114
316-283-4543

National Association of Childbearing Centers (NACC)
3123 Gottschall Road
Perkiomenville, PA 18074
215-234-8068

Public Citizen's Health Research
(for information on C-sections and VBAC)
1600 20th Street NW
Washington, DC 20009

Breastfeeding Information

Best Start
3500 E. Fletcher Avenue, Suite 519
Tampa, FL 33613
800-277-4975

FDA's Breast Implant Information Line
800-532-4440

La Leche League
1400 North Meacham Road
Schaumburg, IL 60173-4840
800-LA-LECHE or check local telephone directory
for information

Medela, Inc.
P.O. Box 660
McHenry, IL 60051
800-TELL-YOU

National Maternal and Child Health Clearinghouse
2070 Chain Bridge Road, Suite 45
Vienna, VA 22182
703-821-8955, ext. 254

Wellstart
4062 First Avenue
San Diego, CA 92103
619-295-5192

Information for Parents of Multiples

Center for Loss in Multiple Birth
c/o Jean Kollantai
P.O. Box 1064
Palmer, AK 99645
907-746-6123

Center for Study of Multiple Births
333 E. Superior Street, Room 464
Chicago, IL 60611
312-266-9093

Mothers of Supertwins (M.O.S.T.)
(triplets or more)
P.O. Box 951
Brentwood, NY 11717
516-434-MOST

Multiple Births Foundation
Queen Charlotte's and Chelsea Hospital
Goldhawk Road
London, England W6 OXG
081-748-4666, ext. 5201

National Organization of Mothers of Twins Clubs, Inc.
P.O. Box 23188
Albuquerque, NM 87192-1188
505-275-0955

Triplet Connection
P.O. Box 99571
Stockton, CA 95209
209-474-0885

Twin to Twin Transfusion Syndrome (TTTS) Foundation
Mary Slaman-Forsythe, Executive Director
411 Longbeach Parkway
Bay Village, OH 44140
216-899-8887

Twin Services
P.O. Box 10066
Berkeley, CA 94709
510-524-0863

The Twins Foundation
P.O. Box 6043
Providence, RI 02940-6043
401-729-1000

Twins Magazine
5350 S. Roslyn Street, Suite 400
Englewood, CO 80111
800-328-3211

Information for Parents of Premature Infants

ECMO Moms and Dads
c/o Blair and Gayle Wilson
P.O. Box 53848
Lubbock, TX 79453
806-794-0259

Intensive-care Parenting (magazine)
ICU Parenting
RD #10, Box 176
Brush Creek Road
Irwin, PA 15642

Children with Special Needs, Birth Defects

American Cleft Palate Foundation
1218 Grandview Avenue
Pittsburgh, PA 15211
800-24-CLEFT; 412-481-1376

CARESS
(information on services for parents of children
with disabilities)
P.O. Box 1492
Washington, DC 20013

**National Information Center
for Children and Youth with Disabilities**
P.O. Box 1492
Washington, DC 20013-1492
800-695-0285

National Association for Rare Disorders (NORD)
P.O. Box 8923
New Fairfield, CT 06812

National Down Syndrome Society (NDSS)
666 Broadway
New York, NY 10012-2317
800-221-4602

After the Baby's Birth

Depression after Delivery
P.O. Box 1282
Morrisville, PA 19067
800-944-4773 (answering machine only)

Children's Problems

Allergy and Asthma Network
3554 Chain Bridge Road, Suite 200
Fairfax, VA 22030
800-878-4403

National Reye's Syndrome Foundation
426 North Lewis Street
Bryan, OH 43506
800-233-7393
800-231-7393 (Ohio only)

Safety for Your Baby

The Danny Foundation
(information on crib dangers)
3158 Danville Boulevard
P.O. Box 680
Alamo, CA 94507
800-83-DANNY

SafetyBeltSafe USA
123 Manchester Boulevard
Inglewood, CA 90301
310-673-2666

Child Abuse Information

National Child Abuse Hotline
800-4A-CHILD (800-422-4453)

Glossary

abortion. Termination or end of pregnancy; giving birth to an embryo or fetus before it can live outside the womb, usually defined as before 20 weeks of gestation. Abortion may be spontaneous, often called a *miscarriage,* or induced, as in a medical or therapeutic abortion performed to terminate a pregnancy.

acquired immune deficiency syndrome (AIDS). Debilitating and frequently fatal illness that affects the body's ability to respond to infection. Caused by the human immune deficiency virus (HIV).

aerobic exercise. Exercise that increases your heart rate and causes you to increase your oxygen intake.

afterbirth. Placenta and membranes expelled after the baby is delivered. See **placenta.**

alpha-fetoprotein (AFP). Substance produced by the unborn baby as it grows inside the uterus. Large amounts of AFP are found in amniotic fluid. Larger-than-normal amounts are found in the maternal bloodstream if neural-tube defects are present in the fetus.

amino acids. Substances that act as building blocks in the developing embryo and fetus.

amniocentesis. Removal of amniotic fluid from the amniotic sac; fluid is tested for some genetic defects or fetal lung maturity.

amniotic fluid. Fluid surrounding the baby inside the amniotic sac.

amniotic sac. Membrane that surrounds baby inside the uterus. It contains the baby, placenta and amniotic fluid.

anemia. Any condition in which the number of red blood cells is less than normal. Term usually applies to the concentration of the oxygen-transporting material in the blood.

anencephaly. Defective brain development combined with the absence of the bones normally surrounding the brain.

angioma. Tumor, usually benign, or swelling composed of lymph and blood vessels.

antigen. Substance formed in the body or introduced into the body that causes formation of antibodies, which interact specifically with the substance.

anti-inflammatory medications. Drugs to relieve pain or inflammation.

Apgar score. Measurement of a baby's response to birth and life on its own. Taken 1 and 5 minutes after birth.

areola. Pigmented or colored ring surrounding the nipple of the breast.

arrhythmia. Irregular or missed heartbeat.

aspiration. Swallowing or sucking a foreign body or fluid, such as vomit, into an airway.

asthma. Disease marked by recurrent attacks of shortness of breath and difficulty breathing. Often caused by an allergic reaction.

atonic uterus. Uterus that is flaccid or relaxed; lacks tone.

baby blues. Mild depression in woman after delivery.

back labor. Pain of labor felt in lower back.

bilirubin. Breakdown product of pigment formed in the liver from hemoglobin during the destruction of red blood cells.

biophysical profile. Method of evaluating a fetus before birth.

biopsy. Removal of a small piece of tissue for microscopic study.

birthing center. Facility in which a woman labors, delivers and recovers in the same room. It may be part of a hospital or a freestanding unit. Sometimes called LDRP, for *labor, delivery, recovery* and *postpartum*.

blood pressure. Push of the blood against the walls of the arteries, which carry blood away from the heart.

bloody show. Small amount of vaginal bleeding late in pregnancy; often precedes labor.

board certification. Doctor has had additional training and testing in a particular specialty. In the area of obstetrics, the American College of Obstetricians and Gynecologists offers this training. Certification requires expertise in care of women.

Braxton-Hicks contractions. Irregular, painless tightening of uterus during pregnancy.

breech presentation. Abnormal position of the fetus. Buttocks or legs come into the birth canal before the head.

carcinogen. Any cancer-producing substance.

cervix. Opening of the uterus.

Cesarean section (delivery). Delivery of a baby through an abdominal incision rather than through the vagina.

Chadwick's sign. Dark-blue or purple discoloration of the mucosa of the vagina and cervix during pregnancy.

chemotherapy. Treatment of disease by chemical substances or drugs.

chlamydia. Sexually transmitted venereal infection.

chloasma. Extensive brown patches of irregular shape and size on the face or other parts of the body.

chorionic villus sampling (CVS). Diagnostic test done early in pregnancy. A biopsy of tissue is taken from inside the uterus through the abdomen or the cervical opening to determine abnormalities of pregnancy.

chromosomal abnormality. Abnormal number or abnormal makeup of chromosomes.

chromosomes. Thread in a cell's nucleus that contains DNA, which transmits genetic information.

clomiphene-challenge test. Way of testing for ovulation using a drug that stimulates the ovaries.

colostrum. Thin, yellow fluid that is the first milk to come from the breast. Most often seen toward the end of pregnancy. It is different in content from milk produced later during nursing.

condyloma acuminatum. Skin tags or warts that are sexually transmitted, caused by HPV, human papilloma virus. Also called *venereal warts.*

congenital problem. Problem present at birth.

consanguinity. Being related by blood to the person you are married to.

constipation. Bowel movements are infrequent or incomplete.

contraction stress test. Response of fetus to uterine contractions to evaluate fetal well-being.

contractions. Squeezing or tightening of uterus, which pushes the baby out of the uterus during birth.

corpus-luteum cyst. Normal cyst on ovary after ovulation.

cystitis. Inflammation of the bladder.

cytomegalovirus (CMV) infection. Group of viruses from the herpes-virus family.

D&C (dilatation and curettage). Surgical procedure in which the cervix is dilated and the lining of the uterus is scraped.

developmental delay. Condition in which the development of the baby or child is slower than normal.

diastasis recti. Separation of abdominal muscles.

differentiating. Changing, especially because of growth.

dilatation. Opening or stretching of the cervix during a baby's birth.

dizygotic twins. Twins derived from two different eggs. Often called *fraternal twins*.

due date. Date your baby is expected to be born. Most babies are born near this date, but only 1 of 20 are born on the actual date.

dysplasia. Abnormal, precancerous changes in the cells of the cervix.

dysuria. Difficulty or pain urinating.

EDC (estimated date of confinement). Baby's anticipated due date. Calculated from the first day of the last menstrual period, counting forward 280 days.

eclampsia. Convulsions and coma in a woman with pre-eclampsia. Not related to epilepsy.

ectopic pregnancy. Pregnancy that occurs outside the uterine cavity.

Edwards' syndrome. See **trisomy 18.**

effacement. Thinning of cervix.

electronic fetal monitoring. Use of electronic instruments to record the fetal heartbeat.

embryo. Organism in the early stages of development.

embryonic period. First 10 weeks of gestation.

endometrium. Mucous membrane that lines the inside of the uterine wall.

enema. Fluid injected into the rectum for the purpose of clearing the bowel.

engorgement. Congestion, as filled with fluid.

epidural block. Type of anesthesia injected around the spinal cord during labor or some types of surgery.

episiotomy. Surgical incision of the perineum (area behind the vagina, above the rectum). Used during delivery to avoid tearing of the vaginal opening and rectum.

estimated date of confinement. See **EDC.**

expressing breast milk. Manually forcing milk out of the breast.

external cephalic version (ECV). Procedure done late in pregnancy, in which doctor manually attempts to move a baby in the breech position into the normal head-down position.

face presentation. Baby comes into the birth canal face first.

Fallopian tube. Tube that leads from the cavity of the uterus to the area of the ovary. Also called *uterine tube.*

false labor. Tightening of uterus without dilatation of the cervix.

false-negative test result. Result indicates negative outcome, but it is actually positive.

false-positive test result. Result indicates positive outcome, but it is actually negative.

fasting blood sugar test. Blood test to evaluate the amount of sugar in the blood following a period of fasting.

ferrous gluconate. Iron supplement.

ferrous sulfate. Iron supplement.

fertilization. Joining of the sperm and egg.

fertilization age. Dating a pregnancy from the time of fertilization; 2 weeks earlier than the gestational age.

fetal anomaly. Fetal malformation or abnormal development.

fetal arrhythmia. See **arrhythmia.**

fetal distress. Problems with the baby that occur before birth or during labor, requiring immediate delivery.

fetal monitor. Device used before or during labor to listen to and record the fetal heartbeat. Monitoring of the baby inside the uterus can be external (through maternal abdomen) or internal (through maternal vagina).

fetal period. Time period following the embryonic period (first 10 weeks of gestation) until birth.

fetal-growth retardation (IUGR). Inadequate growth of the fetus during pregnancy.

fetus. Refers to the unborn baby after 10 weeks of gestation until birth.

forceps. Special instrument placed around the baby's head, inside the birth canal, to help guide the baby out of the birth canal during delivery.

fragile-X syndrome. Abnormal X chromosome.

frank breech. Baby presenting buttocks first. Legs are flexed and knees extended.

fraternal twins. See **dizygotic twins.**

full-term infant. Baby born between 38 and 42 weeks of pregnancy.

gene regulation. Gene that regulates the operation of another gene.

genetic counseling. Consultation between a couple and specialists about genetic defects and the possibility of presence or recurrence of genetic problems in a pregnancy.

genital herpes simplex. Herpes simplex infection involving the genital area. It can be significant during pregnancy because of the danger to a newborn infected with herpes simplex.

gestational age. Dating a pregnancy from the first day of the last menstrual period; 2 weeks longer than fertilization age. See **fertilization age.**

gestational diabetes. Occurrence or worsening of diabetes during pregnancy (gestation).

globulin. Family of proteins from plasma or serum of the blood.

glucose-tolerance test. Blood test done to evaluate the body's response to sugar. Blood is drawn at intervals following ingestion of a sugary substance.

glucosuria. Sugar in the urine.

gonorrhea. Contagious venereal infection, transmitted primarily by intercourse. Caused by the bacteria Neisseria gonorrhea.

group-B streptococcal infection. Serious infection occurring in the mother's vagina and throat.

habitual miscarriage. Occurrence of three or more spontaneous miscarriages.

heartburn. Discomfort or pain that occurs in the chest, often after eating.

hematocrit. Determines the proportion of blood cells to plasma. Important in diagnosing anemia.

hemoglobin. Pigment in red blood cell that carries oxygen to body tissues.

hemolytic disease. Destruction of red blood cells. See **anemia.**

hemorrhoids. Dilated blood vessels in the rectum or rectal canal.

heparin. Medication used to prevent excessive clotting of the blood.

high-risk pregnancy. Pregnancy with complications that require special medical attention, often from a specialist. See **perinatologist.**

human chorionic gonadotropin. Hormone produced in early pregnancy. Measured in a pregnancy test.

hydramnios. Increased amniotic fluid.

hydrocephalus. Excessive accumulation of fluid around the baby's brain. Sometimes called *water on the brain.*

hyperbilirubinemia. Extremely high level of bilirubin in the blood.

hyperemesis gravidarum. Severe nausea, dehydration and vomiting during pregnancy. Occurs most frequently during the first trimester.

hyperglycemia. High blood-sugar levels.

hyperkeratosis. Increase in the size of the horny layer of the skin.

hypertension, pregnancy-induced. High blood pressure that occurs during pregnancy. Defined by an increase in the diastolic or systolic blood pressure.

hyperthyroidism. Elevation of the thyroid hormone in the bloodstream.

hypoglycemia. Low blood-sugar levels.

hypoplasia. Defective or incomplete development or formation of tissue.

hypotension. Low blood pressure.

hypothyroidism. Low or inadequate levels of thyroid hormone in the bloodstream.

identical twins. See **monozygotic twins.**

immune globulin preparation. Substance used to protect against infection with certain diseases, such as hepatitis or measles.

in utero. Within the uterus.

in vitro. Outside the body.

incompetent cervix. Cervix that dilates painlessly, without contractions.

incomplete miscarriage. Miscarriage in which part, but not all, of the uterine contents are expelled.

induced labor. Labor started or speeded up by the healthcare provider, usually by using a medication.

inevitable miscarriage. Pregnancy complicated by bleeding and cramping. Usually results in miscarriage.

insulin. Peptide hormone made by the pancreas. It promotes the body's use of glucose.

intrauterine-growth retardation (IUGR). See **fetal-growth retardation.**

iron-deficiency anemia. Anemia produced by lack of iron in the diet; often seen in pregnancy. See **anemia.**

isoimmunization. Development of specific antibody directed at the red blood cells of another individual, such as a baby in utero. Occurs when an Rh-negative woman carries an Rh-positive baby or when she is given Rh-positive blood.

jaundice. Yellow staining of the skin, sclera (eyes) and deeper tissues of the body. Caused by excessive amounts of bilirubin.

ketones. Breakdown product of metabolism found in the blood, particularly in conditions of starvation or uncontrolled diabetes.

kidney stones. Small mass or lesion found in the kidney or urinary tract that can block the flow of urine.

Klinefelter's syndrome. Abnormal number of chromosomes, XXY.

labor. Process of expelling a fetus from the uterus.

laparoscopy. Surgical procedure performed for tubal ligation, diagnosis of pelvic pain, diagnosis of ectopic pregnancy or for other diagnoses.

leukorrhea. Vaginal discharge characterized by a white or yellowish color. Primarily composed of mucus.

lightening. Change in the shape of the pregnant uterus a few weeks before labor. Often described as the baby "dropping."

linea nigra. Line of increased pigmentation running down the abdomen from the bellybutton to the pubic area during pregnancy.

lochia. Vaginal discharge that occurs after delivery of the baby and placenta.

mammogram. X-ray study of the breasts to identify normal and abnormal breast tissue.

mask of pregnancy. Increased pigmentation over the area of the face under each eye. Commonly has the appearance of a butterfly.

meconium. First intestinal discharge of the newborn; green or yellow in color. It consists of epithelial or surface cells, mucus and bile. Discharge may occur before or during labor or soon after birth.

melanoma. Pigmented mole or tumor that may or may not be cancerous.

meningomyelocele. Congenital defect of the central nervous system of the baby. Membranes and the spinal cord protrude through an opening or defect in the vertebral column.

menstrual age. See **gestational age.**

menstruation. Regular or periodic discharge of a bloody fluid from the uterus.

microcephaly. Abnormally small development of the head in the developing fetus.

miscarriage. See **abortion.**

missed miscarriage. Failed pregnancy, without bleeding or cramping. Often diagnosed by ultrasound weeks or months after a pregnancy fails.

monilial vulvovaginitis. Infection caused by yeast or monilia. Usually affects the vagina and vulva.

monozygotic twins. Twins conceived from one egg. Often called *identical twins.*

morning sickness. Nausea and vomiting, with ill health, found primarily during the first trimester of pregnancy. Also see **hyperemesis gravidarum.**

mucus plug. Secretions in cervix; often released just before labor.

natural childbirth. Labor and delivery in which no medication is used, and the mother remains awake to help deliver the baby. The woman may or may not have taken classes to prepare her for labor and delivery.

neural-tube defects. Abnormalities in the development of the spinal cord and brain in a fetus. See **anencephaly; hydrocephalus; spina bifida.**

nonstress test. Test in which movements of the baby felt by the mother or observed by the healthcare provider are recorded, along with changes in the fetal heart rate.

nurse-midwife. Nurse who has received extra training in the care of pregnant patients and the delivery of babies.

obstetrician. Physician who specializes in the care of pregnant women and the delivery of babies.

oligohydramnios. Lack or deficiency of amniotic fluid.

omphalocele. Congenital hernia at the bellybutton.

osteopathic physician. Physician who has trained in osteopathic medicine, a system of treating medical ailments based on the belief that ailments generally result from the pressure of displaced bones on nerves and are curable with manipulation. Osteopaths rely on physical, medicinal and surgical methods, much as their medical-doctor counterparts.

ovarian cycle. Regular production of hormones from the ovary in response to hormonal messages from the brain. The ovarian cycle governs the endometrial cycle.

ovulation. Cyclic production of an egg from the ovary.

ovulatory age. See **fertilization age.**

oxytocin. Medication that causes uterine contractions; used to induce labor. Also, the hormone produced by pituitary glands.

palmar erythema. Redness of palms of the hands.

Pap smear. Routine screening test that evaluates presence of premalignant or cancerous conditions of the cervix.

paracervical block. Local anesthetic for cervical dilatation.

Patau's syndrome. See **trisomy 13.**

pediatrician. Physician who specializes in the care of babies and children.

percutaneous umbilical blood sampling. Removal of blood from the umbilical cord while a baby is still inside the uterus.

perinatal death. Death of a baby around the time of delivery.

perinatologist. Physician who specializes in the care of high-risk pregnancies.

perineum. Area between the rectum and the vagina.

phenylketonuria. Hereditary disease that prevents oxidation of phenylananine (an amino acid) into tyrosine. Left untreated, brain damage may occur.

phospholipids. Fat-containing phosphorous. The most important are lecithins and sphingomyelin, which are important in the maturation of fetal lungs before birth.

physiologic anemia of pregnancy. Anemia during pregnancy caused by an increase in the amount of plasma (fluid) in the blood compared to the number of cells in the blood. See **anemia.**

PKU. See **phenylketonuria.**

placenta. Organ inside the uterus that is attached to the baby by the umbilical cord. Essential during pregnancy for growth and development of the embryo and fetus.

placenta previa. Low attachment of the placenta, very close to or covering the cervix.

placental abruption. Premature separation of the placenta from the uterus.

pneumonitis. Inflammation of the lungs.

polyhydramnios. See **hydramnios.**

postdate birth. Baby born 2 weeks or more past its due date.

postmature baby. Pregnancy of 42+ weeks gestation.

postpartum blues. See **baby blues.**

postpartum depression. Depression after delivery.

postpartum hemorrhage. Bleeding more than 15 ounces (450ml) at delivery.

postterm baby. See **postdate birth.**

pre-eclampsia. Combination of symptoms significant to pregnancy, including high blood pressure, edema, swelling and changes in reflexes.

pregnancy diabetes. See **gestational diabetes.**

premature delivery. Delivery before 38 weeks gestation.

prenatal care. Program of care for a pregnant woman before the birth of her baby.

prepared childbirth. Woman has taken classes to know what to expect during labor and delivery. She may request pain medication if she feels she needs it.

presentation. Describes which part of the baby comes into the birth canal first.

preterm birth. Baby born before 38 weeks of pregnancy.

products of conception. Tissue passed with a miscarriage.

proteinuria. Protein in urine.

pruritis gravidarum. Itching during pregnancy.

pubic symphysis. Bony prominence in the pelvic bone found in the midline. Landmark from which the doctor often measures during pregnancy to follow growth of the uterus.

pudendal block. Local anesthesia during labor.

pulmonary embolism. Blood clot from another part of the body that travels to the lungs. Can cause closed passages in the lungs and decrease oxygen exchange.

pyelonephritis. Serious kidney infection.

quickening. Feeling the baby move inside the uterus.

RDA. Recommended dietary allowance; an amount of a substance as established by the Food and Drug Administration.

Rh-negative. Absence of rhesus antibody in the blood.

Rh-sensitivity. See **isoimmunization.**

RhoGAM®. Medication given during pregnancy and following delivery to prevent isoimmunization. See **isoimmunization.**

round-ligament pain. Pain caused by stretching ligament on the sides of the uterus during pregnancy.

rupture of membranes. Loss of fluid from the amniotic sac. Also called *breaking of waters.*

seizure. Sudden onset of a convulsion.

sexually transmitted disease (STD). Infection transmitted through sexual intercourse or other sexual activity.

sickle crisis. Painful episode caused by sickle-cell disease.

sickle-cell anemia. Anemia caused by abnormal red blood cells shaped like a sickle or a cylinder.

sickle-cell trait. Presence of the trait for sickle-cell anemia. Not sickle-cell disease itself.

skin tag. Flap or extra buildup of skin.

sodium. Element found in many foods, particularly salt. Ingestion of too much sodium may cause fluid retention.

spina bifida. Congenital abnormality characterized by a defect in the vertebral column. The spinal cord and membranes of the spinal cord protrude outside the protective bony canal of the spine.

spinal anesthesia. Anesthesia given in the spinal canal.

spontaneous miscarriage. Loss of pregnancy during the first 20 weeks of gestation.

stasis. Decreased flow.

station. Estimation of the baby's descent in the uterus in preparation for birth.

steroids. Group of hormone-based medications. Often used to treat diseases. Includes estrogen, testosterone, progesterone, prednisone.

stillborn. When the baby is born, it is not alive.

stress test. Test in which mild contractions of the mother's uterus are induced; fetal heart rate in response to the contractions is noted.

stretch marks. Areas of the skin that are torn or stretched. Often found on the abdomen, breasts, buttocks and legs.

surfactant. Phospholipid present in the lungs that controls surface tension of lungs. Premature babies often lack sufficient amounts of surfactant to breathe without assistance.

syphilis. Sexually transmitted venereal infection caused by treponema pallidum.

systemic lupus erythematosus (SLE). Connective-tissue disorder common in women in the reproductive ages. Antibodies made by the person act against person's own tissues.

Tay-Sachs disease. Inherited disease characterized by mental and physical retardation, convulsions, enlargement of the head and eventually death. Trait is usually carried by Ashkenazi Jews.

telangiectasias. Dilatation or swelling of a small blood vessel; sometimes called an *angioma*. During pregnancy, another common name is *spider angioma*.

teratogenic. Causes abnormal development.

teratology. Branch of science that deals with teratogens.

term. Baby is considered "term" when it is born after 40 weeks. Also called *full term*.

thalassemia. Group of inherited disorders of hemoglobin metabolism, which results in a decrease in the amount of hemoglobin formed. Most commonly found in people of Mediterranean descent.

threatened miscarriage. Bleeding during the first trimester of pregnancy without cramping or contractions.

thrombosis. Formation of a blood clot (thrombus).

thrush. Monilial or yeast infection occurring in the mouth or mucous membranes of a newborn infant.

thyroid disease. Abnormality of the thyroid gland and its production of thyroid hormone. See **hyperthyroidism; hypothyroidism.**

tocolytic agents. Medications to stop labor.

toxic shock syndrome. Overwhelming reaction to poisons made by bacteria.

toxic strep A. Bacterial infection that can cause severe damage to mother; usually starts in a cut on the skin, not as a sore throat, and spreads very quickly. It can involve the entire body.

toxemia. See **pre-eclampsia.**

toxoplasmosis. Infection caused by toxoplasma gondii.

transverse lie. Fetus is turned sideways in uterus.

trichomonal vaginitis. Venereal infection caused by trichomonas.

trimester. Method of dividing pregnancy into three equal periods of about 13 weeks each.

triple screen. Measurement of three blood tests to determine fetal well-being.

trisomy. Extra chromosome.

trisomy 13. Extra chromosome at site 13.

trisomy 18. Extra chromosome at site 18.

Turner's syndrome. Missing one chromosome, 45X.

umbilical cord. Cord that connects the placenta to the developing baby. It removes waste products and carbon dioxide from the baby and brings oxygenated blood and nutrients from the mother through the placenta to the baby.

ureters. Tubes from the kidneys to the bladder that drain urine.

urinalysis. Test of the urine. Doctor tests urine during pregnancy to check for signs of disease or infection.

uterus. Organ an embryo/fetus grows in. Also called a *womb.*

vaccine. Mild infection given to cause production of antibodies to protect against subsequent infections of the same type.

vacuum extractor. Device used to provide traction on fetal head during delivery; used to help deliver a baby.

vagina. Birth canal.

varicose veins. Blood vessels (veins) that are dilated or enlarged.

vascular spiders. See **telangiectasias.**

vena cava. Major vein in the body that empties into the right atrium of the heart. It returns unoxygenated blood to the heart for transport to the lungs.

venereal warts. See **condyloma acuminatum.**

womb. See **uterus.**

yeast infection. See **monilial vulvovaginitis; thrush.**

Index

The ideal companion to
Your Pregnancy After 30 . . .

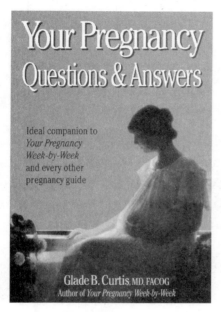

ISBN 1-5561-077-3
$12.95 US, $16.95 Canada

Your Pregnancy Questions & Answers, also by Glade B. Curtis, M.D., is a separate, easy-to-read guide to help you find answers to your questions and concerns when you need them. A great companion to any pregnancy book!

Dr. Curtis answers more than a thousand questions pregnant women ask most often. He includes questions you worry about but may feel are "not important enough to bother my doctor," or are too personal to discuss—and he knows how critical the answers are to you.

Questions are arranged by subject and grouped logically into 20 chapters. Discusses how to prepare for pregnancy through labor and delivery, to babyproofing your home and taking care of your new baby. A detailed glossary explains terms your doctor and health professionals use, and helps you formulate questions you may want to ask your own doctor. Beautifully illustrated and easy to use.

Available at bookstores everywhere.

The #1 bestselling doctor-authored pregnancy title!

ISBN 1-55561-068-4
$12.95 US, $16.95 Canada

A unique book divided into each week of pregnancy, with important information about the developing baby and the changing mother-to-be.

A popular, fact-filled book with helpful, clear advice. This best-selling guide to pregnancy has been improved for a new generation of babies and mothers. Includes a new section, "Before You Become Pregnant," to help you increase the odds of having a healthy baby.

Also available in Spanish!

Su Embarazo Semana a Semana — the Spanish language version of the best-selling *Your Pregnancy Week by Week* — is now available. How does a baby grow in pregnancy? What kinds of changes can the mother expect in her own body? How do her activities affect her health and well-being or her growing baby? Week-by-week format offers answers to these and other questions in this popular fact-filled book. Helpful, clear advice.

ISBN 1-55561-061-7
$12.95 US, $15.95 Canada

Available at bookstores everywhere.